DISCIPLINARY LITERACY INQUIRY & INSTRUCTION, SECOND EDITION

JACY IPPOLITO

CHRISTINA L. DOBBS

MEGIN CHARNER-LAIRD

HARVARD EDUCATION PRESS

CAMBRIDGE, MASSACHUSETTS

Paperback ISBN 9781682539019

Library of Congress Cataloging-in-Publication Data
Names: Ippolito, Jacy, author. | Dobbs, Christina L., author. |
    Charner-Laird, Megin, author.
Title: Disciplinary literacy inquiry & instruction / Jacy Ippolito,
    Christina L. Dobbs, Megin Charner-Laird.
Description: Second edition. | Cambridge, Massachusetts : Harvard
    Education Press, [2024] | Includes bibliographical references and index.
Identifiers: LCCN 2023054172 | ISBN 9781682539019 (paperback)
Subjects: LCSH: Language arts—Correlation with content subjects. |
    Content area reading. | Literacy.
Classification: LCC P53.293 .I67 2024 | DDC 418.0071—dc23/eng/20240129
LC record available at https://lccn.loc.gov/2023054172

Published by Harvard Education Press,
an imprint of the Harvard Education Publishing Group

Harvard Education Press
8 Story Street
Cambridge, MA 02138

Cover Design: Ciano Design
Cover Photo: Martial Colomb/via Getty Images

The typefaces used in this book are Classica Pro, Open Sans, and Clasica Slab.

DISCIPLINARY LITERACY INQUIRY & INSTRUCTION, SECOND EDITION

As always, to Victoria, my best friend and greatest thought partner. Also to my two budding authors, Milo and Emily, may you be writing your own dedications soon.

–JI

To my mom, Larinda, and my nieces Rosey, Bonnie, and Lucy, who inspire me to imagine a world that could be. And to everyone who wants to be a teacher.

–CD

Katie, Quinn, and Wylie, thank you for being my forever team. To the Brain Trust, thank you for providing the foundation of lifelong learning, exploration, and love.

–MCL

CONTENTS

FOREWORD

For the foreword to this second edition of *Disciplinary Literacy Inquiry & Instruction (DLI&I)* we invited two long-time teachers and leaders, as well as collaborators of ours—Jenee Uttaro and Jenelle Williams—to talk about their work with disciplinary literacy, why disciplinary literacy (DL) is still critically important in schools today, and how they see the second edition of *DLI&I* supporting educators moving forward. After a long career in secondary school teaching and leadership, Jenee is currently the Director of Equity and Curriculum at a small independent school in Massachusetts. Jenelle started her career as a middle school English teacher and now works as a state-level literacy consultant, providing support to teachers and school and district leaders around adolescent literacy. Given that both educators have spent years in and across schools and districts supporting DL work, we thought it only right to begin this second edition with their voices from the field. Below is an edited version of our conversation with them about disciplinary literacy inquiry and instruction.

Q: **How did you first start thinking about and working with the idea of disciplinary literacy?**

Jenee: When I moved into teaching ninth grade at Brookline High School (MA), I noticed that a number of our rising ninth graders, particularly our linguistically and culturally diverse students, were struggling and needed that bridge from eighth grade English to ninth grade. But we were noticing this in all content areas. So, obviously, we didn't just have students who were struggling or underperforming in terms of English language arts, but it was across the board. I thought about founding a summer program that had us looking at those basic literacy skills that you (Jacy, Christina, and Megin) talk about in the book, and then the intermediate literacy skills.

So, we designed a program to look at how to address some of those strategies that cut across all disciplines. That's when Jacy, Christina, and Megin helped us think about—how do we go from content area literacy to thinking more about true disciplinary literacy, and what could that look like? It was 2009 when I started The Literacy Project, and then maybe around 2011–2012 that we began to work with teacher teams across the disciplines in the high school, thinking about disciplinary literacy. And this was kind of new for these educators, who sort of said, "I'm not an English teacher. I don't teach literacy."

But then they were so excited to come together and think about teaching and learning in terms of their disciplines, to think about what we really mean by disciplinary literacy, and how to help all our students, not just our students who had been underperforming. What I loved about that project was that it was interdisciplinary in nature. It required inquiry, collaboration, discussion, action research, and reflective practice…all the elements of disciplinary literacy that had a direct impact on the students that I originally was interested in supporting.

Jenelle: Coming into my current role as a district-level literacy consultant, work was ramping up in Michigan around literacy in general. Our literacy scores were not great, and our track record in terms of meeting the needs of historically marginalized communities was one of the worst in the nation. We definitely recognized that we were at a crisis point with supporting literacy from birth through grade 12. At the same time, work had been taking place around a few Right to Read cases in the Detroit area, with students bringing cases against their school districts, indicating that their needs were not being met. And Dr. Elizabeth Moje, at the University of Michigan, was asked to testify and gather research about what it takes to really support the literacy of adolescents across the board. Ultimately, I became part of and was then asked to lead that statewide work, partnering with 6th–12th grade educators and leaders, building their capacity around not only the instructional pieces but also the systems pieces that need to be in place.

For me, that's what I've really appreciated about the work of Jacy, Christina, and Megin—you know, they are a powerhouse team, where you have the lens of effective professional learning communities and inquiry cycles; you have the lens of thinking about adolescent literacy development; and you have the leadership lens. And that was what really was exciting to me, not only about this book, but their other work too. I found their work to be really helpful because the work that I do is also systems work and building capacity, taking the work to scale across the state. And the equity piece, the social justice piece–that's the part that I think really keeps grounding me in the work, even though it's hard. It's been challenging through the pandemic. But knowing the *why* for the work, the equity piece, is really powerful.

Q: Why was disciplinary literacy originally important to you? Why is disciplinary literacy still important in schools today?

Jenee: I have always brought an equity lens to this work. So, for me, literacy has always meant liberation. That was how I grew up. I was an English language arts teacher, so that's what I care about, right? But also, I honestly couldn't quite solidify it in my mind until I started working with Jacy, Christina, and Megin, and doing my own reading. To me, by its very nature, disciplinary literacy supports equitable literacy instruction, within and across disciplines, across all grade levels. And because I was in a K–8 school teaching middle school, I got to see what was happening with our early learners, and I realized that disciplinary literacy could even draw on students' own funds of knowledge and their own cultural backgrounds, their own sort of schema, so that they could at some point even contribute to the disciplinary fields themselves within their own rich learning environments. Again, Jacy, Christina, and Megin talk about this in their disciplinary literacy inquiry and instruction framework.

But as I learned more and more about disciplinary literacy strategies and instruction, I thought about the culturally sustaining pedagogies that I cared so much about, and even though it didn't seem like there was a lot of direct discourse around that several years ago, I felt like we were right there on the cusp of it. And so, all that critical thinking and the power of relevance and proximity and engagement that are so important for our marginalized learners and for all of our learners, it seemed critical that when moving forward with disciplinary literacy we know that inequities are embedded within the disciplines.

As we talk about whether it's the academic language, or who is in the canon…who we're reading and what those language structures are…

I felt like disciplinary literacy could allow us to produce empowered readers and critical thinkers, critical readers, and social justice workers. As we move forward, postpandemic, knowing how the pandemic impacted our students and all of us, whether it's the social isolation, the loss of executive functioning, the social emotional learning–it has all ramped up postpandemic, the mental health needs of students and adults too. They were much more exacerbated and spotlighted by the pandemic. Now we can't look away from what those inequities were and are.

Also, the RAND framework–texts, tasks, students, culture–is so much more relevant now. So, why is disciplinary literacy still important? Well, I think that after the murder of Mr. George Floyd, and after the pandemic, it seems to me that our students are clamoring for and desperate for the relevancy, the motivation, and the engagement that disciplinary literacy can provide, that sort of real-worldness. With meaningful evidence and artifacts and the opportunity to apply real world lived experiences; it feels really important now.

Jenelle: I think initially I was drawn to this work because of two things: disciplinary literacy is truly about loving and honoring and making space for all the unique and wonderful ways of knowing and being in our world. And I think maybe that's my International Baccalaureate background speaking. But if you're truly doing disciplinary literacy, you are saying, "We need people who can think in ways that scientists think. We need people who can see the beauty in mathematics. We need all of that." And by setting the stage in school through disciplinary literacy work, we're making that a possibility. That, in and of itself, is starting to provide equity in a system that was not built for equity.

So, I think just honoring that beauty and uniqueness and the identity that educators bring to this work. And the passion, for me, is really powerful. Not only does DL center teachers' identities, but it helps center important student identities. So yes, of course, you're gaining the content. And it's worth noting that we can't gain content without language. This work is about being really intentional around the language of your content. But it also centers students' identities by saying each student that comes through the classroom door is worthy of these opportunities and able to engage in this. So, there is a presumption of competence that shifts how teachers think about things–it truly lives into an asset-based pedagogy.

Then why is disciplinary literacy still important? Where do I think it's going? I think we're in a very divided state right now, in education. And whenever people frame things as either/or, or black or white, I usually turn to polarity management. Because when I think about the decisions that the districts that I support are making, they're thinking: "Do we focus on social emotional learning (SEL), or do we focus on instruction? Do we focus on equity, or do we focus on instruction?" These are not either/or problems to be solved. These are interdependent pairs. You can't truly be doing SEL work without effective instruction. You can't truly be working toward equity without these practices. It's a matter of how we manage that, knowing we need both. They're interdependent.

Jenee: If we could get our minds around and understand the intersection of these pieces, and how foundational and fundamental disciplinary literacy actually is, it could totally change the game. That's another great thing about this book, is that Jacy, Christina, and Megin talk about real reflective practice, adult learners learning disciplinary literacy, and how we can best teach it. And then, you know, how to model that for kids. And then it's a learning journey for them. It's not binary. There's culturally sustaining pedagogy in there. Then we've got learners who are loving it. We've got educators who are learning and loving it. I just think it's super powerful.

Jenelle: For me, I think it's an opportunity for all of us to experience joy in teaching again.

Jenee: Yes!

Jenelle: And that means you have to make a shift as a teacher, right? You have to be willing to make yourself vulnerable and not be the expert. And that's hard, but it's also really exhilarating when you suddenly have students interested in what's happening in your classroom. By foregrounding the things that students are interested in, foregrounding issues in their communities and then centering the learning around that, you have a greater chance for them to be experiencing joy and learning, but also for you to experience joy. I don't think that can be underestimated. When we start working with schools and disciplinary literacy, it is often leaders that come to us and say, "We want to do disciplinary literacy because we need our kids to be reading better." Okay. That's great that you're wanting that, and we want that too. And also, are you willing to rethink secondary education? Because that's really what this is calling for. This is calling for you as leaders to be willing to step aside and just be the remover of obstacles, and to empower teachers to really set the direction for the work.

But what I appreciate not only in this book, but in the others from Jacy, Christina, and Megin as well, is the belief in the professional knowledge and judgment of teachers to know what their students need best, with a little bit of support and research-driven practices, empowering teachers to do the work that needs to be done. And that is not where we've been the past several years. We need that.

Q: Where do you see disciplinary literacy work headed next?

Jenee: I like to call it the marriage of disciplinary literacy and culturally sustaining pedagogies. I like to say that when content-area teachers teach in culturally responsive ways, they can help students better leverage discipline-specific knowledge to negotiate this world that privileges some at the expense of others. And, by the way, our students, our high school students and our elementary students, are desperate for contemporary content. Like, how do we navigate #metoo? How do we navigate Black Lives Matter? How do we navigate gender and sexual identities? All of these pieces that you could argue twenty years ago weren't so much at the forefront. Even though they should have been. We were thinking about it. But this is what kids are contending with right now and thinking about right now.

So, to me, that is why teaching is the hardest job in the world, and the most exciting job in the world, because we're constantly evolving too. But the language is changing. That's the beauty of language. We need to learn new literacies, and to me, I think DL work is headed next in the direction of making explicit the fact that we're not talking about binaries here and that we've got a new generation of learners, in our postpandemic context. It's just different. And we need to adapt and adjust. I think disciplinary literacy is crystallizing for me even more, where we can really sort of see how to empower our students and be social justice warriors alongside them, thinking about our learners who learn differently. All of those pieces feel really important. That's what I'm thinking about.

Jenelle: Yes! All of that! As always, there's a lot of work to be done around issues of diversity, equity, inclusion, and social justice. And I think that we're in a very challenging space in education with navigating those issues. At the same time there are educators who remain committed to those ideals and their students, and who care deeply about them and want the opportunity to have a voice in the world that they've been thrust into. And so I hope that more work continues to be done around culturally sustaining disciplinary literacy. The role of criticality and supporting students in pushing back against some of those historical norms. You know, what do we mean by "academic language," and who decided, and for whose benefit?

I don't see that as telling students what to think. It's making space to honor the thoughts they are already having. It makes space for criticality. And this work is happening, you know, not only in Michigan, but in other states, where people are coming together and asking the question, "How do we make the learning experience better for students at the secondary level?" There are a lot of people that are thirsty to have that conversation and to move in a different direction. So, it's really just a matter of having the right tools to do it.

Q: How might this second edition of *DLI&I* support educators in engaging in the type of disciplinary literacy work you're describing?

Jenelle: I think that the stories from the field in this book are incredibly helpful. We have instructional practices. We've got schoolwide practices that talk about systems pieces. Yeah, but boots on the ground, what are some ways that disciplinary literacy is actually happening? What are some examples? That's where I always lean on this book. And I plan to continue to lean on it because it takes a lot of time to articulate those stories. And they're gold, especially for a lot of secondary level educators who haven't had a lot of time for professional conversations around disciplinary literacy. It can feel like a whole new world. So, the examples in this book become the mentor text, and I think that's really helpful. And the new chapters about professional learning systems, and then the role of the school leadership. I think those are really important too, to have up-to-date, reality-driven examples and guidance. Because, you know, leaders get really frustrated if they go to something that says, "Well, just do this particular thing" and then they're asking, "How am I going to make that work?" So, it's really, really important to be able to work through the models in this book within our current context. Then you know what it can look like to work towards success.

Jenee: I'm so excited for this second edition. You can see the Heifetz book[1] on my shelf, over my left shoulder here. And Jacy, Christina, and Megin talk about Heifetz and the adaptive work of disciplinary literacy in their book. But in his book, Heifetz said, "If we're going to implicate ourselves in the solution, we have to implicate ourselves in the problem." And I'm inspired by the idea that this new *DLI&I* book is a second look, thinking about the lessons from last time, and how our landscape has changed, and what more we need to do, and where some new things are that we should consider. And that's what adaptive work is all about, right? You know, there are no technical solutions, right? And so, as we grapple with the RAND framework in this new context and think about the stories of the educators in the book, and sort of apply this same lens in a new context, I think it is super powerful.

And as Jenelle mentioned, I think educators are hungry, *thirsty*, for some of that learning. Like *somebody*, please speak to this moment, right? Like, the other moment has passed. Who is helping us meet this current moment? We've all heard about how difficult it is to be an educator and how many educators are leaving the field. So how can we continue to move forward? I know that in this new, second edition the *We Used to Think and Now We Think* protocol in the preface just makes it so concrete. It will help teachers in the trenches, if you will, on the ground doing this work. Gosh, you know what, I used to think that way too! It's helpful to have somebody sort of say it like that, because that's how I've been thinking. And including those stories from the field again, using the RAND framework, the leadership pieces that we talked about, and obviously the culturally sustaining pedagogy pieces. Those are really going to speak to what educators are dealing with right now. And for those reasons, I think this book is potentially more practical than it ever was. I love this evolution. It's right alongside my own growth, as I contend with my new reality. So, I love that.

PREFACE TO THE SECOND EDITION

Do the best you can until you know better.
Then when you know better, do better.
~MAYA ANGELOU

WHEN THE FIRST EDITION of *Disciplinary Literacy Inquiry & Instruction* (*DLI&I*) was published in 2019, we viewed the book as the natural extension of our 2017 book, *Investigating Disciplinary Literacy* (*IDL*). We intended for *DLI&I* to pick up where *IDL* left off, helping individual teachers and teams of educators to chart their own paths forward in learning about and enacting disciplinary literacy (DL).

Toward that goal, we enlisted the help of teachers and specialists with whom we had collaborated to share their own stories of DL professional learning and teaching. We were thrilled to share their stories in 2019, alongside our own experiences and a framework for digging into the work of DL professional learning. When the first edition arrived, we imagined that we would immediately launch into using the book with teachers and teams across settings.

Of course, in the fall of 2019, we never could have anticipated that only months later COVID-19 would sweep across the world. All preK–12, higher education, and professional learning work shifted dramatically or halted. Like all schools and classrooms in the United States and beyond, our own work was interrupted, and we wrestled with how to navigate teaching and learning in less familiar virtual environments. Although we did receive words of excitement about the 2019 edition of *DLI&I*, we were disappointed not to find ourselves in schools alongside teachers using the book and forging ahead with DL work.

Now, flash-forward five years. Having mostly weathered a global pandemic alongside equity-driven societal upheaval and all the uncertainty and change brought by that time, we are thrilled by the opportunity to expand and reissue *DLI&I* with Harvard Education Press. This opportunity has allowed us to look at *DLI&I* with fresh eyes, to provide updates that speak to the current context of schooling, and to more explicitly connect these ideas to our previous work, as the full companion to *Investigating Disciplinary Literacy* that we always envisioned.

To begin this second edition, we three (Jacy, Christina, and Megin) came together for one of our favorite types of conversations, an "I used to think . . . now I think . . ." conversation in the tradition of one of our mentors and beloved teachers, Richard Elmore.[1] We sat together (virtually, of course, because like the rest of the world, we have learned the power of videoconferencing), and we discussed elements of the first book, and the field of DL, that remain just as relevant today as five years ago. We then touched upon ways in which our thinking and work have evolved since 2019–notions reflected both in this preface and across this second edition.

Thus, we begin this second edition with highlights from our conversation, framing this book and hopefully supporting you, the reader, who may also be carefully considering the ways in which your own thinking and work, related to DL and beyond, are continually evolving.

WE USED TO THINK . . . AND NOW WE THINK . . .

We used to think that excellent DL professional learning focused predominantly on supporting teachers in inquiring into and then adopting or adapting new instructional strategies to bolster students' literacy and content knowledge and skills.

Now we think that excellent DL professional learning must support *both* teachers' acquisition of new instructional skills *and* must foster hope, authentic engagement, and collaboration among teachers in order for their work to truly flourish.

Why is this important? We are living through a time in which teachers, as professionals, are being told to follow scripts and cede decision-making power, as if they don't know their own students best. While it continues to be critical for teachers to participate in ongoing preparation and professional learning that follows the latest research in both literacy and content teaching and learning, we have begun to worry across and beyond the pandemic that most teacher professional learning undervalues teacher professionalism and expertise. For many, such professional learning robs teachers of both the hope and authentic collaborative work (with colleagues and students) that drew them into the teaching profession in the first place. Therefore, in this second edition of *DLI&I*, we strengthen our original arguments about how educators across grade levels can and should be given the tools needed to adopt, adapt, invent, and share DL instructional practices that work well for their own students. As we learned in our own studies of teacher professional learning across the pandemic, when faced with extraordinary social, epidemiological, and technological challenges, teachers turned primarily to each other to learn how best to support students. In this new edition, we encourage that same spirit of collaboration in service of bolstering teacher expertise and hope for creating not only a technically proficient but also a more informed, accepting, adaptable, and creative citizenry.

We used to think that it was important to communicate to teachers that the progression of students' literacy skills from basic, to intermediate, to disciplinary literacy is more layered and interwoven than originally presented;[2] therefore, we created our own 2019 model illustrating greater overlap and interconnection among those three teaching and skill development areas.[3]

   Now we think that it is *even more important* to help teachers understand the complexity of how teaching and learning within and across those three areas (basic, intermediate, disciplinary literacy) overlap and intertwine across all levels of K–12, particularly as we consider the increasingly wide array of learners in our classrooms (e.g., multilingual students who are learning English; neurodivergent learners; all who experienced interrupted schooling across the pandemic; etc.) as well as newer models of literacy learning that emphasize the complexity of literacy learning, such as Duke and Cartwright's active view of reading.[4]

   Why is this important? While much within the world of education is presented as quite linear and stepwise, living through the era of COVID-19 has reinforced for us the notion that there are no silver bullets, no quick and easy or foolproof solutions. During an age when we are all grappling with a renewed focus on the teaching of strong foundational literacy skills, we cannot be seduced into believing that phonics and decoding skills alone will translate seamlessly into later sophisticated comprehension and DL skills (what some have called the "vaccination" model of literacy).[5] As we hope we have all have learned across the pandemic, vaccines are critical, but alone they are not enough to guarantee long-term success.

Therefore, in this second edition, we reiterate the importance of all K–12 educators understanding the ways in which basic, intermediate, and disciplinary literacy can be layered and reinforced across grade levels in developmentally appropriate ways. As we have observed firsthand, teacher teams who strive to focus on DL ultimately merge and layer literacy skills across basic, intermediate, and disciplinary areas to meet students' diverse learning needs.[6] Moving forward, and especially as we continue to navigate the effects of disrupted schooling for all, we want to continue encouraging teachers across all grade levels to embrace complexity and engage in professional learning and practices that interweave basic, intermediate, and disciplinary literacy skills simultaneously. We need to shy away from assumptions about simple, linear progressions of skill development. We hope that this second edition of *DLI&I* will play a small role in helping educators to build a strong foundation across areas of literacy, as the overlap and interweaving of literacy domains are more important now than ever.

We used to think that school, district, and community contexts were important in designing and carrying out both DL professional learning and teaching initiatives.

Now we think that DL inquiry and instruction is *even more context sensitive* than we first imagined. School leadership, existing professional learning systems and structures, and teacher- and student-level factors are just a few of the elements that can shape DL inquiry and instructional ventures.

Why is this important? Both the Black Lives Matter movement and the COVID-19 pandemic opened our eyes to the multitude of ways in which literacy professional learning ventures need to be context specific and tuned to the teachers, students, and communities in which they take place. This may seem obvious in some ways, and yet professional learning is so often pitched as teacher-proof and scalable in ways that disregard important differences among our school communities. While some schools and communities may be ready to design and launch into larger, multistage DL ventures such as those we detailed in our 2017 book *Investigating Disciplinary Literacy*, we reinforce across this second edition of *DLI&I* the notion that much DL professional learning and teaching can be small in scope and hyperlocal in its attention to students, texts, tasks, and culture. Over the past five years, we have learned the power of a both/and approach to DL professional learning that embraces both larger-scale efforts and individual or team-based hyperlocal ventures, each attending carefully to what their contexts could support. We present examples of teachers collaborating within larger ventures as well as teachers working alone or in smaller teams across this second edition, to illustrate the ways in which teachers are pursuing DL inquiry and instruction in context-sensitive ways. We have revised and added chapters in this second edition to support educators in intentionally strengthening their school contexts to better support DL inquiry and instruction (e.g., ways in which leaders can directly support; concrete examples of DL professional learning models; etc.). Finally, we now more explicitly include connections to culturally sustaining pedagogies and critical perspectives of DL in this book. Thinking contextually about DL means honoring students' home literacies, their funds of knowledge, and the ways in which they begin to make new meaning and carve out new space within the disciplines. Contextually responsive DL provides students with the instructional opportunities they need to thrive in an ever more complex world.

We used to think that the shift from a more traditional apprenticeship model of DL (i.e., DL in service of helping apprentice students into disciplinary communities) would logically and naturally lead into more critical kinds of DL work in which teachers would help students both enter disciplinary communities and also question the purposes, norms, foundational texts, ways of communicating, and boundaries of those communities.

Now we think that *critical disciplinary literacy* work, in which the ideas from DL are expanded, revised, and interwoven with critical, culturally sustaining, and antiracist pedagogies *will require much more deliberate effort.*

Why is this important? In our 2019 first edition of *DLI&I*, we briefly touched on the notion that the ultimate goal of DL work was to both induct students into various disciplinary communities and to help them craft personal and professional identities that move beyond historic disciplines, such that students could begin to step back from those disciplines and question them through a critical and culturally sustaining lens. Now, however, as we continue to wrestle with the effects of the Black Lives Matter movement and pandemic on schooling, we are even more convinced that a theory and practice of critical DL is what our students need.

Equity and antiracist work in schools is far from the norm, with great pushback from multiple corners of the United States and world. As a result, in many places, students are being taught disciplinary content and skills without opportunities to engage in critical conversations about historical power dynamics, systemic inequalities, racism, classism, sexism, and so on. Students in many places are being taught content without opportunities to develop a critical stance, without tools to ask questions about why and how we got to where we are and the related changes needed to create a more equitable future. Our initial thinking in these areas was perhaps a bit naïve, assuming that all schools and leaders would naturally want to push toward these critical perspectives over time, thus creating more equitable opportunities and outcomes for all students. However, we now realize that this work requires much more effort over a longer period of time. We begin that work here, in this second edition of *DLI&I*, connecting more clearly to culturally sustaining DL work across the book. However, we also invite readers to turn to our forthcoming book, *Critical Disciplinary Literacy*, for a much deeper dive into this territory.

While there is much more that we *used to think … and now think …* when it comes to DL inquiry and instruction, we offer these four reflections here because they neatly shape the ways in which we sought to expand and revise this second edition. It is our sincere hope that this new edition provides you with the inspiration and resolution to launch into renewed DL work in your own school and community. May we all commit to continuing to revisit and expand our thinking over time, always in service of the students who deserve the best of us. May we make spaces and communities where we can learn to be better, and then do better.

~Jacy, Christina, and Megin

CHAPTER 1

The Case for Disciplinary Literacy

As NEW TEACHERS, we were told that *every teacher is a teacher of reading*. This mantra has echoed within schools across the United States since the early 1900s, and for some teachers, like the three of us, it became a mantra that defined our teaching.[1] Whether teaching first and fifth grade in California (Megin), fifth through eighth grade in Massachusetts (Jacy), or high school English in Texas (Christina), we each saw our primary role as helping students acquire the literacy skills they needed to succeed.

This was an easy frame for us to adopt. As an elementary school teacher, a middle school reading specialist, and a high school English teacher, we never questioned that a core component of our work was to be teachers of reading. Early in our careers, "teaching reading" meant different things to each of us. For Megin, it meant immersing her young students in reading and writing workshop experiences. She assumed that these workshop structures would provide students much, if not all, of what they needed to be strong readers. For Jacy, teaching reading meant helping his middle school students adopt and perform the comprehension strategies (e.g., predicting, visualizing, connecting, and questioning) that he assumed would help them become fluent readers. Meanwhile, at the high school level, Christina assumed that her students already were strong readers, coming into her classes ready to analyze texts at high levels. She often wondered what she could possibly do to support students who weren't ready to meet those challenges. This was one of the reasons she later enrolled in a graduate program to become a reading specialist.

Given that we each saw some part of our teaching roles as supporting students' literacy skills, we alternately focused on reading and writing workshop structures, comprehension strategies and routines, and literary analysis. We pored over books like *Strategies That Work* (Stephanie Harvey and Anne Goudvis), *Mosaic of Thought* (Ellin Oliver Keene and Susan Zimmermann), and *Craft Lessons: Teaching Writing K–8* (Ralph Fletcher and JoAnn Portalupi).[2] We applauded our own work when students were able to effectively summarize and analyze the books that populated our classroom libraries. After several years of classroom instruction, however, each of us realized that "teaching reading" could and should mean something much larger. In fact, we use our own experiences as the initial cases in this book in order to paint a picture of the inquiry and iteration that is a cornerstone of disciplinary literacy (DL) instructional practice.

THE BEGINNING OF OUR OWN DISCIPLINARY LITERACY INQUIRY AND INSTRUCTIONAL WORK

As a newly minted literacy coach, Jacy naïvely went into seventh- and eighth-grade math, science, and social studies classrooms and began extolling the virtues of general comprehension and note-taking strategies, such as K-W-L charts, double-entry journals, and concept maps.[3] As you may guess, he was met with a range of responses–from curiosity and confusion to irritation and frustration. "How are students going to make a text-to-self connection when reading the equation for a straight line?" asked the math teacher, reasonably. The science teacher wondered aloud, "How will asking students to write about what they already *know* and what they *want to learn* in a K-W-L chart work when learning about mitochondria? Students have never heard of mitochondria before!" The social studies teacher saw some value in general reading comprehension strategies, but he was also quick to say that his primary goal was to help students understand and remember specific historical events and their relationship to current events. He was much less interested in creating all-purpose strong readers. It was only in partnership with content-area colleagues–designing new reading, writing, and discussion routines that targeted the discipline-specific skills those teachers prized–that Jacy began to adopt a differentiated way of teaching literacy in content-area classrooms.

Meanwhile, Christina was trained as a traditional high school English teacher, majoring in English and studying a common list of classic texts through high school and college. Then she became a teacher with mostly students of color in a school whose curriculum rarely presented these students with any representations of themselves, or of Christina herself for that matter. She soon gravitated toward independent reading for students, who often expressed displeasure with their prior experiences with reading in school. Her minilessons were focused on skills specific to English language arts (ELA), like identifying theme or tone. She always felt as though students had to be good readers prior to entering her classroom, and if they were not reading as well as they might, she did not have many tools to help. If she was going to help students become more confident and engaged readers, she had to find a broader, all-purpose toolbox of instructional tools to use. No one had really taught her to be a teacher of reading, and she was surprised to find that she needed to be one.

As an elementary teacher, Megin was quick to see that the comprehension strategies that, with fiction allowed her elementary readers to make connections with the text, did not have the same impact with informational texts. For example, when encountering a scientific text, though students were quick to make connections that demonstrated their excitement–"Oh! I've been to a museum and seen a planet display!" "My uncle likes to show me the stars when we go camping!"–comprehension strategies, such as making connections, did not on their own help students to access scientific texts effectively. Instead, Megin discovered that she needed to teach about the informational text features used in science writing at the elementary level. She realized that teaching students the importance of looking carefully at diagrams, reading the labels on those diagrams, and paying attention to headers and bolded words was necessary to help them begin to read and ultimately write like scientists. This type of instruction spread across content areas as Megin began to define the different ways to work with students around reading and writing, depending on the content that she was teaching, as she endeavored to help students learn how to approach and feel comfortable with literacy work across a variety of disciplines.

Each of us, in turn, encountered the possibilities and challenges of being teachers of reading and writing in the various ways we defined our roles. Ultimately, we each needed to become something more. Lots of teachers are teachers of other things, like quadratic equations and cell structures and civil wars. Most notably, elementary-level teachers find themselves teaching one discipline and then another from one hour to the next. Across K–12 contexts, when it came to teaching content, we each began to realize that reading, writing, and discussion were not ends unto themselves.

These literacy skills were a means of learning complex content and communicating in ways that authors, historians, mathematicians, scientists, and so on would understand and value. The goal for the social studies teacher isn't just promoting enjoyment of a historical narrative; it is something closer to helping students learn a new way of thinking about connections between past, present, and future events. The math teacher may feel successful when students understand when, how, and why to apply particular formulas and flexibly represent their answers in multiple forms. The science teacher may feel successful when students successfully craft open-response answers on lab reports that include the precise language used to describe cell structure and function. The ELA teacher may see success as a stack of elegantly written student essays about the use of symbols in a novel. Moreover, beyond these core academic areas, a wide variety of visual and performing arts teachers, world language teachers, technology and vocational teachers, librarians, and more all focus on a wide array of both discipline-specific and cross-cutting content and process goals for their students. The sheer number and variety of disciplinary goals for students across classes and grade levels can become a bit dizzying.

For the elementary teacher, the goal may be for students to seamlessly toggle between different ways of reading, writing, and speaking, depending on the subject area–to develop flexibility as readers and writers and tackle a social studies text with as much ease and confidence as they would a novel. Each of these goals requires literacy skills, and some of those skills are fundamentally related. However, the layered instruction of both shared literacy skills across areas and highly differentiated and discipline-specific literacy skills was never made clear to any of us early in our careers.

INITIAL INQUIRIES INTO DISCIPLINARY LITERACY

For each of us, it would be several years before we first read the phrase "disciplinary literacy" in the now-classic 2008 *Harvard Educational Review* article "Teaching Disciplinary Literacy to Adolescents" by Timothy and Cynthia

Shanahan.[4] Through reading this article and reflecting on past dilemmas of practice in our own classrooms and beyond, we slowly developed a new focus in our teaching and coaching. Content-area teachers weren't being stubborn or unreasonable. They were rightly defending their own instructional goals. They were signaling that thinking and working as an actor, biologist, American historian, literary critic, string musician, physicist, and so on require specialized and fundamentally different literacy skills than the basic or general literacy skills presumed necessary across all contexts. Transporting general reading comprehension skills, historically designed and tested in ELA classes, into content-area classes, was clearly not going to inspire content-area teachers to become "reading teachers." Nor were traditional ELA-focused comprehension strategies, without a good deal of adaptation, going to help elementary and content-area teachers and their students achieve goals such as representing data using tables, figures, and words; comparing bias across multiple primary sources; writing formal lab reports; or identifying themes across multiple fiction and informational texts.

When Shanahan and Shanahan published "Teaching Disciplinary Literacy to Adolescents," it seemed like the perfect time to reframe "every teacher [as] a teacher of reading."[5] *Time to Act* would be published two years later, coinciding with the release of the Common Core State Standards.[6] Both *Time to Act* and the Common Core emphasized the need for teachers across grades to focus on college and career readiness for students, which included a greater emphasis on advanced and discipline-specific literacy skills. The Common Core boldly stated that all teachers across grades and content areas needed to use "their content area expertise to help students meet the particular challenges of reading, writing, speaking, listening, and language in their respective fields."[7] Suddenly, DL seemed to be the answer to the age-old question of "Whose responsibility is it to teach students to read, write, and communicate in school?" We all need to teach literacy skills, but a DL framework offered a more nuanced way to understand that charge.

Proponents of a DL instructional framework are not asking all teachers to be general reading teachers; instead, they are asking all educators to teach the discipline-specific literacy skills students need to succeed in college and the workplace, such that students can enact their own visions of their future selves. Students need their teachers, across grades and content areas, to be their mentors for how to read, write, and communicate like authors, historians, mathematicians, scientists, and so on. This can span from kindergarten teachers helping their students learn to observe and describe the world like biologists to high school math teachers helping their students discuss and write about mathematics using the succinct, specific language of the field.

As the first decade of the twenty-first century came to a close, the field of disciplinary literacy roared to life.

A BOOK TO BOLSTER TEACHER INQUIRY, INSTRUCTION, AND EXPERTISE

We have revised and expanded the second edition of this book with quite a different mindset than that which we held at the beginning of our respective teaching careers. We have written this book as professors and designers of literacy professional learning projects, having collectively engaged in disciplinary literacy research and practice for over fifteen years. We have written this book to support teachers and leaders who are eager to help apprentice all students across grade levels into the advanced literacy subcultures that exist within each of the disciplines. Moreover, we hope that this book helps prompt some thinking about what lies beyond apprenticeship. We envision students becoming not just expert communicators within the disciplines but also critical consumers of those disciplines. We see students begin to imagine new disciplinary and transdisciplinary futures that are broadly representative of all backgrounds, literacies, and funds of knowledge.

This is the book we wish we had read as new teachers working K–12. This is the book we wish we had given to our colleagues when we began working as reading specialists and literacy coaches. We hope this book falls into your hands at just the right time in your own professional work.

A QUICK NOTE ABOUT RESEARCH

Before delving more deeply into the evolving concept of DL, we wish to share a quick note about how we conceptualize research. As teachers first and then as teacher leaders, coaches, and professors, we have often heard and used the term *research* in a variety of ways—as encouragement to implement particular practices, as a rationale to change the practices of others, and sometimes, as we heard when we were teachers, as a means to encourage us to stop asking questions. Often the term *research* has been used to imply that the case is closed, the facts have been found, and the path is now clear. As we became researchers ourselves, we came to a slightly different understanding of what this term means. We think it is important to share our understanding with you here as we begin to describe some of the DL research base and then encourage you to both consume and create research through your own inquiries.

As we discuss research in this book, we are going to reference some of the formal research on DL that has been published over the past decades. We think this work has value in documenting and assessing various practices, making space for new ideas to be considered, and comparing classroom work across contexts. But there are a few key points we would like you to remember as you consider this research in relationship to your own work:

- Research is useful but limited. Many topics, disciplines, and contexts have not been explored formally, and there is still much work to be done in a wide array of areas. We want you to know that, in some cases, you may seek research that does not exist yet, and we don't want that to feel discouraging.
- Some research has taken deficit views of the students, schools, and communities that we love and serve. We understand the pain that can come from these presentations. It is okay to skip over such studies or to take only what is useful from them and to ignore the ways that the work does not see the beauty and potential in all communities.
- We would love for you to take a broad view of research, focus on what makes sense, adjust what does not quite fit, and leave aside what does not help you to achieve your goals. DL is still such a new field of inquiry that we don't want you to feel restricted by the boundaries of the relatively small research base. Instead, we want you to feel free to use research in service of improving your own classrooms and schools.
- Formal research is just one source of information. It can be put alongside the vast experience developed by practitioners who have not written about their work. It can be added to the knowledge and experience of your own students to ensure that your instruction becomes more fine-tuned and context specific in ways that help you achieve your own improvement goals. Formal research is powerful, but it is not the only way of knowing what works.
- We think of teachers as experts, with expertise that is different than that of researchers but is expertise nonetheless. You are an expert in your disciplines,

in understanding your context, and in understanding your students. The inquiry work you may do in the course of improving your own instruction will generate new techniques and new ideas, and these insights deserve to be shared. You can share with others from your team, school, district, and beyond. The work you do in these cases is teacher-driven action research worthy of an audience because it can assist others in answering questions similar to the ones you have asked.

We hope that these quick notes are encouraging and provide a sense of how much we respect and learn from teachers' work. We have seen the greatest success in schools where teachers both consult formal research and then systematically study their own classroom-based work as part of continual improvement efforts.[8] Therefore, throughout this book, when we talk about research, we use that term in its broadest sense, including your important classroom experiments.

Having provided this quick overview of how we think about research-based work, we now turn our attention to unpacking DL—what we have learned from formal research and the classrooms of the teachers with whom we've collaborated.

WHAT DO WE MEAN BY *DISCIPLINARY LITERACY*?

Defining Disciplinary Literacy

In 2024, sixteen years after the publication of "Teaching Disciplinary Literacy to Adolescents," more than four hundred articles have been published in peer-reviewed literacy and content-area journals describing DL as a framework for instruction.[9] As part of our own content analysis of the term *disciplinary literacy* in top-tier literacy journals alone, we found a range of definitions.[10] Broadly, researchers define disciplinary literacy as the habits of reading, writing, and communicating that are discipline specific and are used to construct and disseminate knowledge within the disciplines. Most of the articles we reviewed referenced McConachie and Petrosky, Moje, and Shanahan and Shanahan when defining the construct of DL.[11] We have provided a handful of definitions and ways of thinking about DL in table 1.1, just so that you might compare some of the more popular and widely cited characterizations of the concept.

TABLE 1.1   Common definitions and characterizations of disciplinary literacy

Reference	Definition of disciplinary literacy
Shanahan, T., & Shanahan, C. (2008). Teaching Disciplinary Literacy to Adolescents: Rethinking Content-Area Literacy. *Harvard Educational Review*, 8(1), 40–59.	"Specialized reading routines and language uses . . . literacy skills specialized to history, science, mathematics, literature, or other subject matter" (p. 44).
McConachie, S. M., & Petrosky, T. (2010). *Content Matters: A Disciplinary Literacy Approach to Improving Student Learning*. John Wiley & Sons.	"A discipline's content and habits of thinking always go hand in hand. Habits of thinking occur in disciplinary ways of reading, writing, reasoning, and talking. So the big questions for schooling have to do with the ways in which teaching in the core disciplines supports students as they work on problems situated in the content and habits of thinking of the disciplines" (pp. 6–7).
Shanahan, T., & Shanahan, C. (2012). What is Disciplinary Literacy and Why Does It Matter? *Topics in Language Disorders*, 32(1), 7–18.	"Disciplinary literacy . . . is an emphasis on the knowledge and abilities possessed by those who create, communicate, and use knowledge within the discipline" (p. 8).
Moje, E. B. (2015). Doing and Teaching Disciplinary Literacy with Adolescent Learners: A Social and Cultural Enterprise *Harvard Educational Review*, 85(2), 254–278.	"To teach disciplinary literacy, teachers need to involve learners in inquiry that allows the learner to gain insight into how questions are asked and examined and how conclusions are drawn, supported, communicated, contested, and defended" (p. 257).
Rainey, E. C., Maher, B. L., Coupland, D., Franchi, R., & Moje, E. B. (2018). But What Does It Look Like? Illustrations of Disciplinary Literacy Teaching in Two Content Areas. *Journal of Adolescent & Adult Literacy*, 61(4), 371–379.	"Disciplinary literacy practices are shared language and symbolic tools that members of academic disciplines (e.g., biology, philosophy, musical theater, architecture and design, psychology) use to construct knowledge alongside others. All disciplinarians engage in cycles of inquiry that enable knowledge production; inquiry includes articulating questions or problems for pursuit, investigating those questions using discipline-specific methods, communicating results of investigations to specific audiences, and evaluating one's own claims and those of others" (p. 371).

Note that many popular definitions of DL share a few common themes:

- Advanced literacy skills are needed to create and share knowledge within and across the academic disciplines and their related professions (e.g., the study of biology as a disciplinary field in college or graduate school and later specialized professional work as a marine biologist).

- Students need to be inducted into various disciplinary discourse communities, each of which includes specialized vocabulary, written genres, norms for communication, and standards for inclusion or exclusion.
- DL instruction is about more than just teaching advanced reading skills. It is about supporting students in acquiring and flexibly using specialized vocabulary and language structures; acquiring and using specialized reading, writing, and communication skills; and acquiring and creating knowledge with an awareness of the sociocultural norms of the discipline (e.g., while mathematicians might write poems to share their latest proofs, they would be doing so with the understanding that this practice is an exception to the historical norm of publishing new mathematical discoveries in peer-reviewed journals).

Interestingly, fewer than a dozen articles in our original content analysis included a critical element in their definition, with DL pedagogies being used to question existing disciplinary boundaries and norms.[12] While more researchers have begun considering a critical element to DL since 2020, our findings still suggest that few researchers and authors have focused on evaluating, critiquing, or changing the nature of the disciplines through participation in DL instructional work. Given this gap, we would like to push the field by adding a fourth theme that we see as emerging and quite powerful:

- DL instructional frameworks can nudge students beyond mere apprenticeship into existing disciplinary communities and cultures; they can be used to critique and reframe existing disciplinary communities. If carefully introduced, a critical DL instructional framework can help students see, understand, adopt, and eventually change the norms within any disciplinary subculture. Such instruction can expand students' notions of who may be included in each discipline, what counts as knowledge, and which modes of representation and communication are valued. In this way, a critical DL framework can provide students with the tools they need to continually question, reframe, remix, and remake disciplinary boundaries. We might even go so far as to say that DL instructional work offers one of the greatest potential pathways to creating more equitable and just classrooms, workplaces, and societies.

Building upon our content analysis and how the teachers with whom we have worked talk about DL, we therefore define DL instruction within this book as follows:

- DL is the intentional apprenticeship of students into the specialized ways of reading, writing, thinking, and communicating associated with both academic disciplines and their related professions.
- Effective DL instruction offers students opportunities to apprentice themselves into particular disciplinary communities by
  - acquiring and generating knowledge in discipline-specific ways
  - engaging in authentic inquiry using the particular habits of mind and norms of practice associated with each discipline
  - uncovering and practicing the linguistic and cultural norms associated with particular discourse communities
  - reading, sharing, and producing texts and artifacts in discipline-specific genres and modalities
- Ultimately, DL and critical DL instruction hold the potential to also help students question, critique, and change the norms of disciplinary subcultures, making room for ever-more-inclusive ways of creating and communicating disciplinary knowledge.

While this definition is long, we intentionally include text, task, student, and cultural elements that all foreshadow the model of DL inquiry and instruction introduced in chapter 2. This definition and model guide the rest of the inquiry and instruction stories and recommendations throughout this book.

If you are interested in reading more of the literature on DL, we recommend looking at appendix A, "Further Reading on Disciplinary Literacy." However, for you to more fully understand DL as a frame for teaching and learning, it is critical to review some of our core beliefs about DL as an instructional approach. These beliefs are grounded in both emerging research and our own experiences working with teachers across grade levels.

OUR CORE BELIEFS ABOUT DISCIPLINARY LITERACY WORK

Disciplinary Literacy Instruction Is Not the Same as Content-Area Literacy Instruction

Existing definitions of DL, and the common themes that arise from them, often contrast sharply with previous definitions and practices related to content-area literacy instruction. As a field of inquiry and practice, content-area literacy has existed for over a hundred years and focuses on students' acquisition and application of general reading comprehension strategies across disciplines to support reading and writing.[13] The focus, as you might have guessed from the term "content-area literacy," is squarely on general literacy skills that help students acquire content knowledge.[14] Shanahan and Shanahan reframed some of this cognitive work as "intermediate literacy," or the understanding and use of general comprehension strategies, such as inferencing, questioning, summarizing, and visualizing, all-purpose strategies that indeed may be acquired by students in late elementary and middle school.[15] These "intermediate" strategies, they argued, could be useful to a point but would not ultimately help students master the truly advanced and specialized ways of communicating within academic disciplines and professions.

Thus, we see the introduction of DL instruction into K–12 teachers' repertoires as a both-and rather than an either-or proposition. We compare disciplinary with content-area literacy simply to suggest why a DL approach is so important now, in the twenty-first century, as college and workplace demands, evolving educational standards, and increasingly thorny global problems (e.g., climate change, global pandemics, economic and social inequities) call for a very different way of engaging in literacy teaching and learning activities in schools.[16] See table 1.2 for a detailed comparison of disciplinary and content-area literacy.

We argue throughout this book that educators need to add a layer of DL instruction to a strong foundation of content-area literacy instruction to best support students' advanced literacy work in high school, college, and beyond.[17] Notably, DL instruction can begin in the very early grades, and the layering of basic, intermediate, and DL instructional practices can ripple throughout a student's K–12 education.

While the differences between content-area literacy and DL instructional models may seem subtle at first, they have far-reaching implications for both how teachers make sense of their roles in classrooms and how students see themselves as budding artists, authors, historians, mathematicians, musicians, scientists, and more.

Layering Disciplinary Instruction with Intermediate and Basic Literacy Instruction Is Key

In their 2012 article "What Is Disciplinary Literacy and Why Does It Matter?," Shanahan and Shanahan state, "The major premise of content area reading proponents has been that the cognitive requirements of learning and interpreting any

TABLE 1.2   Comparing content-area literacy with disciplinary literacy

Content-area literacy instruction . . .	Disciplinary literacy instruction . . .
Highlights and privileges foundational underlying cognitive processes (e.g., making connections, inferencing, summarizing, visualizing, and so on) that may be similar across disciplines	Highlights the specialized ways of reading, writing, and communicating unique to each discipline
Introduces general comprehension strategies that can be applied across content-area and disciplinary boundaries	Utilizes interactive approaches to reading and writing to help support students in adopting the habits of mind and ways of working associated with each disciplinary subfield
Supports the effective reading of text-books and pedagogical materials used primarily in schools	Supports the effective reading of primary sources and age-appropriate authentic texts valued by each disciplinary community
Values text primarily as a source of information to be learned	Values text primarily as a model for how experts create, share, and use knowledge in the discipline
Focuses on the instruction of general academic language for wide reading success	Focuses on both general academic language and more specialized vocabulary and grammatical features associated with each discipline
Focuses on the acquisition of content-area knowledge	Focuses on authentic inquiry and the creation and use of knowledge in discipline-specific ways

kind of text are pretty much the same, no matter what the subject matter."[18] Therefore, it follows that if the requirements of reading any text are fundamentally similar, then all students would be well served by learning intermediate comprehension strategies, such as predicting, visualizing, connecting, questioning, and so on. They continue, "For the past couple of decades, research has been revealing that disciplines differ extensively in their fundamental purposes, specialized genres, symbolic artifacts, traditions of communication, evaluation standards of quality and precision, and use of language."[19] Given emerging research into the specialized ways of reading, writing, and communicating in the disciplines, a new focus on DL across grade levels *in addition to* intermediate and all-purpose comprehension strategies makes a great deal of sense.

To clarify, we are not suggesting that the teaching of basic or intermediate literacy skills should be jettisoned in exchange for a sole focus on discipline-specific instruction. Instead, having followed teacher teams working on DL instruction, we recommend a layering of literacy instruction.[20] We have seen effective teams of high school teachers toggle back and forth between intermediate comprehension instruction and more discipline-specific work. Similarly, one would expect that elementary teachers would toggle between basic, intermediate, and DL instruction. This layering is intentional and necessary to meet an ever-widening variety of student needs. This is perhaps even more true now than ever before, as teachers across grade levels seek to meet the needs of multilingual students, students with neurodivergent cognitive profiles, and all students who experienced disrupted schooling experiences during the COVID-19 pandemic.

DL work and understanding grow over the K–12 grade span, with students slowly developing the academic language, ways of working, and habits of mind that are increasingly specialized and specific to each discipline. At the elementary level, students might still be learning to decode or comprehend complex text while simultaneously learning to make meaning of an age-appropriate science article, given the particular discipline-specific style of the article. At the middle or high school level, this layering might entail the shoring up of foundational skills, such as summarizing and predicting, while simultaneously pushing forward with more complex reading skills, such as corroboration, sourcing, and contextualizing in a history class.

Therefore, we encourage you to look for strategies and vignettes throughout this book that push your thinking about how to interweave and layer basic, intermediate, and disciplinary literacies into your everyday instruction, regardless of your grade level or subject area focus.

Disciplinary Literacy Is for More Than Just Adolescents

While DL instruction has most often been conceptualized as appropriate for adolescents and adults, an increasing number of researchers and teachers are seeing value in DL work beginning in the earliest grades.[21] In our own work with teachers across districts, we have seen a wide variety of effective DL instructional practices across K–12 classrooms; therefore, in this book, we take the approach that DL instruction can and should be a component of instructional work starting in kindergarten.

As represented in figure 1.1, we see the earliest grade levels focusing primarily on what Shanahan and Shanahan term *basic literacy skills*: phonics,

FIGURE 1.1   **Disciplinary literacy instructional focus across the grades**

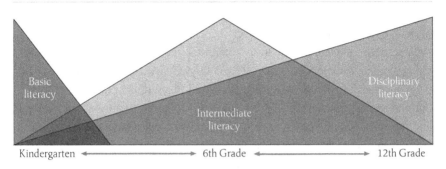

decoding skills, basic comprehension work, reading fluency, and so on.[22] How-ever, while this might be the primary focus of instruction at these grade levels, we see great value in teachers beginning to introduce some intermediate com-prehension strategies, such as making predictions, summarizing, and question-ing. For anyone who has met a kindergartner, you are fully aware that five- and six-year-olds love to predict and ask questions. These skills can be fostered and shaped.

We believe that DL ways of thinking and working can also be taught in age-appropriate ways as early as kindergarten. Throughout this book, we share exam-ples of classroom instruction in which young students are asked to begin thinking, reading, and writing like authors, historians, mathematicians, scien-tists, and so on, in order to adopt habits that can later be refined and shaped in middle and high school. Ultimately, we see the focus on DL growing steadily across grade levels, with intermediate skill instruction peaking during the middle school years and then tapering toward the end of high school.

To be clear, we are not expecting kindergartners to suddenly become sophis-ticated microbiologists, but it is important to increase the rigor in how students are engaging in disciplinary tasks, with disciplinary texts and artifacts, across all grade levels. For example, our youngest learners can practice the skills of close observation and description used by scientists.[23] Practicing these skills and then communicating what they observe with great detail through writing, speaking, or drawing embodies the type of DL work that can be found in a kindergarten classroom.

Disciplinary Literacy Is About More Than Knowledge Acquisition

Moje is right to point out that an effective DL instructional framework must consider students' developing identities–identities as students, as citizens, as social beings, and as knowledge creators.[24] Each disciplinary subculture prizes specific ways in which knowledge is created and shared. Playwrights, chemists, historians, mathematicians, musicians, and so on each touch on some truths about the world and the human condition; they each generate knowledge and share it in quite different forms. Therefore, we need to be careful when adopting and promoting DL instructional frameworks so that we are not just focusing on passive apprenticeship or receptive uptake of content-area facts and figures.

An effective DL instructional framework can help students try on different identities as poets, dancers, musicians, biologists, Americanists, statisticians, and so on, both to discover and to hone their own voices and to eventually reshape the boundaries of those identities and fields to be more inclusive and diverse. As we have begun to write about elsewhere, a *critical* DL framework may be needed to support both teachers and students in developing identities and practices that move beyond historic notions of disciplinary norms and boundaries.

Moving forward, to create a more just and equitable future, we need a critical DL framework to both apprentice students into the disciplines and to prepare them to question and reframe those disciplines over time. Ultimately, students need more than just a toolbox of graphic organizers or rote instructional strategies; they need tools to create within, question, and sometimes dismantle the disciplines as traditionally conceived.

Disciplinary Literacy Is More Than Strategy Instruction—It Requires Cultural Work

Elizabeth Moje further defines DL by focusing on sociocultural elements. Moje writes:

> This conceptualization of disciplines as cultures or discourse communities draws attention to the need to help youth learn to navigate from their home, community, and national cultural practices and discourses to and from those disciplines they are expected to learn in school. Disciplines are highly specialized–and fairly exclusive–cultural groups,

and just as one has to learn the conventions and practices of a new culture, so does one have to learn the conventions and practices of a discipline.[25]

By framing DL instruction as the teaching of "cultures or discourse communities," Moje further enriches our thinking about how DL instruction must move beyond intermediate and all-purpose comprehension instruction toward instructional experiences that help students adopt and eventually adapt the languages, genres, and modalities prized by each professional disciplinary community. This provides space for students to develop identities as participants in various communities, beyond simply adopting and using the literacy strategies of those communities.

For many students, and particularly multilingual students, students of color, neurodivergent students, and others who have been historically minoritized, DL may provide a powerful avenue for trying on and creating new personal and professional identities. As we have seen firsthand, it is one thing to de-level a traditional high school system of tracked, hierarchical classes. It is a completely different endeavor to provide students across classes with opportunities to see themselves as future artists, authors, mathematicians, musicians, scientists, and so on. This is cultural and identity work, and it can and should be part of excellent DL instruction.

Disciplinary Literacy Supports Equity and Social Justice Work

As we have engaged in DL work across districts, we have received some feedback from educators and educational leaders suggesting that DL may be all well and good for wealthy, majority-White suburban school districts with lots of resources—but that it's not an effective approach for majority-minority urban schools trying to increase standardized test scores. We could not disagree more strongly. We have seen, and continue to advocate for, a DL approach for all students in service of equity and opportunity for youth across all racial, linguistic, socioeconomic, gender, and cultural boundaries. If we were to deny particular students in certain communities or of certain backgrounds access to discipline-specific literacy instruction, we would be perpetuating inequalities that have already led to majority-White professions and institutions of higher education. We see DL instruction across all grades and all schools as a way to begin changing the (literal) face of professions and universities and thus the way that they fundamentally operate. This is the very foundation of what we have come to term "critical disciplinary literacy" in our latest work.

Disciplinary Literacy Teaching and Learning Requires Both Adult and Student Learning

Finally, through our research on DL professional learning over the past fifteen years, we have come to understand that effective DL instruction is the product of ongoing and interconnected adult and student learning.[26] All too often in schools, we make the incorrect assumption that students are the ones who need to do all the learning. In fact, what we have seen is that students are better equipped as learners when the adults in a school (both teachers and leaders) are actively, collaboratively, and publicly learning as well.[27] When teachers are engaged in self-reflective inquiry work focused on how best to reveal the ways of working and thinking in their respective disciplines, students see not only models of how to work as a mathematician or scientist but also models of how to become lifelong learners. This is why we have framed the rest of this book around professional learning that is *collaborative, founded in inquiry,* and *guided.* Thus, our framework is designed to support robust DL inquiry and instructional work across grades K–12.

OKAY, DISCIPLINARY LITERACY SOUNDS GREAT . . . NOW WHAT?

A Glimpse of the Rest of the Book

Having reviewed some of the basic ways that we have come to understand DL in chapter 1, we now move into chapter 2, where we outline our framework for DL inquiry and instruction. In chapter 2, and throughout this book, we argue that to effectively teach DL, educators must focus first on their own professional learning and inquiry so that they may then design and lead authentic DL experiences for their students.

The framework outlined in chapter 2 explains how DL inquiry and instruction can productively focus on texts, tasks, students, and sociocultural contexts. We then illustrate our framework across the next four chapters (chapters 3–6) at the core of the book. Each of these core chapters illustrates how collaborative inquiry cycles of professional learning can focus alternately on texts, tasks, students, and culture and can guide both adult inquiry and instruction for students.

Finally, we end with three chapters focused respectively on: leadership and contextual factors to consider when engaging in DL work (chapter 7); extended cases of how to design and implement professional learning to support DL work (chapter 8); and a final exploration of how DL inquiry and instructional work has fundamentally changed our own practice and how, we believe, it can lead to promoting equity and social justice for all (chapter 9).

At the end of each chapter, we provide guided opportunities for readers to pause and reflect on the content presented and suggestions for how to try out the ideas from the chapter in different school settings. At the end of each inquiry and instruction core chapter (chapters 3–6), we also provide explicit connections to the International Literacy Association's *Standards for the Preparation of Literacy Professionals 2017.*[28] We talk a bit more about these standards in chapter 2.

Finally, we offer here a quick note on specific language choices we have made in this book. Throughout, we use the gender-neutral pronouns "they," "them," and "their" to refer to individual teachers and students. Additionally, we interchangeably use the terms "English learners" (ELs) and "multilingual learners" across this book to refer to students who are learning English as an additional language. In specific vignettes contributed by teachers, we retain the language that teachers have used to speak about this population (and others), to honor their voices and particular contexts.

PAUSE AND REFLECT

- After reading chapter 1, how would you define "disciplinary literacy" for yourself, your classroom, and your school?
- What big differences do you see between a DL approach and a content-area literacy approach to instruction?
- In what ways could the layering of basic, intermediate, and disciplinary literacy instructional practices best support various learners in your classes? How could adopting an additional layer of critical DL support your students in questioning or even redefining historical disciplinary boundaries?

- Which units, lessons, or activities have you already tried that seem to focus more on DL? How did it go? What are you hoping to learn and try as a result of reading this book?

TRY IT OUT

- On your own, or with a colleague, take a look at a unit, lesson, or activity recently completed. What would it look like to shift that unit/lesson/activity toward DL instruction or to weave in DL instruction?
- Select one or two of the resources mentioned in this chapter or from appendix A, "Further Reading on Disciplinary Literacy." Read the text(s) alone or with colleagues and select one or two ideas to test out in your classroom or school. What happened as a result of your experiment?

CHAPTER **2**

Learning to Teach Disciplinary Literacy

Connecting Inquiry and Instruction

Having led many teacher workshops, graduate courses, and ongoing professional learning experiences about disciplinary literacy (DL), we consistently hear from teachers some version of the following: "Disciplinary literacy sounds good—just tell us how to do it!" If only it were that simple.

Like many complex instructional practices, learning to teach DL requires more than a technical change.[1] A technical change is one in which both the problem and solution are clearly defined and well known. This does not mean that making technical changes is easy. For example, adopting and using a well-researched phonics program in an elementary school may be a technical change; however, it could still take more than a year of dedicated and collective effort to achieve anticipated results because of the complex nature of the endeavor.

Disciplinary literacy, as a newer area of research and set of instructional practices, is less well understood than other areas of literacy research and instruction, such as vocabulary or phonics. As a result, learning to teach DL requires teachers to tackle an adaptive change.[2] An adaptive change is necessary when a dilemma is less well defined and may have no clear solution. Invention and adaptation are therefore necessary. Undertaking the work of adaptive change requires us to question fundamental assumptions, let go of familiar patterns, and engage in deep learning in order to come to new ways of thinking and working.

All too often in schools, we tend to characterize all changes as technical, when really many educational dilemmas require adaptive learning and change, if not larger reinvention.[3] For example, some school communities, when trying to meet the needs of a rapidly expanding population of English learners, simply provide teachers with workshops on general comprehension and vocabulary strategies. While this may be a necessary part of the work (a first step of sorts), it is ultimately a technical solution to an adaptive challenge, and it is unlikely to be sufficient in effectively supporting a wide range of English learners. More than likely, a great deal of adult learning is needed—surfacing and reframing cultural assumptions, understanding and shifting traditional patterns of classroom discussion, sharing and honoring all students' linguistic communities and traditions, and so on—in order to truly begin meeting students' needs.

Learning to teach disciplinary literacy is a similar adaptive challenge. It requires a great deal of adult learning, individually and collectively. As we have argued before, we believe that truly effective DL instruction is the result of collaborative inquiry led by teacher leaders within professional learning communities.[4] When teachers are able to pose questions about their practice, investigate potential solutions, and pilot and assess new practices together, they are well positioned to make meaningful and lasting changes in classroom instruction that also bolster student learning.

To underscore the connections between adult and student learning that support DL work, we have written this book to focus on the ways that adult inquiry can lead to productive classroom instruction. In this way, we offer a way forward for teachers hungry to bring DL work into their classrooms. We don't offer silver-bullet solutions or page after page of tips and tricks. Instead, we invite teachers reading this book to ask their own questions, to investigate their own disciplinary habits of mind and ways of working, and to design and pilot their own context-specific DL practices.

In this book, we provide research-based frameworks, guiding questions and examples, and lots of stories from teachers who have already walked this path. Ultimately, this is a book for educators who want to take ownership of their own learning, alongside like-minded colleagues, and bring disciplinary literacy to life in their schools.

While we understand all too well the natural instinct to treat disciplinary literacy as a technical set of strategies that can simply be adopted and quickly put to use, what we offer instead is a framework that will lead educators to a deeper, longer-lasting, and more context-specific set of practices. We provide here the tools to undertake adaptive change. Let's begin by turning to the two powerful models that support our inquiry and instruction framework.

A MODEL OF READING THAT CAN GUIDE DISCIPLINARY LITERACY INQUIRY AND INSTRUCTION

Just as the new millennium was beginning, the RAND Corporation brought together world-renowned literacy researchers and scholars and tasked them with collaboratively illustrating the reading comprehension process, given all that was known at the time about the cognitive and sociocultural components of reading. This RAND Reading Study Group met, discussed many competing models, and ultimately crafted the seminal white paper *Reading for Understanding: Toward an R&D Program in Reading Comprehension.*[5] In this paper, the authors shared a simple model, arguing that every instance of reading comprehension could be characterized as the interaction of a particular reader, engaged in a particular reading activity or task, with a particular text, all within a particular sociocultural context (see figure 2.1). And while newer models of reading comprehension have emerged in recent years that explain reading comprehension in interesting and nuanced ways (e.g., the Active View of Reading Model, Duke and Cartwright), the RAND model still captures the highly interactive and context-dependent process of meaning-making in a simple and highly functional form that directly connects to how teachers might approach change in their own classrooms.[6] Our work in schools has shown us that the RAND model is an effective change model for teachers to consider as they work to implement DL, which we describe in more detail here.

Many educators have used the RAND model to make sense of when and why a lesson involving a literacy task may not have worked so well with students. The model prompts us to reflect on the nature of the "text" being read: Is it too complex? Does it contain a great deal of unfamiliar vocabulary, complex grammar, or abstract content? Is the text a traditional book, or a nontraditional text, such as an online article, a series of images, a multimodal text, a graphic novel, or even a

FIGURE 2.1 **RAND model of reading comprehension**

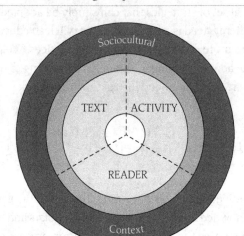

Source: Originally printed in RRSG, 2002, p. xiv.

three-dimensional artifact that students are being asked to "read." The model then focuses us on the reading, writing, or disciplinary literacy task at hand: Is this a school-based assignment or pleasure reading? Is there pressure to read on a certain time schedule? Is this reading simply a step along the way to completing another task, such as writing an argumentative essay? Is writing student-generated or prompted and scaffolded more clearly by the teacher? The model then reminds us to consider each student's individual funds of knowledge, life experiences, reading history, and motivation. Is the student interested in the text and motivated to engage with it? Does the student have prior experience reading or writing this kind of text? Finally, the model prompts us to consider all of the sociocultural factors at play for a student. In what time and place was the text created, and in what time and place is the student engaging with the text? Does the text mirror any aspects of the student's life? Does the student identify with the language, culture, and ideas in the text? How familiar or foreign to the student are the worldviews, assumptions, and biases embedded in the text? All of these sociocultural factors influence how a student may make sense of the text. See table 2.1 for common questions that emerge when considering each domain within the RAND model.

Given these prompts and questions, we have found the RAND model to be effective at helping us tease apart factors when a student is struggling or

TABLE 2.1   Questions about reading that emerge from the RAND model

Text-focused questions

How complex is the vocabulary in the text?

How complicated are the grammar and syntax?

Is the text informational or narrative?

Does the text follow a traditional structure?

How clear is the text structure?

How long is the text?

Is the text digital or in print?

Task-focused questions

Did the student choose the text, or was it assigned by a teacher?

Is the text being read in school or outside of school?

Is there a time limit or deadline for completing the reading?

Is the student reading alone or with a partner or group?

Must the student read the entire text to complete the task?

Is the student being asked to read in order to write?

Student-focused questions

What do we know about the student's reading history?

Which languages does the student speak, read, and/or write?

What is the student interested in, and does this text match those interests?

How old is the student?

How does the student identify (race, language, culture, gender, sexual orientation, and so on)?

What do we know about the student's home life and in-school peer group?

Sociocultural context-focused questions

Which multiple identities does the student bring to the table when engaging with the text?

Which of the student's many identities (race, language, culture, gender, sexual orientation, and so on) are represented in the text, and which are absent or challenged?

What identities and experiences are represented within the school context in which the text is being read?

In what time and place is the text being read, and how does that context shape the reader's understanding of the text?

succeeding as a reader, writer, and learner. Now, as we turn our attention to DL and connecting adult learning with classroom instruction, we have found a new and important use for the model.

In our work with teacher teams on inquiring into and designing DL instructional routines, Christina first noticed that the teachers were often following similar thought patterns. The teachers were asking questions and designing instruction related to the four main components of the RAND model, because they were likely to think of one of the four pieces of the model as something they could understand better and potentially change.

We went back through our field notes and descriptions of teachers' collaborative inquiry work, and we found a distinct pattern of inquiry that led us to believe that the RAND model may be an excellent guide for teachers wondering where to start their own investigations into disciplinary literacy work. As a result, now when we work with teachers and teams on DL instruction, we explicitly prompt them to begin their investigations in one of the four RAND domains. We ask them to first consider texts, tasks, students, or culture as a starting place. We prompt them to ask questions, design instruction, and reflect on one domain at a time and then to slowly connect domains as they become more confident in their work. In this way, teachers can focus their investigations and resulting instructional designs primarily on text-, task-, student-, or culture-focused questions.

However, to truly bring to life this process of investigation and instructional design, we need to interweave another powerful process—the inquiry cycle. The inquiry cycle process is what connects adult professional inquiry with the design, implementation, and refinement of related instructional practice. Like our framework for DL inquiry and instruction, it is collaborative, grounded in inquiry, and guided.

INQUIRY AND INSTRUCTION AS PART OF THE SAME CYCLICAL PROCESS

Collaborative inquiry can be a powerful engine to drive both disciplinary literacy investigations and instruction.[7] Teacher inquiry work has long been known to be one of the ways in which individuals and teacher teams investigate and then design context-specific instruction to meet students' educational needs.[8] While inquiry work can take many forms, we have adopted the five-step model shown in figure 2.2 as the basis for our thinking about individual and team-based

FIGURE 2.2   **Steps in an inquiry cycle**

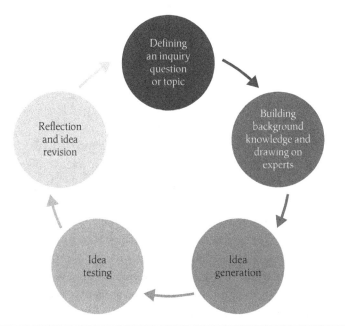

Source: Adapted from Dobbs, Ippolito, and Charner-Laird, *Investigating Disciplinary Literacy* (2017), p. 35. Reprinted with permission of Harvard Education Press.

engagement in inquiry cycles. We explain each of these phases of inquiry briefly in the following sections.

Defining an Inquiry Question or Topic

Defining an inquiry question or topic is perhaps one of the most important phases of inquiry work. Often an idea for inquiry comes directly from a classroom dilemma. The dilemma may focus on a surprising student response to instruction, patterns of student behavior, or the identification of instructional practices that don't seem to be meeting students' needs. In this early phase of inquiry, a topic such as "promoting mathematical discussion" or "supporting students in asking more rigorous questions in science classes" may be turned into productive inquiry questions simply by adding a "How can we …" to the beginning of the topic at hand. The result is an inquiry question that guides investigation and design work, such as "How can we promote mathematical discussion?" A question such as this is broad enough to allow for multiple entry points, suggesting investigations into the literature on topics ranging from classroom talk and mathematical discussions to teacher-student and student-student discussion routines, and so on. However, the question is also narrow enough to allow for a deeper investigation of just a few territories, as opposed to trying to tackle all aspects of reading, writing, and communication at once.

Building Background Knowledge and Drawing on Experts

After having defined an inquiry question, individuals and teams can begin investigating their question through multiple simultaneous means. Teachers may begin reading research and practice literature related to their topic. They may reach out to veteran teachers in their building or across their district to learn more about others' practices. They might consult experts in the field, either in person (if locally available) or online through social media, email, online modules, or webinars. Sometimes, depending on available funding and school professional learning structures, a group of teachers may gather formally in a series of workshops or a summer institute focused on the inquiry area at hand. Alternately, a group of teachers may gather informally in a book study group or to collectively read through a series of journal articles that touch on the topic at hand. Regardless of the mode of inquiry, this phase of the process is focused on gathering information, sifting and sorting findings in search of what may work in a particular context, and doing a bit of early translation work to begin adapting existing ideas and practices into context-specific routines.

Note that sometimes the exact inquiry question or topic chosen (e.g., DL assessments in biology) may not be immediately accessible through a slew of journal articles or stack of existing books. This is often the case in DL inquiry cycles where discipline-specific questions are asked. In these cases, we recommend two things:

1. Teachers may choose an inquiry focus that is a bit broader (e.g., effective assessments in science classes) as a way to start their inquiry, knowing full well that they will eventually need to do a bit more tailoring of the discovered strategies to fit their needs.
2. Teachers may choose multiple adjacent topics to investigate and then focus on synthesizing their findings (e.g., effective assessment practices, different types of science assessments, discipline-specific skills needed in the field of biology).

In these ways, teachers can still focus their inquiry without fretting that their specific topic has not been thoroughly explored yet in the research and practice literature.

Idea Generation

This stage of the process is all about brainstorming new instructional practices and routines while keeping in mind the new information gathered, sorted, and synthesized during the previous phase. The idea-generation phase is characterized by what we call the "improv philosophy" of making sure to say, "Yes, *and*..." when kicking around ideas. Instead of immediately shutting down suggestions (from yourself or from others), as can sometimes happen in brainstorming sessions, it is critical here to build momentum and encourage yourself and others to say, "Yes, and..." while thinking about how new practices could be built and layered on top of one another. The "Yes, and..." strategy allows individuals and groups to build on and layer ideas and practices instead of immediately forcing an either/or mentality. This phase of the inquiry should be less about judgment and more about entertaining all possibilities of what new instructional practices may achieve.

Idea Testing

The idea-testing phase of the inquiry and instruction cycle is when teachers, individually or collectively, try out new ideas in their classrooms. While this sounds straightforward, there are several important suggestions we give teachers during this phase. First, we encourage teachers to document their classroom experiments so that they can more accurately reflect on the efficacy of their new practice. Without some form of documentation, teachers run the risk of not being objective enough about classroom interactions to determine whether a new practice is worth keeping or is better modified or abandoned.

Documentation can be done in one's own classroom or in pairs or groups when teachers document each other's practices through observation and feedback cycles. Video recording classroom instruction, taking careful field notes, and gathering student work all support later analysis of the effects of instruction. We also suggest that teachers pilot a new practice for a little while— not just in one class, one time. New practices that involve routines, such as science vocabulary journals, sophisticated mathematical discussions, or identifying sources of bias in primary documents, rarely go smoothly the first time they are attempted. Remember that these are new routines for teachers and students alike. We recommend trying a new practice at least three or four times before stepping back to analyze potential effects.

Finally, we recommend that teachers in this phase of inquiry engage in what photographers call *bracketing*. Photographers will often take the same picture several times, but each time, they will change one factor slightly (e.g., increasing aperture size with each shot, or slowing down the shutter incrementally). In this way, the photographer is able to secure a great shot and will have a better sense of which factors (like aperture size and shutter speed) work best for that particular context. The same can hold true for teachers. When piloting a new practice, teachers can change just one element of the practice or lesson at a time, with the same group of students or with different groups at the secondary level. This allows teachers to discover, in a more fine-tuned way, which parts of the new instructional routine are most and least effective.

Reflection and Idea Revision

Finally, the last phase of inquiry focuses on reflection and the revision of instructional ideas. Again, this may be done individually or as part of a group; however, key to this work is looking back at documentation from the piloting phase and sifting through teacher moves and related evidence of student learning. The reflection phase is when ideas for new practices cohere. Notes and records produced in the idea-testing phase come in handy at this stage for making decisions about how to move forward. For example, if teachers are figuring out how to incorporate vocabulary instruction while teaching hands-on science, their notes about different approaches will be useful as they decide on a practice to build into their ongoing science routines in the classroom. Through the process of reflection, as teachers solidify and clarify new practices, they may look back on the idea-testing phase to ask the following questions:

- Which approaches that I tested seemed most effective?
- Which new practices seemed to most effectively build disciplinary literacy skills for my students?
- Which new practices can I integrate effectively into my instructional approach?

Answers to these questions will depend on which specific measures each teacher is using to judge efficacy, whether formal student assessments (e.g., analysis of student writing, scores on formal or informal tests, and so on) or more subjective teacher analysis of classroom documentation. As one source of support in answering the question "Are my students *doing disciplinary literacy*?," we provide a simple rubric in appendix B.

In addition to considering which new ideas teachers will implement, it is important to consider next steps in the inquiry process. This often involves revising practices, adding a new layer of questions to the inquiry, or deepening new practices that teachers have tried. It is at this point that a series of next step questions can be asked:

- Which new practices do we keep? Which do we abandon?
- Which practices do we modify and continue to test?
- Who else may want to pilot these practices, in or across schools in our district, so that we may better learn about their effects?
- What new inquiries do we wish to engage in, having learned a bit more about this last question or topic?

As may be obvious from figure 2.2, inquiry work is cyclical and never-ending. One inquiry cycle easily begets another. As new ideas are tested, adopted, and adapted, new dilemmas arise and necessitate new inquiry cycles. However, beyond the five main phases of inquiry and instruction outlined here, we also wish to highlight five accompanying structural elements that influence the shape and outcomes of inquiry work:

- focus of inquiry
- duration
- intensity
- individual versus collaborative inquiry
- facilitation

Let's look at each of these elements individually.

STRUCTURAL ELEMENTS THAT INFLUENCE INQUIRY WORK

Focus of Inquiry: Choosing, Shifting, and Layering over Time

Some teachers and teams worry about choosing a particular inquiry focus or question. What if they choose the *wrong question*? In these cases, we remind teachers that inquiry work is iterative and layered. There is never a wrong question, only questions that lead to other questions.

Instead, we invite teachers to consider sequencing inquiry work in an order that helps them consider which areas of teaching and learning are just within reach, which feel further away, and which feel a bit scary. We sometimes encourage teachers to create a three-column chart with columns labeled "Initial Inquiries," "Inquiries for Later This Year," and "Inquiries for Next Year." Mapping out potential inquiries in this way reinforces the idea that you *can* do it all…just not *all at once*. It is a nice way to ease anxiety, and it can also solve potential disagreements among team members by allowing for commitment to certain inquiry cycles later in the year.

Another method is to carefully consider which of the RAND model domains (texts, tasks, students, culture) teachers and teams feel that they can genuinely influence. A team of teachers tackling science instruction with required texts may not feel that they have much influence in choosing new books or lab experiments; however, they may begin inquiry work by delving into the specific reading, writing, and discussion tasks that are assigned alongside those texts and labs. In this way, teachers can choose appropriate inquiry topics that feel productive and actionable, as opposed to immediately facing roadblocks related to limited resources, school or district mandates, and so on.

Take time to map out for yourself or your team a series of inquiry topics at the beginning of the school year, and then, when the time is right, you will have a menu of related but new topics to delve into.

Duration of Inquiry: Maintaining Momentum

Inquiry cycles can vary a great deal in terms of length of time. Moreover, the component steps of inquiry can each vary, with some steps taking a single day (e.g., choosing a focus question) and others taking weeks or months (e.g., idea testing). Here, we simply want to say that each teacher and team should openly discuss the planned duration of a particular inquiry cycle, stay flexible about that timing, and keep checking in to make sure that the work feels productive. Maintaining momentum is important. When momentum wanes, it is often time to ask, "Should we move on to the next step?" or "Has this cycle run its course?"

We have seen teachers engage in as many as five or six inquiry cycles per academic year, moving quickly and with enthusiasm from topic to topic and question to question. We have also seen teachers focus on just one area of inquiry across an entire year, delving deeply into a rich territory, such as disciplinary and interdisciplinary discussion routines. One suggestion we give to teachers is to think of a pie chart made of two pieces, one piece representing enthusiasm and one exhaustion. As the exhaustion piece grows, there will come a tipping point when it probably makes sense to move on from a particular inquiry cycle to another question or topic. Sometimes teachers feel reluctant to move on because they feel like they haven't completely plumbed the depths of a topic or instructional area. In this case, we still recommend moving on and then circling back to the same topic or inquiry cycle at a later date, rather than hitting a wall of exhaustion and losing interest in engaging in the inquiry and instruction work altogether.

Intensity of Inquiry: Regulating the Heat

Different teachers engage in inquiry with different levels of intensity. Some want to investigate, generate new ideas, and test those new ideas all within a single week. Others wish to spend a lot more time investigating and brainstorming—weeks or months—before they bring fully formed new practices into their classrooms. Either model can work, although we do urge teachers to *just try it* more often than not, as we have found that overly long deliberations rarely result in significantly more effective practices.

We nod to the work of Heifetz, Grashow, and Linsky once again and their notion of "regulating the heat."[9] This is a simple phrase we use with teachers to remind them that they have the ability, in many inquiry cases, to intensify the work (i.e., turn up the heat) by speeding up the investigation, generation, and testing phases of the work and by changing large-scale aspects of instruction. They also possess the ability to slow down (i.e., turn down the heat), fall back on tried-and-true methods, and tackle microchanges as opposed to wholesale shifts. Whenever teachers find themselves anxious or frustrated within inquiry cycles, we remind them that they can regulate the heat for themselves.

Individual Versus Collaborative Inquiry: The Pros and Cons of Collaboration

To be totally transparent—we have a strong, research-based inclination toward collaborative inquiry, and we continue to highlight collaboration as a core component of DL inquiry and instructional work across the various cases in this book.[10] We have seen the power of collaborative inquiry transform DL instruction across teams and schools. However, we also recognize that collaborative inquiry is not always possible or necessarily productive across all contexts. Therefore, we want to clearly state that all of the inquiry ideas presented in this book are also adopt-able by individual teachers. The rhythm of the work may feel a little different, but the outcomes of the inquiry and instruction work can be similar–new DL prac-tices that are context specific.

Like anything, the choice of working together in teams versus alone has trade-offs with advantages and disadvantages that we want to acknowledge, despite our thinking that collaboration can be particularly effective. The process of inquiry work in teams can be impactful and important, but it requires material resources, such as time and shared space, administrative support, and the capacity to col-laborate as a group. It can become a space with conflict or lack of engagement if enthusiasm wanes or other initiatives encroach. Working on inquiry alone can have benefits, such as the autonomy to make quick and personalized decisions, but it can also make more work for an individual when surveying the research base and tackling other larger tasks (e.g., analyzing resulting student work). But regardless of the potential drawbacks, in many cases, working independently on inquiry is the only option available in some schools, and we definitely think it is a better option than not doing the work at all.

A final note on this point–in chapter 8, we present multiple extended compos-ite cases drawn from our work with schools to demonstrate how both groups and individuals/pairs of educators can successfully move through cycles of inquiry and related DL professional learning in various configurations. We offer those cases as illustrations of the multiple paths to success in DL professional learning.

Facilitation of Inquiry: The Power of Teacher Leadership to Guide Inquiry Work

If engaging in collaborative inquiry, we strongly recommend that one of the teach-ers in the group takes the role of facilitator or team leader. By designating a facili-tator, a point-person to help guide colleagues through inquiry and instructional work, you increase your chances of keeping the group on track, of holding on to new knowledge over time, and of spreading new practices farther into adjacent classrooms and schools.[11] Facilitators can help to create and facilitate consistent agendas, and they can easily connect with other facilitators of nearby inquiry groups and teams to compare notes. We also find that facilitators can support the documentation of inquiry work and regular communication with school admin-istration. If you choose not to designate a single facilitator, we recommend that each member of a group take on different specific roles, such that important work isn't overlooked (e.g., documentation, creation of materials to share with other teams, and so on).

COMBINING MODELS INTO A NEW FRAMEWORK: WHERE THE MAGIC LIES

Clearly inquiry is a core and critical part of our DL inquiry and instruction framework. However, the real magic can be found when teachers and teams focus their inquiry work using the RAND model as a starting place. When teams and individuals iteratively inquire into the texts, tasks, students, and cultural aspects of DL instruction, the results are more coherent visions of disciplinary and interdisciplinary reading, writing, and communication instruction.

This focus on adult professional learning, in service of new practices for students, is exactly what the International Literacy Association (ILA) has called for in their latest set of standards—*Standards for the Preparation of Literacy Professionals* 2017.[12] These standards outline the literacy skills and knowledge required by literacy specialists, coaches, and coordinators. They also provide guidance for what principals and classroom teachers need to know and be able to do to support students' literacy growth. A new focus on teachers' comfort with and use of DL is highlighted as one of the major changes in these standards:

> Given the emphasis on learning from informational text and the need for associated high-level skills and knowledge of academic vocabulary, disciplinary literacy in the service of content learning is now embedded in these standards. It is expected that candidates will be able to facilitate students' ability to work with content materials.[13]

The standards further emphasize (across roles and grade levels), in Standard 6, that ongoing and job-embedded professional learning is necessary to both jumpstart and sustain innovative classroom practices, such as those associated with DL work. As a result of this new emphasis in these and other standards (such as the Next Generation Science Standards and National Council for the Social Studies Standards), we have deliberately made connections to the latest ILA standards at the end of each of our four core chapters on inquiry and instruction into texts, tasks, students, and culture. These connections will help readers and preparation programs zoom in on the must-have literacy and professional learning skills related to DL inquiry and instruction.

In this chapter, we quickly reviewed why we believe the RAND model for thinking about reading comprehension, when viewed through the lens of teacher inquiry work, can be an effective framework for learning about and implementing disciplinary literacy in schools. We focus the rest of this book on not only explaining how teachers can productively engage in disciplinary literacy inquiry and instruction but also showing what this work looks like. We illustrate our own suggestions with stories from teachers and teams engaged in various stages of DL work.

The following four chapters each concentrate on one component of the RAND model—texts, tasks, students, or culture—and demonstrate how teachers can productively inquire into disciplinary literacy teaching and learning practices related to each area. We have organized the chapters around the inquiry process, with five distinct sections in each chapter mapped onto the five broad phases of inquiry: defining an inquiry question, building background knowledge, idea generation, idea testing and reflection, and idea revision. The five sections of each chapter illustrate what the inquiry steps can look like when focused around each component of the RAND model.

We have organized these chapters in a particular sequence—texts, tasks, students, and then culture. This mirrors the order in which we have seen many teams successfully engage in inquiry and instructional work. We have found that teams of teachers often feel that they have the most authority and influence over texts and tasks, whereas student- and culture-related inquiry questions can feel a bit trickier to ask and answer. However, we suggest that you read the next chapters in whatever sequence makes the most sense to you as a reader and perhaps as part of a professional learning community. The sequence of your own inquiry work will likely depend on the composition of your teaching team, larger professional learning systems and structures in your school, and a variety of other school-specific contextual factors (which we consider further in chapters 7 and 8). For you and your team, questions of culture may feel most critical; if so, please start there. We also suggest that, while reading the chapters sequentially at first may make sense, you then may wish to use these chapters as resources later (and out of order) when you begin to engage in specific inquiry and instruction work related to texts, tasks, students, and culture.

Finally, we provide guidance and cautions in each chapter based on our own experiences leading inquiry and instruction work in schools. As briefly mentioned before, we illustrate our guidance with stories from some of the K–12 teachers with whom we've worked over the years, showing how these educators have successfully engaged in DL inquiry and instruction work across grades and content areas. We have included the voices of educators across the K–12 continuum representing a variety of disciplines. In this way, we hope that you find illustrations of work that simultaneously feel within your reach and also challenge you to take on new inquiries.

As you begin to read the next chapters focused on inquiry and instruction examples, we offer you a simple interactive reading organizer (see table 2.2) to help you take some notes and consider which aspects of the stories and ideas in the following pages may best guide your own disciplinary literacy inquiry and instruction work.

Now, we turn to chapter 3, in which we describe DL inquiry and instruction focused on text-related questions and instructional experiments. We start here because many teachers and teams consider the texts component of the RAND model to be one of the areas over which they have a good deal of influence. This makes it a good starting place when considering DL inquiry work.

PAUSE AND REFLECT

- After reading chapter 2, how would you summarize the RAND model to a friend and colleague? How would you summarize the inquiry cycle?
- Which of the RAND elements (texts, tasks, students, or culture) do you naturally wonder about most? Which elements are more difficult for you to consider?
- When have you engaged in inquiry work similar to that described in this chapter? What went well? What would you like to do differently as a result of reading this chapter?

TRY IT OUT

- On your own, or with a colleague, spend five minutes brainstorming an initial list of literacy-focused inquiry cycle questions. Look over your list, and see

TABLE 2.2 Inquiry and instruction organizer

Inquiry steps and guiding questions to consider for all inquiry cycles	Focus of inquiry	Important ideas to remember for future work
Defining an inquiry question		
How broad or narrow is our question?		
Is this a discipline-specific or cross-disciplinary question?	Texts	
How is this question related (or not) to other inquiry questions?		
Building background knowledge		
What do we already know about this area?		
What have we already tried?		
Who are the local experts in our school and district we might consult?		
Which online and print resources do we need to consult?	Tasks	
How will we organize and share our findings?		
Idea generation		
Which researched and newly generated ideas seem best to pilot?		
Which ideas might we save for later?		
Who is best positioned to pilot new ideas and with which students?	Students	
How might we know if these new ideas are working?		
Idea testing		
How will we document our classroom pilots?		
How will we share the products of our pilots?		
How will we document and evaluate changes?		
Which new ideas are proving most successful, as demonstrated by student learning and behaviors?		
Reflection and idea revision		
Looking back, what seemed most successful and why?		
Where do we see room for further tweaking?		
Which new practices will we keep, and which will we retool or abandon?		
How might we share successful new practices with colleagues?	Culture	
What might we investigate next?		

if you can begin to sort the questions into the four categories suggested by the RAND model (texts, tasks, students, and culture). Which bin has the most questions? Which questions cut across bins? Which questions might be the most productive starting points, given our advice about not aiming for questions that are too broad or too narrow?

■ If you were going to engage in an inquiry cycle alone, where would you start and why? If you were going to engage in an inquiry cycle with colleagues, whom would you want to invite and why? Talk with colleagues, and ask them to create their own lists of potential inquiry questions. Compare notes and discuss the benefits and potential pitfalls of collaborating on an inquiry cycle soon.

CHAPTER 3

Texts as a Focus for Disciplinary Literacy Inquiry and Instruction

Having outlined a framework for connecting disciplinary literacy (DL) inquiry and instruction in chapters 1 and 2–intertwining the RAND model and the five core steps of teacher-led inquiry–we now turn our attention to illustrating this framework in action. We begin with a look at teacher inquiry and instruction focused on texts as a rich starting place for DL work. Throughout this chapter, we introduce teachers who have positioned texts as the central focus of their inquiry work. You will meet:

- Alisa Conner, a high school Spanish teacher who reimagined text use in her classes
- Lisa Collins, a kindergarten and first-grade teacher who expanded her definition of science texts to include many hands-on materials
- Evan Mousseau, a high school ELA teacher hoping to make summer reading more meaningful for students
- Julie Padgett, a high school math teacher focused on introducing new text types in math classrooms
- Christopher Alba, a high school physics teacher focused on how to write engaging lab reports

Let's begin with a snapshot of Alisa's work.

Alisa teaches Spanish at Brookline High School in Brookline, Massachusetts. She participated, as part of a professional learning community, in DL inquiry and instructional design work across two years. In the following snapshot, note how Alisa talks about text as one of the primary drivers of both inquiry and instruction in her DL work.

ALISA CONNER
Focusing on Texts in High School World Language Instruction

I was attracted to the idea that different skills might be required for literacy in different content areas, and I had the notion that I might be able to learn something about how to better support heritage Spanish learners. I also keenly felt the dearth of good readings for my students—the ones in the textbooks seemed like isolated selections with little connection to surrounding curriculum. Having gone through CRI [the Content-Area Reading Initiative disciplinary literacy professional learning project], I can affirm without exaggeration that it transformed my teaching.

So how has my practice been transformed? Allow me to name the big-picture questions that now form the frame for all my decisions about curriculum and instruction. I ask myself:

Will, and how will, this text engage students?

The motivation/engagement triangle (autonomy, relatedness, competence) frames everything. Can students do this and feel successful (competence)? How will it build their skills? Can students relate to this material? Do they have room to explore their own personal experiences and opinions through this (relatedness)? Do they have some choice in what/how they read (autonomy)? Not every reading activity hits every point of the triangle. But throughout a unit, a quarter, a year, I try to keep these questions in mind.

What is the meaningful context for teaching this material?

No one learns vocabulary well in isolation (or grammar either, for that matter), so many of my colleagues and I have tried to move away from thematic lists of words. Instead, we pull vocabulary—particularly high-frequency words—from the texts. Students learn the words they need to understand and talk about the text. We also learned that for students to learn new vocabulary in the context of a text, upwards of

90 percent of the text needs to be comprehensible. So, while we do use authentic texts (particularly in my Spanish 4 Advanced classes), for other levels, we are conscious about choosing or creating level-appropriate texts that provide lots of repetitive, comprehensible input (which is a foundational approach in world language teaching). CRI was instrumental in guiding us to the research that backs up this approach.

What do I want my students to do with this text? What do I want them to get out of it?

The "old school reading approach" is to have students read a text and then answer comprehension questions about it. Boring! It's not that I never do that, but that's only one kind of engagement with a text. Another option is to offer a much larger menu of activities for engaging with a text.

In our CRI departmental team, we developed a number of documents that now help me consider what texts to use and which activities to ask students to complete. First, we have a list of questions for teachers to use to determine the purpose in choosing a text (our "Determining a Purpose" document is posted here: http://wlspanishcontentreading .weebly.com/essential-questions.html). This reminds me to check in with that motivation/engagement triangle as I plan activities. We also created a giant menu of different kinds of vocabulary strategies to employ with texts. Many of these have made it permanently into my curriculum. Finally, we adapted a set of world language-specific "habits of mind" that we came across in our research (posted here: http://wlspanishcontentreading.weebly.com/habits-of-mind.html). I review these specifically with my students at the beginning of the year and refer to my homemade classroom posters often, and they guide every reading activity either implicitly or explicitly.

For those new to DL inquiry, the work that Alisa describes may seem daunting. However, it is important to note that this kind of inquiry and instruction work is not atypical. When given time, resources, and support, teachers are able to dive into deep inquiry work around texts, tasks, students, and culture in order to create discipline-specific and long-lasting instructional routines.

In this chapter, as foreshadowed by Alisa's work, we highlight how teachers can productively consider possibilities for changing instruction centered on the texts they use. Choosing and using a wide array of texts (and text types, broadly defined) across disciplines and grade levels are critical to the effective teaching of content and supporting the identity development of students into particular disciplinary discourse communities.

As we move through the five steps in the inquiry process across this chapter, we illustrate some of the possibilities for using, changing, and manipulating text as a means for changing instruction and assessment to be more disciplinary in nature.

INQUIRY STEP #1: CENTERING TEXTS AS THE SUBJECT OF OUR INQUIRY WORK

Often, as we begin the work of asking teachers where they may like to start DL inquiry work, they choose to start by considering the texts they use with students. Because texts are relatively concrete and central to many teachers' approaches to instruction, it can make sense to start with considering which texts we use and why.

As we have guided teachers and teams through the process of settling on an inquiry topic, we have found that text can make good sense for a few potential reasons:

- Texts used in disciplinary classrooms/subjects often reflect many of the habits of mind we hope to foster in students as they do the work of the disciplines. They present an opportunity to consider how participants in various disciplines read, how they present information (both substantively and in terms of format, such as texts, figures, or graphs), what they consider important, and how they dissect information differently depending on the discipline.[1]
  - For example, using a primary source in a history classroom presents an opportunity for students to practice historical thinking and reading skills, such as sourcing (analyzing historical documents and considering who wrote the text and why they may be invested in a particular narrative of events).
  - Similarly, using smaller samples of complex text, images, graphs, and real-world objects in a lower-elementary math or science lesson presents an opportunity for students to practice reading data, observing artifacts, and developing fluency with the language of science and mathematics.

- Sometimes texts used in classrooms can seem disconnected to the disciplinary habits we hope to foster among students. Teachers sometimes lament the textbooks they must use, often having had no part in choosing them or determining when new ones may appear. These texts can still be worth exploring to better emphasize the habits of a disciplinary subject, even though they are more centered on synthesis.

  - Science teachers we have worked with sometimes talk about feeling a disconnect between reading science in a textbook and doing science in a more lab-type setting. But the science textbook presents chances to learn from diagrams or other models of phenomena, which are important means of communicating in the sciences, a collection of disciplines with many discursive norms.[2]

  - Elementary teachers may similarly be asked to work with textbooks or informational texts that feel inauthentic or don't include full texts or rich descriptions of scientific phenomena. These instances provide opportunities to take a critical stance, encourage implementation of text sets in which multiple artifacts and texts are used to glean information, and to teach students about text features, such as bold type, glossaries, tables of contents, and so on in order to equip elementary readers with the skills to navigate longer texts with multiple components (including textbooks themselves).

- Sometimes teachers feel compelled to explore texts through inquiry cycles because they are puzzled by how students respond to those texts in the classroom. When students seem to resist reading texts or express that they feel disengaged with a particular text, they are often giving us important information about themselves as readers and what may better support them.[3] It is often an opportunity for inquiry into how to make the text more meaningful and connected to the work of the discipline. Notice how this is exactly what Alisa Conner did within her DL inquiry professional learning community.

- Finally, texts can occasionally be relatively easy to change within a curriculum. Sometimes a text, especially a textbook, is not movable because of strict curricular guidelines, limited availability of texts, or expense issues. But in other cases, shifting texts can be straightforward, especially in cases of short texts or text sets, leaving lots of space to build new opportunities for students to explore and expand their thinking. In such cases, beginning inquiry by asking questions about replacing or adding new texts can be incredibly productive.

Choosing texts as the focus of a DL inquiry cycle often makes great sense for individual teachers or teams as they begin investigating DL. As one initial resource, we recommend that teachers consider Phillips Galloway et al.'s notion of a "continuum from less- to more-disciplinary texts."[4] Phillips Galloway and colleagues suggest that texts vary along a continuum of disciplinary-ness, from pedagogical texts, such as textbooks, to highly disciplinary texts that only professionals in specific fields would use.[5]

Talking about this continuum with colleagues and making sure that students are working with age-appropriate texts all along the continuum is one productive way to move from designing an inquiry question around text into the next step of building teacher background knowledge about text types, features, and uses. Figuring out how to articulate a curriculum across K–12 within a discipline means thinking about the types of texts that are appropriate, across the grades, in order to ultimately build facility for all students to access highly disciplinary texts by graduation.

At the youngest grade levels, such as kindergarten, this may mean adopting more real-world artifacts to be used as texts to help students begin practicing ways of thinking and working that will later translate into work with complex discipline-specific texts. For example, consider this snapshot of practice from Lisa Collins, a kindergarten and first-grade teacher in the Horace Mann Lab School in Salem, Massachusetts.

LISA COLLINS
Introducing Real-World Artifacts in Kindergarten as a New "Text Type"

The focus of our science inquiry each year is Salem Harbor and its surrounding ecosystem. Since taking daily trips off of school property is not a reality during the school year, I began to look for ways to bring experiences into the classroom. I looked at each science unit and the essential questions that could guide student learning. I tapped into the expertise of our science coach and, together with her and my kindergarten team, created investigations for upcoming units. As a kindergarten team, we often struggle with the idea of being developmentally appropriate, now that kindergarten has become so much more academically rigorous. I began to think of more ways to bring hands-on activities into my classroom that are developmentally and grade-level appropriate but still require high-level thinking, reading, and writing. I thought if I explicitly taught students how to observe, draw, and write like a scientist they could become the experts and teach others what they had discovered and learned.

With interactive reading, writing, and authentic science experiences in mind, I created a Discovery Center in my classroom that students could visit anytime during literacy, science, or choice time. In the Discovery Center, I placed hands-on materials as a new type of "text type" for "reading" and observation. For example, in the fall, I had leaves, acorns, pinecones, and so on in the Discovery Center. During our liquids and solids unit, students had access to different solids and liquids, such as dish soap, bubbles, salt, Play-Doh, and oobleck (cornstarch and water). In the spring, students were given soil, seeds, and potting materials.

As they were given time to explore the various materials, they were also given tasks of sketching and labeling their work. I would encourage them to "read" the artifacts, look and look again, and use all five senses while conducting their observations. For the first few visits to the Discovery Center, I modeled what a scientist does during observations, and we used interactive writing to write together about what we had discovered. Once students got the hang of it, the center became independent, and my check-ins with them became less frequent. The Discovery Center became the most anticipated and visited center during literacy centers, especially when new materials were introduced for investigations!

Lisa's inquiry work, investigating ways in which she could bring new and real-world texts and artifacts into her kindergarten classroom, eventually resulted in the creation of a Discovery Center. This Discovery Center provided students ample opportunities to "read" the world and observe and take notes in the ways that young scientists might. Many of these age-appropriate DL skills may then later be translated into work with complex science texts.

Also note that Lisa's definition of "text," which mirrors our own, is much broader than traditional notions of printed words in a bound book. Through the inquiry process, many educators come to the conclusion that a broader definition of text allows students and teachers to focus on habits of mind such as observation, analysis, comparison/contrast, and so on, in increasingly discipline-specific ways. By first practicing discipline-specific skills with objects (e.g., artwork, natural objects, historic artifacts, online museum exhibits, songs, and so on), students with a wide variety of reading and writing skills and experiences can each engage fully in intermediate and DL work.

INQUIRY STEP #2: BUILDING BACKGROUND KNOWLEDGE WHEN INQUIRING ABOUT TEXTS

Once individuals or teams have chosen to focus their inquiry on texts, it is time to consider what teachers may want to learn and explore in this area. In our work with educators, we have found a range of topics to be important when the inquiry is text centered. In table 3.1, we list some of the topics that groups have explored while engaging in inquiry about texts, alongside some of the questions that have been asked in those cycles.

Once an inquiry topic and specific question have been chosen and honed, it is time to begin investigating what is already known about the topic at hand. This is one of the inquiry steps that teachers enjoy most, as it allows for individual or collective exploration of online resources, articles in research journals, books, and even interviews with other knowledgeable teachers (in person or via online networks). Sometimes teachers, such as Alisa and Lisa, employ a combination of investigative strategies, including participating in a structured professional learning experience, gathering and sifting information from online sources and research journals, and sharing the fruits of investigative labors with colleagues. We have found several online tools and scholarly communities helpful in beginning this investigative work. Sites include the following:

- Academia.edu (www.academia.edu)
- Edutopia (www.edutopia.org)
- Eric (www.eric.ed.gov)
- Google Scholar (www.scholar.google.com)
- ResearchGate (www.researchgate.net)
- The International Literacy Association (www.literacyworldwide.org)

K–12 teachers can easily access these websites, which provide a multitude of research-focused articles and papers. Schools often have connections with universities or professors that have been established over time. We have found

TABLE 3.1   Topics explored by groups when inquiring about texts

Topic	Purpose	Sample questions
Vocabulary	Understanding the word-level demands of the texts we use	Which words are our key focus for this lesson? Which general academic words might be barriers to student understanding? Which words will give students more access to the language of this text?
Language structures	Learning about potential language structures, including but also extending beyond vocabulary, that might support or challenge readers in accessing content	How are sentences and paragraphs structured in this text? Have we helped students understand those? What is the stance in this text, and how might it help students understand? What skills beyond vocabulary do you need to access this text successfully?
Text complexity	Developing a toolkit to understand how text complexity is determined and how that relates to reading in particular disciplines	How difficult is this text in terms of readability? What is taken for granted here, and what is explicit? How well does this text reflect the disciplinary skills we hope to foster?
Background knowledge	Understanding how various experiences and prior knowledge can contribute to readers' sensemaking as they read varied texts	What background knowledge do you need to access this text? How do students from a diversity of backgrounds and experiences make meaning here differently? What background knowledge is essential here to take away the lesson goals?
Digital literacy	Learning about how reading differs by being presented in various media and how this shifts the experience of text as well as potential for scaffolding	How does reading on paper differ from reading on a screen? How do we ensure students are reading successfully when reading digitally? What potential scaffolds are gained in a digital version of a text? How can we use tools to build fluency and comprehension online?
Multiple texts	Building sets of texts around particular topics to achieve goals, such as differentiation, or working on skills such as perspective-taking	How can we use an array of texts to generate interest? How can we use a text set to build stronger content knowledge? How can we use text sets to differentiate for readers with different skills and interests?

(continued)

TABLE 3.1   Topics explored by groups when inquiring about texts (*continued*)

Topic	Purpose	Sample questions
Written versus spoken texts	Considering the ways in which spoken language and written language are similar and also quite different in terms of word choice, formality, language structures, etc.	How might we learn with and from oral histories, podcasts, TED talks, and other oral "texts"? How can we use our own speech and conversations (solo or in pairs/groups) as the basis for moving into written texts? How might oral rehearsal (talking aloud and recording oneself; talking with a partner) translate into a more robust written product?
Objects and artifacts as text	Exploring the variety of ways that artifacts, natural objects, two- and three-dimensional art, music, and so on can be considered "text" and used as the basis for disciplinary thinking	How might we "read" an object or an artifact, independently and also as a precursor to reading a more complex text? In what ways are the disciplinary habits of mind and ways of working similar and different when analyzing traditional texts versus artwork or real-world objects? How might engagement with non-traditional texts support our youngest learners, multilingual learners, and others in practicing disciplinary ways of thinking, reading, writing, and speaking?

in our own work that it is wonderful to collaborate and support teachers (with our access to academic libraries) by helping them flesh out their research agendas and find related resources for building background knowledge. We often can locate and share resources connected to teachers' own questions, pointing them in a variety of productive directions. Moreover, school librarians and technology/media specialists often have many of the same resources and access points as academics.

One such story of collaboratively collecting relevant background and research materials comes from a team of high school ELA teachers, librarians, and administrators at Brookline High School, Brookline, Massachusetts. These educators found themselves questioning how to handle the ever-present conundrum of summer reading, and they used an inquiry cycle about texts to examine the possibilities. One participating teacher, Evan Mousseau, described the background-knowledge building that they undertook to determine next steps in their plans for summer reading.

EVAN MOUSSEAU
Exploring Text Options for Summer Reading Work

Our team of librarians, teachers, and administrators was hoping to continue to develop our high school summer reading program. After what we perceived as a largely successful all-school summer reading experience that culminated in an author visit, we wanted to continue to build on this momentum but faced a challenge: it is hard to find a title that hits the sweet spots of interest, accessibility, and rigor for all students, from the most struggling incoming freshman to the strongest rising senior. Furthermore, we wanted to continue to increase student engagement in summer reading and had heard from some students that the "all-school read" hadn't interested them, and they hadn't read it. We valued the common conversations that came with a shared reading experience, but we knew that the perfect all-school read would be hard to find, if it existed at all. How then could we improve engagement while keeping an avenue for a shared school-wide discussion?

As a team, we started by seeking out research. What could the data and experiences of other schools tell us that would refine our search or reshape our thinking? We worked primarily with *Summer Reading: Closing the Rich/Poor Reading Achievement Gap*, edited by Richard L. Allington and Anne McGill-Franzen.

We found ourselves cherry-picking our research for what was relevant to our students and community. Much of the research we found focused on elementary readers and communities whose demographics did not match our own, but we noticed two clear patterns: students engaged more in summer reading if they had choice in the title(s) they read and if they had books in hand when they left for summer.

Complete choice did not pave a way for common class- or school-wide conversations, though, so further compromise with the research was needed. Through a series of conversations, we settled on a school-wide theme of "Young Changemakers," with books where young people try to make a change in their world or have spoken up and taken action on issues that affect them. This choice was inspired by students in our community. Initially, we planned to solicit recommendations from a variety of student groups that would lead to a list of eight to ten titles but realized this would still be constricting that element of student choice more than was ideal. Rather than gathering titles and unveiling them alongside the theme, we decided to unveil the theme and use that to solicit title recommendations through a class activity.

Ultimately, we developed a lesson in which students explored a variety of news excerpts connected to our theme, with the task of discerning the common link. Following their exploration and a class-wide discussion, students were given access to a Google Form that they could use to make recommendations. We collected over 450 recommendations from students in grades 8 through 11. These recommendations were consolidated into a "Top Twelve" list that included titles that were particularly popular or well reviewed, along with a list of over one hundred other titles sorted by genre. Accompanying these lists was a reminder that students could also choose a text that was not included on the list, so long as it fit the theme. This entire endeavor not only led to much greater student engagement with summer reading but also bolstered students' discipline-specific thinking about how we may assemble text sets around culturally relevant themes.

Diving into the research as a key part of background knowledge building is an exciting step in the process. Remember, however, that some of the topics and inquiry questions we may choose have enormous bodies of associated research, and that associated research may span a huge range of content areas. But much existing literacy-focused research has concentrated on the (somewhat arbitrary) "Big-4" disciplines of math, science, social studies, and English language arts. Other disciplines often have far less associated research. In these cases, teachers will have to extrapolate and experiment more as they take what has been learned in some content areas and try to apply it to others. It is our experience, though, that lack of extensive research can be a rich and creative opportunity for teachers to innovate and push the whole field forward. Teachers have unique expertise in considering how best to induct others into their disciplinary communities and to lead others in questioning and critiquing the norms within those communities. In our work, we have often been inspired by what comes of working together to learn both from research and from classroom experiments.

INQUIRY STEP #3: IDEA GENERATION ABOUT TEXTS

Once you have learned a bit about the domains that feel most relevant to the discipline or goals at hand, the next step is to generate ideas about how to shift instruction around the texts being used to better ensure student learning and engagement. Sometimes, though, teachers and teams realize they need to use an assessment process to take stock of their texts prior to generating ideas for what to try. This may include taking stock of the book room or classroom libraries, using text-leveling tools to refine thinking about what may make certain texts more challenging than others, or even surveying students about their experience of the texts.[6]

In our experience, ideas related to changing instruction with texts fall into a handful of common categories of instructional moves. Teachers can do the following:

1. **Change the text.** A relatively simple idea for improving text is to replace one text with another, in order to better achieve the initial learning goal. This includes changing not just the texts that students read but also the ones that they make. It may also include expanding our notion of what counts as text (e.g., including a variety of objects, artifacts, artwork, music, etc. as part of a text set).

2. **Modify current texts to add more scaffolding.** Sometimes teachers modify existing texts by rewriting portions, focusing students' attention on specific passages while eliminating others, or even just changing the format. (Note: Both web browsers and independent websites can be used to enlarge or shrink text and even eliminate distracting ads and graphics from online texts.) In addition to modifying texts, teachers may also scaffold a text more fully, using digital or audio supports, annotations, interactive reading guides, picture walks, introduction of vocabulary beforehand, or other tools that scaffold the text at hand, giving students a stronger foundation from which to read.

3. **Add more texts.** Sometimes an inquiry cycle can reveal that there aren't enough texts in the curriculum to achieve goals related to disciplinary habits of mind, which can lead to the need to include more texts in the disciplinary class. One way to quickly do this is to consider the previously mentioned continuum of less- to more-disciplinary texts.[7] What may happen if we work to add several more texts at different points along that continuum? Similarly, particularly in the lower grades, teachers may turn to objects, artifacts, artwork, and so on, just as Lisa Collins did. In such instances, teachers may ask themselves, "What kinds of text could I bring into my instruction about tide pools, division, concepts of justice, and so on? What real-world artifacts and objects could I use to enrich a text set about these concepts?"

4. **Build text sets.** Beyond simply adding an additional text or two, building an intentional text set can provide students with a much more accessible and cohesive reading experience. A single text is rarely effective for fully

teaching content or for apprenticing all learners into a discourse community. Often, using just one text in a whole-class activity is less effective than using multiple related texts to achieve a more realistic reading environment and set of purposes. This creates a need to build text sets around key topics or skills. Text sets can be intentionally built around particular focus areas:

- content goals (e.g., causes of the US Civil War, ecosystems, number sense)
- authors or figures (e.g., E. B. White, Toni Morrison, Lin-Manuel Miranda)
- nonmajority perspectives (e.g., Black Lives Matter, *Hidden Figures*, *The Laramie Project*)
- concepts or theories (e.g., origin stories, the water cycle, gravity)
- time periods or movements (e.g., Reconstruction, Cubism, the Enlightenment)
- genres and text types (e.g., poetry, graphic novels, word problems, scatterplots)

5. **Prepare more fully for teaching vocabulary.** Sometimes a careful exploration of texts can reveal hidden or unexpected vocabulary challenges. Rather than modify the text, a teacher may decide to focus on preparing students to tackle vocabulary more successfully. Though this is a regular practice in many elementary classrooms, upper-elementary, middle, and high school teachers can sometimes forget that students are continuing to learn vocabulary throughout their school years and that careful attention to teaching vocabulary can effectively scaffold complex texts for students at all levels.

6. **Build background knowledge more effectively.** Student populations are increasingly diverse, and it is necessary to think creatively about building background knowledge, as students with ever-broadening ranges of experience can have more and more varied prior experience, and this creates a need for fuller and more effective scaffolding.

These are just a few of the typical ways that we have seen teachers make changes related to their classroom texts. Once a decision is made to use one or more of these pathways, teachers and teams begin testing their ideas to see how students fare with these sorts of changes.

One team of math teachers at Brookline High School in Brookline, Massachusetts, engaged in DL inquiry and instruction cycles for two years, covering a wide range of topics.[8] One of their key investigations focused on finding and incorporating a host of new texts in their classrooms, which they describe here.

JULIE PADGETT
Introducing New Texts into Secondary Math Classrooms

After starting our inquiry cycle on reading and learning about how to select readings, frame them, and create accompanying questions, we set out to find "good" readings to assign our students. This task turned out to be the hardest of our work by far. The readings we found in textbooks usually matched the content and difficulty of our courses but didn't have much to add beyond what we were already teaching in class. Other readings, such as articles or websites, would have interesting related topics or applications but often would skim over the actual math that was being used. Across all types of readings, we had a hard time finding ones that matched the difficulty level of high school readers with the appropriate content. Readings were often geared toward elementary students or had math that was college level. What "good" readings we did find were saved into a digital library of readings that could be accessed by all teachers in the department. A number of good readings that we found were widely shared within curriculum teams and have become part of the curriculum at all levels and years.

My biggest takeaway from our work around mathematical texts was to understand the importance of asking students to read regularly in math class. As we assign readings of various length, difficulty, and purpose throughout the year, students come to expect it as another aspect of the course. Because I ask them to read (and write) regularly, I don't ever hear, "We aren't supposed to read in math class," anymore. I continue to struggle to find "good" readings to give to students, but every time I come across a good article or reading, I save it into my curriculum files and implement it in my lessons.

INQUIRY STEP #4: IDEA TESTING—IMPLEMENTING NEW TEXTS OR REFINING USE OF EXISTING TEXTS

Once new ideas have been generated, the next step is to pilot these ideas in the classroom to see what happens. This is often one of the most interesting and fun steps in the process, and different teachers and teams reach this step at very different paces. When teachers are working individually, they can implement new ideas relatively easily, but when they are working in teams, they must collaboratively determine what is worth attempting. We have found a few ways to track idea testing around texts that could be useful.

1. **Before trying a new text, or a new strategy with text, look backward.**
   Consider how existing texts you have used in the past worked (or didn't work)
   for students. Look back at student work, ask former students for recollections,
   or journal about your own memories of how effective existing texts were in
   the past. Then consider what may be done next.

2. **Make a plan for trying your new idea.** Different team members may try
   different strategies, or you may try different strategies and texts with different classes or small groups to see what happens. Once these decisions are
   made, consider what you are hoping to see change as a result. What do you
   hope to see from students? What understanding do you hope they will
   have that they didn't have before? What do you want to see happen with
   engagement?

3. **Determine how to collect data before you begin.** This step is often
   skipped, creating a situation in which general impressions are the only tools
   we have to consider how well something worked. Our own impressions are
   useful, but they often don't capture the full picture of how a new instructional approach works for a range of students. Determine the answers to the
   following questions ahead of time:
   - Are you going to track the text discussion to look for particular elements
     or comments?
   - Are you going to collect student work after reading and writing are com-
     plete to see how students are doing?
   - Will you be documenting the work yourself, or will a colleague or two help
     you to capture student information?
   - Will you record (video and/or audio) the lesson to help capture details you
     may otherwise miss?
   - Will you ask students for their perceptions of what has happened?

4. **Consider reading/writing together in the same space.** Often, in secondary classrooms in particular, students read and write for homework and complete other tasks as part of school classwork. But observing students reading
   and writing in class can provide a wealth of information that we wouldn't
   have otherwise. We can see how long students take to read/write a text and
   how their attention varies across a stretch of time. We can visibly notice
   who is disengaged from the reading or writing work. This information can
   be hard to see if students aren't reading or writing in your presence, so you

may consider offering reading/writing time during class, in the same space, to collect valuable and often hidden information.

Meanwhile, please remember—reading and writing skills don't immediately shift for every student with a simple change of text or instruction around text. Even if you don't see a radical shift immediately, you still may have made a difference. Instead, consider what seems different about the new strategy compared to the old one and then think about whether this is the sort of change you are hoping will add up to greater reading or writing skill and engagement over time.

We end this section with a vignette about a new idea that became a fixture in the curriculum for one teacher. Christopher Alba is a physics teacher at Revere High School in Massachusetts. He has worked hard to think through literacy in physics, and as a teacher of color who sometimes felt like an outsider in physics himself, has thought a great deal about ensuring students have explicit teaching in DL to reveal elements of disciplinary discourse that have sometimes been hidden. In doing so, he has found a way of focusing on texts in physics that address and build student skills as well as help students feel less anxious about writing in the sciences.

CHRISTOPHER ALBA
Unhiding Physics Norms and Expectations

I have tried a variety of ways of engaging students in literacy practices in my physics course. For example, I created a set of lessons on how to write a lab report, rather than expecting my students to know how to write one. I found this to be critical because, in the past, I often saw lab reports that had a lot of good stuff but were missing what I considered crucial elements of lab reports. It turns out, after having taught my students how to write one, the reason for these elements being missing was simply because my students were never told that they needed to be there in the first place.

For this particular set of lessons on how to create a lab report, I have students first examine examples from different levels—high school, college, and master's levels; then I ask them to identify common elements in each lab report. My hope is that, by focusing on patterns they see, students recognize that the structures of lab reports aren't all that different in terms of how science is communicated, but they do differ a little bit depending on audience. For example, I discussed with students that, for the master's level lab report, the audience is likely people who are evaluating the research of the master's students or looking to publish their paper; as a result, they are likely to have more of a background in the same field and deeper interest in methodology. The same is not true of a high school or college lab report.

After identifying the key elements of a lab report and discussing audience awareness, students spend some time writing their own lab reports for the most recent experiment they engaged in. I ask them to do this on their own, but they engage in peer feedback of their writing through a protocol in which students spend two minutes giving feedback on what the student receiving feedback requested. In this way, feedback is targeted, and the student receiving feedback knows that they will not receive feedback on something that would heighten their anxiety around their writing, which is something I've found to be commonly experienced among my students.

Notice in this example how Christopher is using both reading and writing tasks, focused on the genre of physics lab reports, to increase students' awareness of disciplinary norms and conventions. The use of traditional lab reports across levels (high school, college, master's levels) as "texts" in his class helps students to analyze and compare/contrast as well as internalize the norms of lab report writing in physics. Ultimately, this shift in practice provides students with greater access to otherwise hidden disciplinary reading and writing expectations. His focus on access and reducing student anxiety not only supports student growth in discrete skills (writing lab reports) but also may translate into longer-lived development of students' identities as young people who can read, write, and engage in scientific discourse.

INQUIRY STEP #5: REFLECTING AND REVISING IDEAS FOR USING TEXTS

Once you have tested a few new instructional approaches and collected a bit of information about the results, the next step in the inquiry cycle is to consider what has happened. What do you want to keep? What do you want to keep tinkering with? What do you think are the results of what you changed?

Of great importance during this step of the inquiry process is the reconsideration of students' DL skills. We often encourage teachers and teams to reflect at this stage on whether the instructional changes they have made are truly supporting students in becoming better general readers, writers, and communicators as well as better discipline-specific readers, writers, and communicators. With the case of instructional changes focused on texts, teachers may agree that modifying texts, introducing text sets, and creating interactive reading guides to scaffold reading and build background knowledge offer students lots of support in becoming better all-purpose readers and writers.

However, at this stage of inquiry a teacher or team may realize that they want to go through a newly refined inquiry cycle focused on similar questions and ideas, in an effort to further tailor thinking and instruction to meet discipline-specific demands. New, more discipline-specific inquiry questions and instructional routines may arise, after an initial inquiry cycle focused on general literacy instructional practices. For example, a team focused on vocabulary instruction may first embark on an inquiry cycle to help themselves become familiar with and implement a few simple, general vocabulary instructional routines. At the end of that first cycle, after having implemented a few new strategies, the team may then embark on a new cycle focused more specifically on how best to teach the highly discipline-specific language found in complex content-area texts. Remember that authentic DL instructional routines may only result after multiple inquiry cycles.

CLOSING THOUGHTS ABOUT INQUIRY AND INSTRUCTION FOCUSED ON TEXTS

As we close this chapter, we return to Alisa's Spanish classroom to hear her takeaways from her team's inquiry cycle about text.

ALISA CONNER
Sharing the Results of Text-Focused Inquiry

So what difference has all this made in my classroom? Here are some of the ways I've changed my approach to texts:

1.   Our "habits of mind" guide everything, and I explicitly teach those as skills. In Spanish 2 Honors, these are more implicitly folded into our units (with both

reading and listening "texts"); in Spanish 4 Advanced, I often use them explicitly to create activities with authentic texts.

2. Students read a lot more—more real-world articles in Spanish 4 Advanced and more leveled readers in Spanish 2 Honors and my beginning Spanish classes. The activities we create ask students to engage with the content of the texts, make personal connections, express personal opinions, and encounter the vocabulary in multiple ways multiple times. We still do some isolated grammar practice, but more and more, I'm trying to introduce and practice "pop-up" grammar in the context of our texts.

3. I offer a lot more independent choice, in a variety of ways:

   ■ In my classroom, I have small, independent reading libraries with a combination of leveled and authentic texts (and, admittedly, I'm still working on different ways to have students engage with these regularly).

   ■ We started to more regularly use level-appropriate magazines designed for language learners as a way to offer students the ability to choose articles on topics that interest them.

   ■ Several times a year, I offer "text sets." Students select a text from a menu of options on a topic and share their discoveries with peers. These can be reading or listening activities and, in Spanish 4 Advanced, are exclusively authentic texts (hooray for the internet!).

   ■ In my Spanish 4 Advanced class, my students often invent the questions they'll use to guide their discussions on a text. The scaffolding I provide for this is inspired by our habits of mind as well as literature circle roles.

   ■ Literacy is not just about reading. I also explicitly teach academic language: those phrases that students need to use when discussing or writing to express opinions, invoke evidence, make transitions, and conclude.

Focusing on texts within our DL inquiry and instruction framework can lead to many benefits for students, as well as shift curriculum to serve students better. We often see teams of teachers use a shift in texts as one way to make the representations in their curriculum more diverse. We also see greater student engagement with text and the related discipline as a result of this work.

When inquiring about texts, just remember, we want to establish a clear purpose for what we hope students will gain, including content and skills, as we move forward into making changes. Helping students better access the texts of particular disciplines can significantly help them begin to understand and critique the ways that ideas are presented in text. In turn, this allows students to better identify with those disciplines as potential pathways in their own lives.

PAUSE AND REFLECT

- After reading chapter 3, which text-focused inquiry questions may be most relevant to your discipline, classroom, department, or grade-level team?
- Which of the steps in the text-focused inquiry cycle would be easiest for you or your team to complete? Which would prove most challenging?
- How do you use texts in ways that build discipline-specific skills versus general literacy skills? Are there ways that you can increase your use of texts to build discipline-specific skills?
- How could you focus text inquiries on creating greater access to and fluency with the sometimes hidden norms in your discipline? How can shifting texts and adding texts create a curriculum that better represents the languages, cultures, and identities of your students, thus forming a bridge between students and the disciplines?
- As you look back at the opening vignette from Alisa Conner, which parts of the text-focused inquiry cycle seemed most important to her? What were some of the big shifts she and her team made as a result? How could this connect with your own work?

TRY IT OUT

- On your own, or with a colleague, conduct a small text-focused self-assessment. Which texts and text-focused activities are working well in your class? Which are proving challenging for students or less effective overall? How could an inquiry and instruction cycle focused on text help? Who may join you in this work?
- Look back across this chapter at the snapshots of practice. Map the teachers' work onto the five steps in the inquiry cycle. Consider what each teacher did (or may have done) in each step. Now, with your own new inquiry question in hand, consider how you may borrow and adapt some of the inquiry and

instructional moves you read about. Which inquiry steps look very similar for you? Which look quite different, and why?

CONNECTING TO ILA'S STANDARDS 2017 FOR CLASSROOM TEACHERS

The International Literacy Association's *Standards for the Preparation of Literacy Professionals 2017* suggest that current and future classroom teachers need a great deal of expertise in selecting and using texts (broadly defined as both print and digital/multimedia artifacts).[9] So essential is the use of text within the standards that the requisite skills do not exist in a single standard or element but are truly spread across all standards.

The standards that connect most closely to our own thinking about texts can be found within Standard 1: Foundational Knowledge; Standard 2: Curriculum and Instruction; and Standard 5: Learners and the Literacy Environment. Here, we highlight a few standards and standard elements that focus specifically on text.

STANDARD 1: FOUNDATIONAL KNOWLEDGE

- For younger learners–1.1: Candidates demonstrate knowledge of major theoretical, conceptual, and evidence-based components of elementary/intermediate reading development (i.e., concepts of print, phonological awareness, phonics, word recognition, fluency, vocabulary, comprehension) and evidence-based instructional approaches that support that development.
- For older learners–1.1: Candidates demonstrate knowledge of major theoretical, conceptual, and evidence-based components of academic vocabulary, reading comprehension, and critical thinking, with specific emphasis on content area and discipline-specific literacy instruction.

STANDARD 2: CURRICULUM AND INSTRUCTION

- For younger learners–2.1: Candidates demonstrate the ability to critically examine elementary/intermediate literacy curricula and select high-quality literary, multimedia, and informational texts to provide a coherent and motivating literacy program that addresses both general and discipline-specific literacy processes.

- For older learners–2.1: Candidates demonstrate the ability to evaluate published curricular materials and select high-quality literary, multimedia, and informational texts to provide a coherent and motivating academic program that integrates disciplinary literacy.

STANDARD 5: LEARNERS AND THE LITERACY ENVIRONMENT

- For younger learners–5.2: Candidates demonstrate knowledge of and the ability to incorporate digital and print texts and experiences designed to effectively differentiate and enhance students' language, literacy, and the learning environment.
- For older learners–5.2: Candidates demonstrate knowledge of and incorporate digital and print texts and experiences designed to differentiate and enhance students' disciplinary literacy and the learning environment.
- For all learners–5.3: Candidates incorporate safe and appropriate ways to use digital technologies in literacy and language learning experiences.

Note how these standards emphasize the wide range of ways that we think about text in the twenty-first century, in print, digital, and various multimedia formats. The definition of text is rapidly expanding as the ways in which we record and communicate information continually expand in the information age.

Also note how expectations around the use of text shift slightly across grade ranges, with greater emphasis on discipline-specific reading, writing, and communicative experiences as students move up through the grades. Skills learned through text early on, such as basic word recognition, blossom into discipline-specific vocabulary acquisition as students move into intermediate and secondary classrooms.

We highly encourage readers to consult the Standards 2017 for grade-specific expectations and recommendations around working with texts. These may prompt rich discussions about shared understandings and expectations among grade-level teams, content-area departments, or entire schools.

CHAPTER 4

Tasks as a Focus for Disciplinary Literacy Inquiry and Instruction

WHILE MANY TEACHERS begin disciplinary literacy (DL) inquiry and instruction work by focusing on questions related to text (the focus of chapter 3), we have also found that a focus on classroom tasks can be equally powerful as a starting place. Questions related to text include questions about genre, number, authenticity, relatability, readability, use, and even what counts as a "text." Alternately, questions related to tasks encourage teachers to surface assumptions and pilot new practices related to what students are doing in the classroom.

Tasks and the purposes behind them are important keys to help students build literacy skills and see themselves as potential members of disciplinary communities through authentic work. As the means by which people read have expanded and the internet has become more and more a part of schooling, what students read has shifted. Moreover, why students read has also changed and expanded.[1] Purposes for reading have an impact on the strategies readers use, their rate, and their focus.[2] Purposes for writing, especially those that are authentic, are similar–they support students with engagement, strategy use, and self-efficacy in writing, especially when those tasks build on students' funds of knowledge.[3]

Many of the questions, inquiry cycles, and resulting new practices related to tasks that we have encountered over the years confront tensions such as the following:

- Which classroom tasks will most closely mirror (in age-appropriate ways) the work of professionals in a particular field?
- How authentic are the classroom tasks? Do they allow students to ask genuinely unanswered questions and engage in age-appropriate research; to read, write, and discuss in both general and discipline-specific ways; and to collaborate with peers to digest existing information and generate new knowledge?
- Which existing classroom tasks may need fine tuning? Which tasks are already successful in supporting students' higher-level and discipline-specific thinking, and which tasks may need to be refined, or retired, given current instructional objectives and shifting classroom contexts (e.g., increasing access to technology, changing student demographics, and so on)?
- Which classroom tasks help students to engage deeply with meaningful regional and national dilemmas of consequence, preparing students to enter into the real world of problem identification and solutions?
- Which classroom tasks reveal disciplinary norms at work and simultaneously provide opportunities for students to question and potentially critique those norms?

When teachers engage in task-oriented DL inquiry and instruction work, they are perhaps most visibly committing to trying new methods in their classrooms. Often, when the wider school community thinks of shifts in instruction, they are thinking about shifts in classroom tasks.

To help illustrate some of the many ways in which teachers can center tasks at the heart of inquiry and instruction work, we introduce you to a handful of teachers in this chapter who have successfully reimagined classroom instruction through the lens of shifting classroom tasks. You will meet:

- Rich Giso, an elementary school teacher focused on providing his first- and second-grade students with more authentic science reading and writing experiences
- Rachel Hayashi, a literacy coach working across several K–8 schools, who first focused on her own teaching and then collaborated with colleagues to

investigate the purposes and tasks we give students when they write about what they read

- Jasmine Juo, a high school biology teacher helping students acquire and use scientific vocabulary
- Eileen Woodford, a middle school social studies teacher who revamped the way she taught and engaged students in studying ancient civilizations

Let's begin with Rich Giso, a multi-age teacher working across kindergarten through third grade. Rich has spent years working closely with colleagues to redesign early-grade science and literacy work. As you read Rich's story, notice how his task-focused inquiry and instruction journey began when he participated in a summer program designed to support young English learners by focusing simultaneously on science and literacy goals. Rich currently teaches at the Carlton Innovation School in Salem, Massachusetts.

RICH GISO
Focusing on Authentic Early-Grade Science Reading, Writing, and Discussion

I was lucky enough to be recruited for the role of multi-age grade 1 and 2 teacher about seven years ago. At this time, Salem State University (SSU) partnered with the Bentley School in Salem, Massachusetts, for a summer program focused on placing learning about science first. Through science learning, our goal was either to advance or to maintain the reading and writing performance of students in a school at risk for state takeover. Most of the young scientists in our program were low achieving. Most had a native language other than English, and most came from homes designated by the state as low socioeconomic status. At this time, I knew we had to do something more than small group guided reading, phonics interventions, looking at data, and reviewing the standards for these young learners. In addition, being a maritime community, we would focus on the ocean (water) as our theme. All of our science content would be relevant to these young scientists. In fact, the ocean was "in our backyard" (across the street). Yet, many of the children had never placed their toes in the sand or noticed that there are tides and that the water doesn't in fact "disappear"!

There was a lot of preparation prior to the start of the program, including two days of training and professional development. My most poignant memory was when a professor from the science department of SSU kicked off the training with a huge, whole-group brainstorm that began with the word "Water" in a web-like graphic organizer on the board. In no time, the board was filled with topics and subtopics that could be chosen to be our science focus either for a week, two weeks, or the whole four weeks of the summer program, depending on grade level. I had no idea how we could all study the same topic but do so in such a different manner. From there, we became the scientists and experimented with fitting as many drops of water on a penny as possible. We each studied a scallop shell, drew it on a white piece of paper, and then had to match each other's shell to our sketches, taking away that detail, to a scientist, is key. It rained, so we ran outside to catch raindrops in a pan of flour to predict the amount of rainfall we would soon face. We managed to get an egg to float in the middle of a tall vase of water. At first, I thought that all of this had nothing to do with our students or our data. It did, however, motivate us, spark our interest, and lead to each classroom picking the science inquiries for the duration of the program. I left the training and introduction to this summer program convinced I had a way to make all the gains in reading and writing happen—and stick!

After the summer program, I discovered that, when beginning writers have things to talk about, they have things to write about. Their motivation to want to communicate their hypotheses and the results of their own experiments was enough to get their thoughts on paper using drawings, labels, and even sentences. The fluidity of their ideas was enough to keep them writing in volumes without even worrying about how to spell a particular word the "correct way." Vocabulary word walls, anchor charts, and lots of books and articles were quick reference tools to help them.

For my new school year, I set up a way to get my new first graders to write about science. Our writing workshop was after gym, art, or music. Before specialists, we would take our lab report (which I devised during the summer program) and record our lab's title and materials. We would write a hypothesis and start an experiment. After specialists, we would discover the results and record our conclusions. Science experiments included melting ice with salt, recording the temperature of hot water over time, designing a bubble wand and predicting the shape of bubble it would produce, and even holding evaporation races by observing the water level of the same amount of water placed in different-shaped containers with different openings. The writing that took place around the science content (which tied directly into our district's first-grade curriculum) was magical. It was "planned magic," but magic nonetheless, as compared to the way my students (and I) viewed writing prior to my experience in the summer program.

We used to see student writing as very formulaic, with little sentence fluency, often written from the first-person perspective, very limited in topic, and often based on an upcoming holiday or season—rarely tied into the content areas. Often, writing work was simply a series of sentence stems students completed because they wouldn't know where to start or would "freeze up."

Now, our new way of teaching writing workshop, integrated with science inquiry, spread fast. In no time, all three members of our first-grade team revamped our schedule, co-planned experiments, shared the responsibility and funding of gathering the materials, and covered more science than we had ever been able to fit in before! Looking at students' increase in writing volume, increase in use of complex vocabulary words, increase of using tools around the room, and increase in excitement over writing was simply amazing!

As you read Rich's story, we hope that many of the elements we have discussed so far in this book come into focus:

- An initial inquiry focus on improving literacy achievement for students–in this case, marrying science and literacy learning more closely
- A period of collaborative and intensive adult learning and investigation–in this case, learning about age-appropriate and authentic scientific inquiry tasks that would lead young learners toward inquiry, reading, discussion, and writing work
- A piloting phase, in which Rich and his colleagues intentionally experimented with new ways of engaging students in scientific inquiry and literacy work
- An iterative phase of spreading the work, sharing new methods with colleagues so that the first- and second-grade teams may engage students in similar ways

The result of this multiyear inquiry and instructional process was not only increased student achievement for a population of students historically considered at risk in many ways but also a series of shared instructional tasks (e.g., weekly hands-on scientific investigations, age-appropriate lab reports, and discussions filled with rich academic language). These tasks are now codified in ways that will solidify students' literacy and scientific ways of thinking and working. This is disciplinary literacy at its best for our youngest learners.

In this chapter, beginning with Rich's story, we outline how teachers can inquire into and design instructional tasks that help students across all grade levels engage in DL work. As we step through the five phases of inquiry across the chapter, we emphasize how a focus on classroom tasks can provide teachers with fertile ground for engaging in inquiry and instructional design work.

INQUIRY STEP #1: CENTERING TASKS AS THE SUBJECT OF OUR INQUIRY WORK

Whenever we are coaching teachers and teams through DL inquiry and instructional work, everyone is quick to consider classroom tasks as an element of school life over which we collectively have lots of control. While many states, districts, and schools set standards for learning outcomes and may even require particular texts, it is rarer for specific classroom *tasks* to be mandated. As a result, *how* teachers achieve common goals and outcomes is largely a matter of individual teacher, team, department, or, sometimes, school decision-making. Having control over classroom tasks can be quite daunting to new teachers. Each of us, as new teachers, remembers facing moments of self-doubt around classroom tasks: Should I ask students to read individually, in pairs, in small groups? For how long? Mostly in-class or mostly at home? What should they be doing while reading: asking questions, taking notes, talking with peers? Where does writing fit in? How much scaffolding should I provide? Is vocabulary and word-work worth the expenditure of class time? And so on.

When we play detective and ask why particular instructional tasks and routines are being used in a classroom (at any grade level), the answers typically center on some version of "That's the way that Teacher X (my mentor/friend) was doing it, so I adopted that structure," or "That's the way that all teachers in our building do this," or "That's what was recommended in my graduate classes," or "I experimented early on with a few different structures, and then I liked this one and so just stuck with it over time." In this way, classroom activities can sometimes calcify and linger far past their usefulness as genuine learning tools.

Just as particular canonical texts can become outdated and should likely receive less of our attention in schools, so can particular classroom tasks. Moreover, some newer practices (such as laptop, tablet-oriented, or virtual practices) may be similarly ineffective and untested. As teachers, we must constantly be asking ourselves the question, "Are the tasks I am designing and assigning the most effective for achieving our teaching and learning objectives?" Whether traditional or brand-new, classroom tasks must be continually assessed to determine whether they are in fact helping us achieve our goals and whether this applies to all students.

In this next case, we meet a teacher and literacy coach in the Brookline Public Schools, Rachel Hayashi, who describes how she came to focus on her students' writing about reading, first in her own classroom and then as part of her broader work with teachers and in professional learning across her district. Her cyclical inquiry work can help us understand how to think about an iterative and increasingly collaborative process for focusing on tasks.

RACHEL HAYASHI
What Are Our Purposes for Writing about Reading?

What made you start thinking about writing about reading and the purposes/tasks we associate with writing about reading?

First, as a focus for myself in teaching . . . When I began teaching seventh grade ELA in Brookline in the early 1990s, I asked students to write Reader Responses and immediately saw that my seventh graders were retelling the stories they read rather than sharing their responses to the stories. Over a couple of years, through working with them very explicitly on the differences between retelling and writing about their reading, students stopped retelling and started writing responses. So then, we moved to varying what responses looked like and how degrees of depth could be explored. What I learned was that their writing could change and grow when I was explicit about my purposes for them and provided them with models for what that writing might look like. Since then, I've grown interested in the possibilities of and been so inspired by the creativity students have shown in written response to text.

Next, as a focus with individual teachers and teacher teams . . . I did work on writing about reading with some individual teachers I coached and some with whom I co-taught. Across grades 3 through 8, I've worked with teachers who are also interested in what it means for their students to write about text, both fiction and nonfiction, and in every case the more we pay attention to it, the stronger students' writing about reading is. When we make time to look across student samples and use them in next-steps instruction, whether in individual conferences, small groups, or whole class lessons, and we are clear about what we see—ask students to tell us what they see, give each other language for describing what we see and how one might have gotten to that writing—student writing grows and changes. Again, seeing student growth in understanding the task and seeing individual creativity and permutations on what we think we are aiming for takes my breath away. Yet, for the most part, the reading units in our curriculum do not provide explicit, in-depth explanations or instructions for teachers on what the writing about reading purposes are, and teachers can be flummoxed as to what to instruct, how much time to give it, how to help students dig into it, and what a progression over the years, grades 3 through 8, would/could/should look like.

Then, as a focus for learning in grades 6-7-8 . . . Most recently, our curriculum coordinator and four middle school literacy coaches designed one aspect of our 6-7-8 monthly meeting structure to be literacy coach-led small-group meetings, with already established coach and teacher pairings. Our first meeting centered on looking at student work—their writing about reading. At that meeting, we saw student writing that reflected a few formats of writing about reading and heard many questions about what our purposes are and what else teachers might ask students to do. Again, I came away understanding that we did not yet have any district-wide or grade-level wide exploration of practice. Therefore, when the opportunity to choose a topic or focus for a sequence of professional development arose, I proposed writing about reading, as I wanted to learn more about it, be better situated to support teachers in their practices with students, and bring the district into an ongoing conversation about what it means and what we think students can gain from it.

As you can see in this vignette, Rachel moved from the first inquiry step of exploring writing about reading tasks in her own thinking and classroom to then exploring a similar focus with a broader range of collaborators. She then bridged to exploring writing about reading as a more common practice in middle school ELA classrooms in her district through her role as a coach. With the added structure and time to meet and explore together with colleagues, Rachel was able to iteratively focus her inquiry in a way that slowly drew in more collaborators across roles and grade levels.

Reassessing round-robin reading provides another quick example of why we need to continually monitor the efficacy of classroom tasks. Remember that round-robin reading is when students spend valuable class time reading aloud from a shared text one after another for long chunks of time. This practice has been widely criticized by literacy experts as being inefficient at best and anxiety-inducing at worst, and many research-based alternatives have been offered, including choral reading, partner reading, reciprocal teaching, and so on.[4] Notice that these are not new citations–in other words, literacy researchers have known that round-robin reading is ineffective for a while. And yet, both research and our own experience in classrooms suggest that round-robin reading is far from dead.[5]

Some classroom tasks stick around despite the existence of better, research-based, and classroom-tested options. Moreover, some traditional and effective classroom tasks (e.g., partner reading) may be glibly replaced, perhaps with seductive digital programs or tools, without deep consideration of potential costs and benefits. Such instructional decisions around tasks need to be made carefully, and ideally incrementally, to allow for careful testing of classroom results.

Fundamentally, DL inquiry and instructional work that focuses on tasks begins with a simple question: "How can we do _____ better if we changed what students were doing with their time in and out of class?" Task-focused inquiry work pulls apart the very fabric of reading, writing, discussion, and hands-on activities to interrogate utility and maximize efficacy. Thus, several straightforward categories of inquiry questions emerge that are related to particular tasks:

- Reading tasks
- Writing tasks
- Discussion tasks
- Hands-on, simulation, or design tasks

Each of these categories maps onto various bodies of research and practice that can prove fruitful for teacher investigation. However, it is the rare classroom teacher who is not already assigning some version of each of these in the classroom. Very few teachers would casually announce, "Oh sure, the students in my class just never read, write, discuss, and so on. Just not worth it." You never hear this. Instead, you often hear that the students are already engaging in all of these tasks on a regular basis.

Therefore, in addition to helping us seek and discover completely new practices, the more common use of task-focused inquiry questions is to help us reframe and reimagine current practices. Task-focused inquiry questions often sound like this:

- **What impact would it have on student learning to shift from whole-class reading and study of a single text to small-group and individual reading of a wider variety of texts?**
  - This is the kind of inquiry question that many teachers ask when they begin thinking about how to build collective knowledge and individual reading capacity quickly (particularly in classrooms where whole-class reading activities have resulted in sluggish progress and widespread student disengagement). Reframing reading work can include focusing more on student choice, analysis of short texts from real-world sources (e.g., online and print newspaper and magazine articles, research article abstracts, newly released survey or statistical findings), and reading with a particular goal in mind (e.g., proving or disproving a class argument). Each of these reframes can dramatically shift the traditional rote task of reading and responding to texts assigned to an entire class.
- **Which kinds of writing tasks would more closely mirror what professionals do in their respective fields? What could an age-appropriate version of a professional writing genre (e.g., lab reports, policy memos, feature articles, and so on) look like, and how could it increase student engagement and motivation?**
  - This kind of inquiry question reframes writing tasks from lackluster responses to text-based questions to more purposeful activities. When students respond to questions in textbooks or worksheets, the task is often to simply complete the assignment as quickly as possible. When students are asked to take a stand, write an op-ed piece for a local newspaper, complete a lab report to guide others who may be engaging in similar experiments, and so on, they find deeper purpose in the task and engage more fully. These kinds of inquiry questions often ask about writing in different genres, shifting the audience for student writing, and reconsidering quality versus quantity.
- **How could shifting when, how, and how much students talk with each other about class content increase students' academic skills? What may happen if we move from a primarily teacher-led discussion format to a more student-led discussion format?**

- We have found again and again that teams of teachers choose discussion as a rich category of classroom tasks to anchor their DL inquiry and instruction work. Discussion-focused inquiry often includes investigations into setting norms for classroom talk; discovering and trying out various talk routines, discussion protocols, and role-based discussion structures; variations on teacher-led, small-group, and partner discussions; students' uptake and use of general and discipline-specific language routines; clear connections between discussion and writing routines; online discussion tools and structures; and investigations into varying the length and placement of discussions in instructional sequences. These kinds of inquiry questions often lead neatly into deeper student-focused questions, such as "Which students are doing all the talking in math class, and why?" and "Which discussion routines promote more equal participation for all students?"

- **How could shifting a rote paper-and-pencil task (e.g., solving a math problem about averages) to a more hands-on task (e.g., researching and calculating the increase in average rainfall for a student's particular town or city to make an argument about climate change) increase engagement and refine students' discipline-specific thinking?**

  - We have found that questions like this are often slower to emerge than those from the other three categories. Much like Rich Giso shared earlier in this chapter, it takes time, collaboration, and sometimes dedicated professional learning time to support a shift toward more hands-on, authentic classroom tasks that simulate those of working professionals. When successful, these questions can lead to productive grant-writing and even the acquisition of new teaching materials. For example, Julie Padgett, the math teacher at Brookline High School introduced in chapter 3, helped her team write a small grant to purchase and assemble math "breakout boxes."[6] The resulting breakout boxes enriched high school math classes. With these boxes, students needed to collaboratively solve complex math problems in particular sequences to gain access to a physical locked box that contained various awards or pieces of information (sometimes as silly and simple as a high school prom photo of their teacher).

Regardless of the category of inquiry question, the key is that task-focused inquiry begins by examining the *how* piece of the learning puzzle—much like text-focused questions examine the *what* and student-focused questions examine the *who*.

INQUIRY STEP #2: BUILDING BACKGROUND KNOWLEDGE WHEN INQUIRING ABOUT TASKS

Building background knowledge about new and different tasks can take many forms: reading widely; watching online instructional videos; talking with trusted colleagues, coaches, and mentors; and participating in online conversations (e.g., social media threads focused on specific educational practices). In many ways, the world of educational literature is filled to the brim with texts focused on new tasks–new strategies to try in your classroom. In this regard, building background knowledge about new tasks can seem straightforward.

However, unlike building background knowledge in response to other types of inquiry questions, which may lend themselves well to print and online textual investigations, task-focused questions sometimes require more collegial conversations to genuinely surface new practices and shift older ones. Partnering with a formal instructional coach at the school or district level or with a colleague who is willing to serve as an informal peer-coach, can produce a wide variety of task-focused inquiry questions and new ideas to try. Bouncing around ideas with a trusted colleague can help surface both assumptions that have kept traditional and perhaps less-effective tasks in place in your classroom as well as generate more effective alternatives to test.

If you consider Rich's story from earlier in this chapter, you can see several important elements of the inquiry and instruction model in action. Together, Rich and his colleagues spent time articulating the instructional challenge at hand–making the curricular learning around water more relevant to the students being taught. From that identified challenge, the group used their professional learning time to consider their dilemma deeply, remembering how to spark curiosity in their own learning and to make connections between these ideas and their own students. While individual teachers may have come to some of the same instructional conclusions on their own, through their independent reading and solo investigations, in this inquiry, the team coming together was a necessary piece of learning how to create community in the classroom. In cases such as this, collaboration may be the fastest way to build background knowledge and begin testing new ideas.

INQUIRY STEP #3: IDEA GENERATION ABOUT TASKS

Once an instructional dilemma and related student needs have been identified, assumptions about time-honored or ineffective practices have been surfaced, and background knowledge into new or different practices has been built, it is time to concretely generate and plan new tasks. We begin with a vignette from Jasmine Juo, a high school biology teacher at Brookline High School in Brookline, Massachusetts, about generating task ideas.

JASMINE JUO PART 1
Adopting and Adapting Vocabulary Routines in High School Biology

In all of our first-year biology classes, students encounter an overwhelming number of new and complex vocabulary terms. Based on a department-designed reading diagnostic that we administered to all science classes as part of our first inquiry cycle, we realized that students would benefit from more time in class to practice the vocabulary with their classmates. In addition to team discussions in our weekly PLC meetings and articles we had collectively read about vocabulary instruction, we talked with other science teachers and experimented with RETELL [English learner] strategies.

For example, in Biology I, an inquiry-based biology class, we typically spend a relatively short time on instruction for human reproductive anatomy before delving into hormones. When a few students came in for extra help, it became evident that they were struggling with the initial step of knowing which structures are found in males versus females. We needed more class time on this vocabulary! Building on the success of an earlier Biology I macromolecule word sort, I developed a new word sort for human reproductive anatomy. Students worked in pairs to sort laminated word cards, using chalk to write category titles on their lab table desktops. Students first sorted the word cards into two categories, male and female, and then into subcategories: gamete travel, hormones, and (male) helper structures. Next, students used the word cards to label a laminated set of male and female reproductive anatomy diagrams. After checking in with me, they labeled and color-coded the diagrams on their handout. Finally, students discussed the functions of those structures within small groups and added this information to their handout.

Another example of successfully modifying a vocabulary strategy is implementing the write-around to review vocabulary. Students silently pass a piece of lined paper among small-group members to generate a list of vocabulary words from the current unit. We share lists and discuss which ones are valid words that belong on the list and remove those that don't belong. We then have a second round in which students in each small group take turns writing definitions of the words listed. As a result, students who perceived themselves as unprepared for an upcoming assessment realized that they were able to contribute to their group's knowledge while better-prepared students benefited by seeing "gaps," what they needed to focus on to improve. I further modified this method to review for larger assessments, switching from lined paper to large poster paper and from only words to include diagrams and explanations of processes. In this case, each small group begins with a different assigned concept within the unit. The poster paper gets passed to another group, with each round focusing on a different task.

Notice in Jasmine's description of her and her team's work on biology vocabulary and content knowledge how she has adopted and adapted several well-regarded practices from various bodies of research. While she has put her own spin on classic tasks, such as word sorts (e.g., adding diagrams to the sorts in addition to vocabulary words), Jasmine has retained many of the original, salient features of the tasks that made them so powerful to start.

Designing new practices can alternately involve developing entirely new ideas or can lean instead on refining evidence-based tasks, as we saw with Jasmine's example. There are a handful of productive ways in which the teams we have worked with have gone about this process. We review each briefly here.

Adopting Already-Proven Tasks

Perhaps the most straightforward move that many teams make is to simply read about, watch, or discuss a proven practice that is new to them and agree that it is worth testing in their classrooms. For Rich and his team, learning from university scientists and adopting previously established ways for students to learn about water were essential components of their plan. After having identified what they believed would be a good set of hands-on tasks, the group moved quickly to implement the tasks and test their efficacy.

Adapting Adjacent Tasks

For other instructional dilemmas, there may be far less available research and fewer widely published best practices. In these cases, we often recommend to teams that they explore widely and then adapt a set of tasks and practices that map closely onto their target. For example, when one team of middle school science teachers was considering how best to support their students in improving technical writing skills, we suggested that they read a bit of the literature on conferencing in writer's workshop. While the conferencing literature is focused primarily on ELA classroom conversations, often with young writers, the science team was able to glean just enough evidence-based practices from that literature to then adapt and apply to their own brief conferences in the science classroom. This resulted in new science-focused mini-conference tasks that students executed with each other and then with teacher mentors to quickly focus on identified writing habits of scientists and improve technical writing skills.

Combining Tasks from Two or More Different Traditions

We sometimes encounter situations in which teachers and teams must consult multiple bodies of literature and then merge best practices to create newly targeted tasks. Take, for example, a high school world language team we coached as they worked to improve their students' Spanish independent reading skills. This team consulted books on independent reading and reading workshop structures from an ELA standpoint; dozens of research articles on effective world language vocabulary and reading instruction; and numerous online resources and research articles about vocabulary acquisition in students' first and second languages. Then, the group synthesized much of what they learned and created team-wide classroom routines that used common informational articles, short stories, portions of books, and so on as part of independent reading work both in and out of class. While the resulting tasks did not exactly mirror any one routine that the team had learned about, the newly blended routines shared the hallmarks of much of what they had read (e.g., modeling for students before independent work time, interactive reading guides, small-group support, reading conferences, and so on).

Designing Completely New Tasks

Finally, there are instances in which teachers and teams must design completely new tasks, often because the identified content area or disciplinary focus is sorely underrepresented in the literature and very few analogous practices exist in adjacent bodies of research. While this happens rarely, we have certainly come across a handful of cases. One example comes from vocational or technical high school settings, where electrical instructors may be devising better ways to help students shift seamlessly between the electrical codebook and real-world modeling and building tasks. This may require a great deal of experimentation, piloting, and assessment of wholly new practices.

To further illustrate these idea-generation pathways, we return to the case of Jasmine Juo, the high school biology teacher. As Jasmine and her colleagues worked on vocabulary, they realized that their current writing instruction was not serving their larger purposes. So, they launched a new inquiry cycle dedicated to studying and better using writing to support learning, which she describes briefly.

JASMINE JUO PART 2
Reframing Writing in High School Science Classrooms

In addition to our focus on vocabulary, the science team spent an inquiry cycle on writing. Having resources from our consultants as well as regular meeting time with the science team was critical to developing and implementing writing strategies in our classrooms. I was intrigued by the idea of "writing-to-learn." I had mostly thought of writing as evidence of learning, and I felt obligated to grade nearly everything that students wrote. Rather, scheduling time to write in class gives students the opportunity to practice the vocabulary terms as well as a way to improve their understanding of important concepts. I created Quick-Write Journal handouts with multiple blank charts with spaces for the date, vocabulary words to use, the prompt, and their written response. I then made a slideshow with the prompts and vocabulary for each Quick-Write Journal entry. I used different prompts throughout the DNA unit as the class learned about DNA replication, transcription, and translation.

The first year that I did this, I noticed that, while most students were able to participate, there were a few who struggled to write anything besides the most basic response. Keeping in mind that for comprehending science readings, it is necessary not only to read the text but also to closely examine the figures and diagrams, I decided to add this element to the writing prompts. I gave students two minutes to write their response using the initial prompt but then showed another slide with diagrams of the process and asked students to add more details to their written response or make any needed changes. This allowed all students to be engaged, including those students who were still learning the vocabulary terms and concepts. The Quick-Write Journals were not assessed for a grade. Instead, as part of reviewing for an assessment, I showed a few student samples anonymously on the document reader so that the whole class could discuss the work and make corrections on their own writing.

Here you can see Jasmine and her team designing new tasks, adapting others, making time for additional classroom tasks, and considering which practices make a difference for students' thinking and work. After building background knowledge and generating several new instructional ideas, Jasmine and her team carefully started implementing and assessing new classroom tasks. This last piece bridges into the testing phase of inquiry work.

INQUIRY STEP #4: IDEA TESTING—IMPLEMENTING NEW TASKS IN THE CLASSROOM

As you prepare to test new tasks with students, it is important to remember that this is a piloting process. Don't expect perfection at first. Give yourself room to iterate and adjust over an agreed-upon period of time before you reflect and ultimately choose to keep, modify, or reject a particular task.

Some of the idea testing advice we gave around text in chapter 3 is applicable to preparing to test new tasks in the classroom. For example, we reiterate the suggestion to "look backward" and clearly articulate what has previously gone well or awry before implementing a new task. This will help you determine whether, when, and how the new tasks are indeed more effective. We also want to remind you how critical it can be to make a plan for trying the new task (e.g., in one classroom, across several, with just one group of students in a single class, and so on), coupled with a clear idea of how you may collect data about how the experiment unfolds. By making a clear implementation plan and collecting just a bit of data about how it goes, you will be well positioned to make crucial decisions about keeping, modifying, or deleting newly implemented tasks.

However, when you try new tasks in the classroom, we also recommend two additional practices to assist in later decision-making about efficacy and next steps.

Use of Video and Audio Recordings

Unlike inquiry and instructional changes focused on text, which often result in students reading quietly for long stretches, changes in classroom tasks can be quite lively and filled with classroom discussions, hands-on activities, and all types of writing conferences. We have seen many teams use video and audio recordings (with appropriate permissions to use the results purely within the school for teacher reflection purposes), which can greatly aid teacher and team reflection and decision-making. Remember that just a few minutes of video or audio recordings can go a long way toward revealing student learning and the efficacy of newly piloted classroom tasks.

Student Check-Out Slips, Surveys, and Other Self-Reports

Again, unlike inquiry into other domains, task-focused inquiry and instructional changes lend themselves to student self-reflection. While it can sometimes be challenging for a student to reflect on differences between reading experiences, or cultural shifts, most students are eager to talk about which activity they liked better. Convening a small focus group of students before and then after introducing a new task can give you a wealth of information about what worked and what didn't. Check-out slips, quick online surveys (e.g., Google Forms), or even reflections built into the task at hand (e.g., a "What was this experience like?" open-ended question at the bottom of a newly designed, collaborative math quiz) can give teachers clues as to what to modify or delete moving forward.

Determining ahead of time how you will document and assess what happens when you pilot a new idea is a key component of successful inquiry. Further, it can sometimes be important to invite colleagues into your classroom to help you capture results. To illustrate, here we meet Eileen Woodford, a middle school social studies teacher in Brookline, Massachusetts, implementing new discussion tasks to teach about ancient cultures. Eileen describes the impetus for the inquiry and then how she tested to determine efficacy.

EILEEN WOODFORD
Helping Students Read and Debate Like Historians

Encountering disciplinary literacy (DL)—its exploration of learning inside of a discipline, along with its strategies and practices—was Nirvana for me. My goal as a middle school social studies teacher, specifically as a teacher of the civilizations of the Ancient Near East and Mediterranean Basin, was to get students to fall in love with ancient peoples. I wanted them to think deeply about the past and be able to compare the workings and doings of ancient societies to their contemporary ever-evolving world. My curriculum had always emphasized deep exploration of a topic concluded by some type of writing exercise, but the results were often mixed. The process could be a drudge at times for the students and the writing disappointing. I wanted a pedagogical road map that would help me get the excellent writing that I considered to be the end result of learning, while truly engaging the hearts and minds of the students. I wanted their whole being present in the learning. DL seemed to offer such a road map.

During the first year of participating in our district's Disciplinary Literacy Initiative (DLI), my incorporation of its practices was restricted to general ideas—sort of the atmospherics of DL, especially as we, as a school-based team, were still learning about it. However, at the beginning of the second year, we decided to dive in using specific strategies focusing on vocabulary building, decoding meaning in texts and visuals, analysis, and fluent written and oral expression. The specific vehicle we chose for our first DL exercise was one that made me, as a teacher, extremely uncomfortable: a debate on the "justness" of Hammurabi's Code, using the DBQ Project's Mini-Q. It wasn't the code that challenged me; it was the debate format. Other than it was "fun," "student centered," and other such vaguely defined education buzzwords, not one of my colleagues could describe what tangible, measurable learning outcomes—mastery of content, analytical thinking, and verbal and written expression—were supposed to ensue from a debate. I saw it as an open invitation for seventh graders to reenact the World Wrestling Federation's SmackDown: loud, raucous, and theatrical. But was it really wrestling?

But dive in I did, because DL had given me the secret decoder ring for setting up an academically rich learning experience that was still fun—and loud and raucous and theatrical. DL clarified a range of possible specific disciplinary outcomes—history vocabulary, close reading, questioning, analyzing, and synthesizing—and, most important, it gave me the strategies for achieving these outcomes. The strategies can be segregated into four areas, three before the debate itself and one after: creating a unified understanding of the topic through the explicit teaching of foundational vocabulary and terms (e.g., What is "the law"?); acting as a reading coach (and behavior referee) rather than a "teacher" to help the debate teams decode and make meaning of the primary source texts; explicitly teaching somatics (instruction on body posture beyond "make eye contact") and delivery (enunciation and metered phrasing) just before the debate—and allowing for in-class practice time; and a whole-class reflection that included both the process of the debate and the discussion of "justness."

Having been involved in preparing the students for the debate, I felt I was not able to judge it by myself, so I asked one of my DL teammates, the librarian, and the principal to serve as judges. They were so impressed by both the content and the oral presentations that they couldn't determine a winner! All students, even my strugglers, became deeply engaged in the material. I could hear them arguing about the justness of Hammurabi's Code—using all the vocabulary and citing specifics in the texts—after they left class. However, the process of using DL strategies to prepare for the debate transformed one student, a girl who never gave herself the space to think through anything because she was so busy with the social dynamics of the class, into a brilliant thinker and eloquent speaker. Her arguments were stunning, insightful, and profound. She went from being Queen Bee to RBG (Ruth Bader Ginsburg) in the space of a week.

The DL value of the debate was not just the debate itself and its afterglow among the students, but how much of the learning process would be internalized by the students and how much of the vocabulary as well as historical thinking skills they would carry forward to the next topic in the curriculum. We held two debates during the year; the first was SERP's SoGen Word Generation unit on whether the pharaohs of Ancient Egypt were oppressors or great leaders.[7] This exercise introduced the element of reading visuals, which was a critical turning point for my struggling readers. This time, the students were able to organize their work in groups more quickly than in the first debate, and the outcomes were strong argumentation and good oral expression. More important this time, though, is that the students retained the vocabulary and used it continually through to the end of the school year. This mastery of historical vocabulary gave them greater confidence in class, especially among my students with learning disabilities. Their posture in class changed: they sat up more and were more open with the way they held themselves. Their speaking voices changed, becoming more assured, and they took more risks in their thinking. The conversation had grit and substance and was intellectually animated. They could extend their meaning-making beyond blurting out the big ideas by rote. They used facts to defend their points.

By the time we undertook the third debate—Stanford History Education Group's Structured Academic Controversy on Athenian Democracy—the students could slip easily into the process of thinking like historians.[8] My role was still as a reading coach, as the primary source texts were challenging for even the best students; however, I no longer had to help them structure their arguments. Yes, even at the end of the year, the debates were loud, raucous, and theatrical, and my classroom still looked like the WWF's SmackDown. But now it really was wrestling.

Notice in Eileen's story that there was uncertainty as to how the class would unfold. She was taking a risk but decided to "dive in." This is exactly how testing new tasks in the classroom may feel. And this is completely normal. Much of DL inquiry and instructional work can (and should!) feel like a bit of a small risk—an attempt to adopt, adapt, and design instructional tasks to better fit the discipline-specific needs of your students across grades. But you can see here how Eileen brought in trusted colleagues to help her understand how students were performing during the actual debate itself. She and her colleagues watched for changes in students' reading, writing, and argumentation skills as potential evidence of success. This is yet another reason, whenever possible, that we recommend that you engage in this work with trusted colleagues, coaches, and mentors.

INQUIRY STEP #5: REFLECTING AND REVISING NEW TASK IDEAS

If you follow our earlier advice in Inquiry Step #4—to make a plan, collect some data, and perhaps even use video/audio recordings or collect student self-reflections—then this final step of reflecting and revising classroom tasks can be incredibly rich and rewarding. All too often in schools, we base our next steps on gut responses and impressions of what went well or awry. Instead, we encourage you, when reflecting on newly implemented DL tasks, to rely on as much concrete evidence of student learning as possible. Whether analyzing student written products, classroom footage of student discourse, or student check-out slips describing how they felt about their reciprocal teaching roles, the best reflections on practice come from collaborative investigations of classroom-level or "street" data.[9] And we use the word "data" here in the broadest possible sense, including all kinds of teacher journaling and record-keeping or student-level reports and comments, in addition to more traditional quantifiable measures.

Coming full circle, we return now to Rich Giso, the teacher from the beginning of this chapter. We end with a few takeaways that Rich sent to us, after reflecting upon his own inquiry and instructional work around science and literacy instruction.

RICH GISO
Reflecting on New Science and Literacy Tasks in Early Grades

Since beginning to teach science and literacy together in more authentic ways, I have several takeaways:

1. At first, I was worried that if I took a science topic and asked the children about questions they had and began my unit from there, I would not be able to cover the required standards. For example, in teaching about the moon, I know I need to teach how it follows a predictable cycle (moon phases). If I introduced our study of the moon and no young scientist was curious about that, what would I do? In no time, I learned that inquiry leads to more inquiry! Starting with a few basic wonderings was okay, because as we researched answers to our questions, did lots of hands-on simulations, and watched lots of media clips, our questions would grow—resulting in my not only covering my required standards and essential understandings but a lot, lot more!

2. The quality of the output in my students' writing is always better when they are writing about science! I have years' worth of rubrics involving the Six Traits of Writing to prove this. The quality of established details, use of content-specific vocabulary, and consideration of audience is so much higher and in-depth when students are motivated to share their content learning with the world via writing.

3. In order for students to write more, they need to research and talk about a topic a lot! Talking with partners, in the whole group, during minilessons, in small groups, and with me in writing conferences all contribute to a greater final product. When we would study the way authors presented the information of the earth's rotation, we would study how the author conveyed the information and brainstorm how we could utilize the same techniques in our own writing.

Notice, in particular, how careful Rich is to connect much of his decision-making about new tasks to data that he has collected over time: writing rubrics, amount of writing produced, amount of talk produced, examples of new content-specific vocabulary students produced in discussions and in writing, and more.

CLOSING THOUGHTS ABOUT INQUIRY AND INSTRUCTION FOCUSED ON TASKS

As we end this chapter, we leave you with a few final reminders and suggestions. First and foremost, if you start your inquiry and instruction work by focusing on tasks, please also consider the interconnectedness of the other domains (texts, students, and culture). Often the tasks we design are inherently related to who our students are, the larger sociocultural environment of our schools and wider communities, and of course the texts that we most want to put in students' hands. Some teams jump at the chance to change classroom tasks, which makes great sense because tasks are perhaps most under teachers' control. However, we do caution that rushing to change tasks, without careful consideration of the other domains, may leave you with tasks that are not as student responsive, culturally embedded, or authentic as you may ultimately wish.

Second, we reiterate the point about collecting data. Today, just the word "data" can send shivers down many teachers' spines (with good reason). In the standards-based and postpandemic era of education, data have been wielded both well and inappropriately, and we must all rightly become critical consumers and producers of classroom- and school-level data.[10] However, we encourage you not to be shy about always asking the question "How will I know if this task or set of routines is *better* than what I was doing before?" Many of the teachers and teams we have coached have asked, "Is this *better*?" over and over, and it has become the fundamental driving force for all of us to plan ahead, collect data in the moment and right after class ends, and collaboratively analyze data to guide next steps.

Last, we encourage you to always use *authenticity* as a high bar for judging whether a new practice is indeed moving you and your students toward more discipline-specific literacy teaching and learning. The more authentic the task, the more closely it mirrors the real-world dilemmas, questions, habits of mind, ways of working, language, texts, and tasks of professionals going about their work. This brings us closer to supporting students in acquiring DL skills.

PAUSE AND REFLECT

- After reading chapter 4, think about which task-focused inquiry questions may be most relevant to your discipline, classroom, department, or grade-level team.
- Which of the steps in the task-focused inquiry cycle would be easiest for you or your team to complete? Which would prove most challenging?
- Which tasks in your classroom are already nudging students to acquire and use discipline-specific literacy skills? Which tasks are bolstering basic or intermediate skills? Which tasks are supporting students in becoming more critical consumers and questioners of the disciplines themselves?
- Who may be your best collaborators in designing, testing, and reflecting on new DL tasks?

TRY IT OUT

- On your own, or with a colleague, conduct a small task-focused self-assessment. Which literacy-focused tasks are working well in your class and truly supporting DL thinking and work? Which are proving challenging for students or less effective overall? How might an inquiry and instruction cycle focused on tasks help? Who may join you in this work?
- Look back across this chapter at Rich's story of early-grade science and literacy instruction. In your opinion, what were the keys to success in that story? What, if anything, would you suggest as next steps for Rich? Which parts of his story may map well onto your own work?

CONNECTING TO ILA'S STANDARDS 2017 FOR CLASSROOM TEACHERS

The International Literacy Association's *Standards for the Preparation of Literacy Professionals 2017* zoom in on the required skills and knowledge that classroom teachers (across grade levels) need to effectively design and refine classroom tasks that support students' reading, writing, and discussion skills.[11]

The standards that connect most closely to our own thinking about classroom tasks can be found in Standard 2: Curriculum and Instruction and Standard 3: Assessment and Evaluation. From Standard 2, current and future classroom teachers are expected to "apply foundational knowledge to critically examine literacy curricula; design, adapt, implement, and evaluate instructional approaches and materials to provide a coherent and motivating literacy program that addresses both general and discipline-specific literacy processes."[12]

This general standard is then broken into four elements:

- 2.1: Candidates demonstrate the ability to critically examine elementary/intermediate literacy curricula and select high-quality literary, multimedia, and informational texts to provide a coherent and motivating literacy program that addresses both general and discipline-specific literacy processes.
- 2.2: Candidates plan, modify, and implement evidence-based and integrated instructional approaches that develop reading processes as related to foundational skills (concepts of print, phonological awareness, phonics, word recognition, and fluency), vocabulary, and comprehension for elementary/intermediate learners.
- 2.3: Candidates design, adapt, implement, and evaluate evidence-based instruction and materials to develop writing processes and orthographic knowledge of elementary/intermediate learners.
- 2.4: Candidates plan, modify, implement, and evaluate evidence-based and integrated instructional approaches and materials that develop the language, speaking, listening, viewing, and visually representing processes of elementary/intermediate learners.

Moreover, elements of Standard 3 (focused on assessment) connect directly with our notions of assessing efficacy and refining instruction accordingly.

- 3.2: Candidates use observational skills and results of student work to determine students' literacy and language strengths and needs; select and administer other formal and informal assessments appropriate for assessing students' language and literacy development.
- 3.3: Candidates use results of various assessment measures to inform and/or modify instruction.

Note how these standards emphasize, as do we, several key ideas–adaptation (not just adoption) of instructional practices; integration (not isolation) of literacy skills, such as reading, writing, and discussion; close observation, assessment, and refinement of instructional practices; and, of course, a focus on both general academic and discipline-specific skills.

Also, as we outlined in chapter 2 of this book, these standards encourage greater emphasis on DL as students move through the grades (with the greatest emphasis placed on high school). However, it is important to note that the standards encourage some degree of discipline-specific instructional attention across all grades. For this reason, we highlight the elementary/intermediate standards here, as a midpoint in the continuum of discipline-specific work.

CHAPTER 5

Students as a Focus for Disciplinary Literacy Inquiry and Instruction

Now that we have explored texts and tasks as the focus of inquiry work, two fairly concrete ways of making changes, we turn our attention to the third element of the RAND model, focusing on students. Because students are ever-changing and individual, this focus of inquiry can look a bit different from the other two, which are grounded in exploring the curricula and associated tasks we present to students. Throughout this chapter, we will meet teachers and teams of teachers who have centered students—their needs, skills, and interests—as the focus of inquiry. You will meet:

- Evan Mousseau, the high school ELA teacher from chapter 3, who is trying to help his ELA students better understand their growth across a year of learning
- Jennifer Rappaport and Lindsey Hutcherson Smith, two middle school ELA and ELL teachers working to explore what was and was not working in their writing instruction for particular students
- Sol Rheem, a high school ESL social studies teacher focusing on instruction that helped her know students better while they are making connections to US history

■ Karen Engels, a third- and fourth-grade teacher working to center students' identities in her teaching

First, we'll read Evan's story of trying to help his students better perceive their reading growth over a year, in order to demonstrate their increasing competence.

EVAN MOUSSEAU
Helping Students Become More Complex Readers

Reviewing student feedback, I found a common pattern of students believing they had improved significantly as writers but not as readers. In spite of this, students had successfully engaged with a series of increasingly challenging reading tasks and increasingly complex texts over the course of the year. I had seen students grow as readers, so why didn't they feel like they had grown as readers?

As I thought about this question, I revisited the work that had informed some of my own thinking about teaching reading and kept returning to the visual of the RAND model, the visual heuristic presented in *Reading for Understanding: Toward an R&D Program in Reading Comprehension*.[1] As I read, I began to suspect that my students saw reading as wholly composed of the relationship between the reader and the text. They were not taking into account the activities they were doing with the text as part of the reading process.

As I reflected further on this idea, that my students were not always thinking about the activity at hand when they thought about reading, I began to notice other ways this pattern was showing up in my classroom—students coming to class discussions saying, "I did the reading, but I don't remember anything"; students expressing frustration when generating ideas for an essay evaluating a character, as they hadn't really been focused on character development when reading; students summarizing rather than responding to assigned articles.

Reflecting on how to get students to read more purposefully, with a focus toward the activity we'd be doing with our reading, I kept coming back to the RAND model. If I used it to guide my thinking about the teaching of reading, why keep it a secret from my students? Why not explicitly teach them to think of reading as a complex task, one they were still learning to perform, and one that included consideration for the reader's purpose in reading as a fundamental part?

This dilemma focuses on a question of not only how we shape student thinking but also how we discover what they understand and whether we have rich and useful information about their preferences, backgrounds, and skills. It also raises a key question about how students are perceiving their work in the discipline of English language arts over time. This type of student-centered inquiry is the focus of this chapter. Setting students as the central focus of an inquiry cycle can lead to fruitful pathways forward and to instruction that is more sensitive to student needs and differentiated toward their various forms of diversity.

A strong connection between students and authentic literacy tasks in content classrooms has long been argued and proven to be a way to support students in their learning and motivation.[2] But this means we must understand and know our students well, in a way that is focused on supporting their motivation to engage with content learning.[3] This sort of design work, which is attuned and attentive to students in a specific way, is challenging and requires what Fairbanks and colleagues term a *thoughtfully adaptive* stance toward instruction.[4] Inquiry work is a nice way to take this sort of adaptive stance, and as we have already discussed, inquiry is an effective approach for tackling adaptive challenges. Throughout this chapter, we focus on how inquiry work can support teachers in adapting instruction for particular students, by focusing on what we know and may still learn about the specific students in our classrooms.

INQUIRY STEP #1: CENTERING STUDENTS AS THE SUBJECT OF OUR INQUIRY WORK

Often as teams or individuals begin to think about improvement, they ask a number of questions about their own students: What do they know? What do they like? What would they like to learn? What is their experience of school, various disciplines, and their teachers? Do they see themselves as full members within disciplinary classrooms? Such inquiries can bolster teachers as they address and refine their approach to an array of nagging dilemmas.

Student-centered inquiry cycles can make sense for a variety of reasons:

- **Exploring Perennial Questions**
  Teachers often have nagging frustrations and questions about how to better engage students in their classes and lessons, feeling as though they don't have enough tools to support and reach all of their students. Simply

designing engaging projects or other authentic tasks is not enough on its own to engage students.[5] Student-centered inquiries help address these questions and stretch our instruction even further–to find out why students feel engaged in particular disciplines, tasks, or activities.

- **Exploring Assumptions**

Teachers sometimes realize that they have made assumptions about students' background knowledge and language that are not manifested as learning takes place, and they want to create a richer and fuller picture of what students know from prior experience.[6] Students may also bring assumptions to our classrooms about their potential in particular disciplines, and their identities may be shaped by those assumptions.[7] As our classrooms become more diverse along a variety of cultural and linguistic dimensions, this is an inquiry that often bubbles to the surface as teams or teachers think through what has worked before and for whom.

- **Exploring Student Interests**

Teachers sometimes have questions about students' interests and preferences that can be addressed through inquiries about these facets of students' lives. In order to better match curriculum to learners, knowing more about their interests can make the pathway clearer and provide lots of useful information for teachers; this knowledge can ultimately support improved student achievement in literacy-related tasks.[8] Often this is the ideal opportunity to partner with librarians, specialists, and other professionals within schools who sometimes have unique windows into students' interests and preferences that don't always emerge within the traditional classroom setting.

- **Exploring Student Skills**

Teachers can sometimes have unclear pictures of students' skills–they may know quite a bit about how students fare in particular subjects, but other less immediately relevant skills may be more hidden, depending on the grade level of students being taught. For example, secondary teachers may have too little information about student reading fluency or basic reading comprehension, or elementary teachers may need more information about a student's discipline-specific skills, depending on the available assessments for younger learners.[9] Additionally, state tests can be poor sources of information about the particulars of student skills.[10] Finding out more detailed information about students' current skills, to better support students in growing needed skills and expanding on their strengths, is often an important focus of inquiry work.

Choosing to center students in our inquiry work often helps teachers meet the always-present but sometimes elusive goal of providing effective motivational support and instructional differentiation for a variety of learners. Here we meet Jen and Lindsey, two middle school teachers from Charles O. Dewey Middle School 136 in New York City, who identified students' writing skills as an ongoing dilemma that they wanted to address in their teaching. First, they needed to engage in a bit of student-focused inquiry work to determine how best to support students.

JENNIFER RAPPAPORT AND LINDSEY HUTCHERSON SMITH
Supporting English Learners (ELs) in Writing

We were having a challenge pushing our students to improve their writing coherence and overall expression of ideas. Students were not growing in the areas they needed to grow in, according to the New York State writing rubric. They made progress with finding and citing strong evidence; however, they continued to struggle with analysis and organization. We were having rich discussions in class but were not seeing on paper what students were expressing orally in class. We offered numerous scaffolds—mnemonic devices, graphic organizers—and followed a consistent organizational format (Claim, Evidence, Analysis). We were left pondering this question: How do we get our students to use the tools we give them to clearly and effectively express in writing what they think and say in class?

Students wrote routinely in our ELA class. We collected numerous samples of student writing. After months of analyzing our students' writing, we noticed that while some students were growing in writing, many (particularly ELs and students with disabilities) were stagnant. We observed several things:

- The tools and scaffolds may have been stifling some students.
- We noticed struggling writers (often ELs) stick to graphic organizers as the product, not as a tool.
- The result was choppy, disconnected, not genuine writing.

Here is an example from Lindsey's class:

Students in an English as a new language (ENL) class were writing drafts of an essay. In order to make sure they had an organized essay, I provided them with an outline for an essay. All they had to do was fill in boxes with things like quotes, transition words, and ideas they had previously written on graphic organizers. Basically, I broke the essay into teeny, tiny parts. All they had to do was fill in the blanks. Easy, right? After two days of the kids and me being confused, angry, and frustrated, we threw the outlines into the garbage and just wrote on paper. This was an "a-ha" moment for me. This tool was not right for my kids. As much as I wanted to impose this structure and strategy on them, it was not working. They had lost sight of the final product by trying to please me and complete the outline. There was no cohesion in thinking, just them trying to fill in the blanks. I learned that it's okay, when we are teaching writing, to be flexible, and we have to hear what the kids are saying. In the end, the scaffolds I was providing were stifling many of the kids.

Jen and Lindsey framed their dilemma clearly, and this led them to reflect on what had happened thus far in their classrooms, as they began the work of generating new ideas to support their students' writing. This is the power of a student-centered inquiry cycle—gaining insight to address ongoing challenges for students. Knowing deeper and richer information about the particular students in a classroom, like Jen and Lindsey gained here, not only can guide the general or overarching lesson planning for a particular group but also opens avenues by which those lessons may be altered to better meet the needs of a wide variety of students.

INQUIRY STEP #2: BUILDING BACKGROUND KNOWLEDGE WHEN INQUIRING ABOUT STUDENTS

Once students have been chosen as a focus for an inquiry, we turn again, toward further learning, digging into a variety of sources that may support teachers in gaining a deeper understanding of their students. The approach, though, can look different from prior inquiry pathways.

First, teachers may pursue some of the topics discussed in prior chapters—those related to texts or tasks—when they are learning to carry out a

TABLE 5.1   Further data collection resources to support student-focused inquiry cycles

Focus	Potential resources
Action research, data collection, & analysis as part of inquiry cycles	*Digging Deeper Into Action Research: A Teacher Inquirer's Field Guide,* by Dana, 2013
	Improving Schools Through Action Research: A Reflective Practice Approach (4th ed.), by Hendricks, 2017
Methodology and design support for data collection	*Living the Questions: A Guide for Teacher-Researchers* (2nd ed.), by Shagoury & Power, 2012
	Survey Methods for Educators: Collaborative Survey Development, by Irwin & Stafford, 2016
Bigger picture thinking about classroom-level research and data	*Street Data: A Next-Generation Model for Equity, Pedagogy, and School Transformation,* by Safir & Dugan, 2021
	The Teacher's Guide to Research: Engaging with, Applying and Conducting Research in the Classroom, by Firth, 2020

student-centered inquiry. If teachers hope to understand more about students' vocabulary, motivation, or fluency, they may work to learn more about those topics and how these skills and concepts can support strong learning. But student-driven inquiries often involve the need for tools and ideas to assess what students know, like, and want to know. This may require delving into sources related to assessment and data, such as the following (see also further resources for inquiring into students' learning in table 5.1).

Using Existing Assessments

Sometimes teams or individual teachers want to learn more about student skills in areas they don't already assess; exploring what measures already exist can be useful. We have seen teams elect to use existing measures of skills such as silent word reading to create a fuller picture of student literacy. Sometimes good, cost-effective, and time-sensitive tools already exist, and a bit of inquiry can help teachers and teams identify and use those. We have seen teachers productively spend time inquiring into how these tools are built and how they can be used to great advantage.

Creating New Assessments

Sometimes teachers want to learn from students about skills for which assessments don't already exist. This can lead to the creation of new, site-specific tools to gain more information. It can also sometimes lead to creating new valid and reliable tools that may be shared more widely across grade levels, schools, and districts. Teams and teachers often have questions about item formats or administration decisions that can lead to better and clearer information, which can be answered by inquiry in this area.

Using Existing Surveys and Questionnaires

Similarly, sometimes the inquiry question is related to students' preferences, styles, interests, and engagement, and teams may want to explore existing tools to glean more information about those areas. Identifying a survey instrument that already exists can help provide useful information, such as information about survey design and purpose, norming for each question, or even ways that various schools or districts have used tools previously. Considering these tools can save time, if teachers or teams find something that meets their needs.

Designing Our Own Scales and Surveys

In the same way that teachers may want to build their own assessments of skills, they may also want to build their own surveys or questionnaires to zero-in on specific information about students' experiences. But often survey design isn't a part of teacher training, so teams and teachers may wish to spend time learning how to build these sorts of tools or rely on a local expert (e.g., an instructional coach, technology teacher, and so on) for support. The benefit of a self-designed tool is the ability to gather just the information needed to guide an inquiry process.

Finding and Building Other Tools

Teachers and teams may also need additional tools to find out more about their students. Teams might find or build observation protocols, interview protocols, focus group questions, and so on. These too can merit time spent exploring, and we always encourage teachers to learn from the prior work of others, in their building or district, who have walked this same path.

Automating Collection of Information from Students

Sometimes, if teams or teachers would like to collect information from a large number of students, it can make sense to do some learning and planning around how to automate data collection to make it less work intensive once collected. Teachers may explore survey tools (e.g., SurveyMonkey), the online tools they use every day or learned to use during the pandemic (e.g., Canvas), or tools from Google (e.g., Google Forms) to learn how to maximize efficiency when collecting, organizing, and analyzing data. Time can be short, and investing in automating data collection during the learning phase of inquiry can buy much more time later to use what has been learned.

Reaching Out to Families for Information

Sometimes teachers or teams are looking to gain a more holistic view of students, and they reach out to families to learn more about students, their preferences, and their experiences in settings outside of school. Partnering with families in this way allows teachers to gather information that further illustrates who students are.

Building a Toolkit of Data Analysis Strategies

The information gathered from students can present a need to learn more about managing and using data, and we have seen teams and teachers embrace this sort of learning. They often learn methods of analysis, ideas for settling on priorities after they analyze information, or structures for action planning, in order to help guide next steps.

Student-centered inquiries often rely on data analysis tools teachers already have and skills they already use. But these inquiries may also require teachers to expand their existing skills or explore what others have done to answer similar questions. As teams and teachers build and expand their data analysis repertoire, they accumulate tools to use in the future, regardless of the inquiry on the table or the particular students they are learning about currently. In this way, teachers can acquire an assessment toolkit that is useful as inquiries grow and shift over time. At times, it is useful to look to local experts for support in growing this toolkit. Data specialists, statistics instructors, and others who make frequent use of student data can be useful guides for this work. We also often recommend the resources in table 5.1 for teachers wishing to grow this particular skillset.

Using Instruction to Learn More About Students

In addition to all the methods already listed, it is also possible and potentially useful to use instructional moves to get to know students better and to gauge their connection to the material being learned on any given day. Building personal connection tasks into instruction can support your work in centering students as a key component of enacting disciplinary literacy (DL).

Here, we meet Sol Rheem, a former high school ESL teacher of US history in Somerville, Massachusetts. Sol is a Korean American with a background in Latin American studies who taught students who were fairly early in learning to use English at school. Somerville High taught US history using a theme-based approach that focused on questions of equity and justice. Sol describes an ongoing dilemma: getting to know students and ensuring they felt as though they could be fully themselves in US history class and then how to address this in her history instruction. Her story shows how she moved from Step #2 to #3 in the inquiry cycle.

SOL RHEEM
Routines to Make Space for Students as Individuals

My goals in teaching immigrant kids were to create a space where they could be themselves and be mixed if we're talking about language use. I found that they used what they wanted, like whatever type of bilingualism, multilingualism, or translanguaging practices that they were using, wanted to use, or wanted to develop. I wanted to make a space where their languaging practices were seen and embraced and then also where they could explore other languaging practices, while also exploring their cultural identities.

I learned the concept of launch questions, which I used every day, from my mentor teacher, Sam Texeira at the Henderson School, when I was doing my student teaching. Each was a question about kids' everyday lives, and they started every single history lesson. The theme of the question was related to our current history theme. But the questions were not warm-up questions that required you to remember anything from the previous day or to have been there on the previous day (because attendance was sometimes spotty). It was a question that anyone could access that was engaging and interesting and that allowed them to tell a story about their lives or about what they think. We started every class with that launch task, with five minutes to write and discuss. Here is one launch example:

> *Risk (Riesgo): Tell me about a time when you took a risk to do something. What was the situation? What was the risk? How did you feel? Were there any benefits or rewards?*

This was from the unit about immigration. We were studying different instances of organizing by Latinx people—their organizing successes in US history. We were going to learn about the grape workers' strike in California that day.

I translated "risk" to Spanish and Portuguese, because at that point those were the two languages represented in my classroom. The purpose of the launch is access, for every single person. Regardless of how you're doing in the class, or how many days you've been in the class, you should be able to answer this question and say something about it.

Sol continued describing how this practice became routine for students and how, in the process of responding to students each day and listening to their discussion, she was able to learn important information about her students— their identities, interests, opinions, and patterns in language use across their multiple languages. She used this routine to keep generating new ideas about and understandings of students and how they may learn history best in her classroom.

INQUIRY STEP #3: IDEA GENERATION ABOUT STUDENTS

The idea generation phase of inquiry, centered on student questions, can operate a bit differently than those centering on texts or tasks, and often it results in two miniphases related to Steps #2 and #4.

First, once teams have inquired into the means they'll use to learn more about students, they will be ready to make a set of iterative decisions about what they know or want to know. This may include choosing to use a tool or survey they've found, designing mechanisms for more student feedback or information, or taking careful stock of what they already know from prior data or teacher knowledge. It may involve collecting new information, looking back at known information or student work, or discussing together what has seemed effective or ineffective for particular students in the past. Once a team or teacher feels comfortable that they have the tools they will need, they can begin the work of making decisions about what they want to do. But there are all sorts of ways that teams could use this phase to reflect and make an informed plan to better center students in their work.

Often teams find that data already exist that they can use during this phase of a cycle, although that isn't always the case. Here we meet Karen, a third- and fourth-grade elementary teacher at the Graham and Parks School in Cambridge, Massachusetts. Karen used instructional activities as a means to highlight student identity and also to gain information about students simultaneously, as her third graders began two years in her looping classroom.

KAREN ENGELS
Highlighting Student Identity in Multimodal Writing Activities

I am privileged to teach in a looping third-to-fourth-grade classroom, where I have the luxury to build relationships with children and families over the course of two years. This allows me to begin each loop with an extended period of getting to know children personally, culturally, and academically. During the early weeks of third grade, our first project is building "identity cubes," little cubes made out of manila folders that include collaged representations of different aspects of each child's identity (names, culture, hobbies, family, friends, and favorite school subjects). Inside, third graders write a letter to their end-of-loop fourth-grade self about their hopes and dreams for the years ahead. During the first month of school, we listen carefully as each student presents themselves to their classmates during our Morning Shares, and by the end of the month, we have begun the long process of forming a multicultural community in which each child feels that their whole self belongs.

Karen's story demonstrates how teachers can begin to seamlessly weave efforts to learn more about students into their curriculum. It also demonstrates how learning about students benefits not only teachers who are aiming to shape their curriculum more effectively but also other students, as these processes can help build or strengthen a community. Note also how multiple literacy skills, such as writing, discussion, and reading, are embedded in Karen's brief activities, with an authentic purpose to communicate aspects of identity both to peers and to students' own future selves. Within the genre of identity discovery and development, this is quite a nuanced (and age-appropriate) DL task.

INQUIRY STEP #4: IDEA TESTING WITH A FOCUS ON KNOWING STUDENTS AND MEETING ALL STUDENTS' NEEDS

Once teachers have determined what they want to know about students and collected that information, teams can move toward idea testing. This phase of the inquiry cycle often focuses on using what has been learned about students to tailor instruction or assessments to better serve their skills, needs, and interests. It often involves what most people tend to call differentiation, but it doesn't have to.

We tend to think about several types of shifts that can be made during this portion of idea testing. Teachers often have some success using self-determination theory to help guide their thinking.[11] This theory, which is a broad psychological one and not just school focused, posits that people are motivated to grow because of three different factors—competence, autonomy, and relatedness—and that everyone has a need for all three.

- **Competence** is a need to experience mastery.
- **Relatedness** is an experience of caring for and being cared for by others.
- **Autonomy** is a need to be an agent and to act on behalf of yourself.

When all three are in place, students often feel an overall sense of well-being.

We have found over time that this theory can be extremely useful in guiding teachers and teams who are generating ideas about student-centered inquiries. It gives them a frame for using the information they have or have collected to try out new instructional choices.

Using the data that we have collected about students usually becomes an answer to a deceptively simple question. The question is a version of "What do students need in order to learn better, engage more authentically, or achieve their own goals more fully?" It requires us to make sense of what we know about students. Self-determination theory can be a useful frame to generate and test ideas around these sorts of cycles, and here are some questions that could be used as a guide to an array of classroom experiments:

- **How can we tailor our instruction (including our texts and tasks) to build a stronger sense of competence among students?**
  - Can we make students more aware of how competent they are? How their skills grow over time?
  - Can we tweak or change our instruction to build competence for students?
  - Can we endeavor to make the hidden expectations of our disciplines clearer for students? Can we give them better tools to use to participate in and even critique various disciplines?
- **How can we grow student relatedness to our curriculum, our disciplines, our classroom communities, and to us as their teachers?**
  - How can we incorporate student interests and preferences, when possible?
  - How can we create more opportunities for students to explore various disciplines? How can we help them see a broader representation of participants in our disciplines?
  - How can we build stronger communities in classrooms, stronger relationships with students, and communities more supportive of risk-taking and growth as students learn?
  - How can we modify our language such that we can help students envision themselves as future and present members of our disciplines, such as seeing themselves as scientists or writers or artists?
- **How can we build more opportunities for student autonomy in our classrooms?**
  - How can we create chances for students to do more of the work of the disciplines, including building habits more in keeping with various subjects?
  - How can we incorporate more opportunities for student choice in our instruction over time?
  - How can we help students become more active in constructing a more complex sense of themselves within various disciplines (e.g., seeing themselves as historians, scientists, and so on)?
  - Can we build pathways by which students can become more seriously involved in various disciplines if they would like to?

In our prior work, we have seen teams and teachers generate all sorts of ideas for adjustments to instruction or assessments they can implement that relate to understanding and supporting students. So, a teacher may decide, for example, to implement literature circles in place of a whole-class novel, to address a few of these needs. They may use literature circles to support student competence by ensuring that various groups of students with different skills are reading a novel that will improve those skills. A teacher may help meet varied interests by grouping students to read texts more related to their own interests and preferences. Or they may use those texts to let students decide what they would most like to read. Of course, it depends on each teacher's goals and how they would like to support students better through a change like this one. They may ultimately use a combination of these choices based on the information they have about their students.

Several of the steps that we discussed earlier—looking backward, making a plan for trying out new ideas, and determining how to collect data before you begin—are all components that are likely still in play as student-centered ideas are generated and tested. You will almost certainly need a clearly articulated plan for this work as you begin testing student-centered changes and assessing the outcomes. To that point, we share here two additional considerations when testing new ideas as part of student-focused inquiry cycles.

Set Goals Carefully

Inquiry cycles that center on students often involve fine-tuning or trying to find good strategies to better support particular groups of students. And, as is typically the case in teaching, few instructional strategies work equally well for everyone. It is usually worth spending some time thinking in these cycles about what your concrete goals are. Sometimes working on differentiation can feel, in the moment, like something isn't working, just because it isn't working for everyone or working immediately. We have found that it can help to think about what your concrete goals are for these sorts of improvements. Do you hope to see progress for certain students? Or even just one student? Do you think this work will need to happen across several days or even weeks in order to see progress? Clarifying your goals ahead of implementing your new instructional strategies can be especially useful in the case of student-centered inquiry work.

Consider Streamlining Processes

Sometimes teams or teachers want to connect their data collection early in the cycle to their collection later in the idea-testing phase. Maybe you created and are using new data collection tools (e.g., focus group questions or survey tools), and you may consider whether you could use similar tools across multiple phases of your inquiry. Doing so may not be possible, as you may have developed an idea that is much more specific than the questions asked of and about students during the second phase of this process. There are advantages to streamlining, though, such as giving you waves of data over time that may help in considering the overall efficacy of instructional moves made on behalf of particular students. This is also a wonderful time to look toward automated data collection tools, such as those mentioned earlier in this chapter.

Student-focused inquiries, like other cycles, can take time to yield results, and they can require tinkering as you try to match strategies with students more effectively. It can help to talk with students about this tinkering, to involve them in the process of trying new strategies and providing feedback on how well they are working. This will help you have clearer information about how things are working, as well as help students refine their reflection and metacognitive skills at the same time.

INQUIRY STEP #5: REFLECTING AND REVISING IDEAS GEARED TOWARD STUDENTS

Once new ideas have been tested and feedback collected, we return to the questions that we have used to close other cycles. What do you want to keep? What do you want to keep tinkering with? What are the results of what you have changed, and for whom? These questions are still the ones that we focus on as we make decisions about keeping new strategies or continuing to try others, continuing the cycle or starting a new one, and considering whether and how to share our new ideas with other teachers and teams.

But previously, where the focus has sometimes been on more discipline-specific skills in other types of cycles, student-centered inquiries can require a broader range of thinking, including whether we have been able to strengthen the foundational and intermediate skills that otherwise might prevent some students from achieving as much as they might. Or we may want to know if we have been able to shift student attitudes or engagement, or whether we have helped students to envision themselves as members of and critical consumers within disciplinary communities.

Now we return to Evan's inquiry to illustrate how his use of an adapted RAND model supported student growth and led to new understanding for him and his students as they defined and refined the purposes for reading more clearly in his classroom.

EVAN MOUSSEAU
Using the RAND Model to Try a Different Approach to Reading

At the start of the academic year, I taught a lesson that explicitly built up the task of reading as a series of interrelated elements taken from the RAND model: the reader, the text, the activity, and the context. Using an excerpt from a YA novel I had book-talked, students noted the relationship between text and reader by seeing that students with different background knowledge accessed the text differently. After this, I distributed a variety of activities to focus their reading of another excerpt from the book. Some students were asked to record details about the character, others to describe the setting, some to analyze the author's use of figurative language, and a few to count the number of times the excerpt used the letter "e." When subsequently challenged to complete tasks that they hadn't focused on during their reading, students were frustrated and, in the case of counting letters, a bit confused. But the activity served to illustrate the point: if you don't read with the purpose in mind, you aren't fully reading. A thought experiment involving how reading the book in different contexts might shape one's understanding helped fill out the "context" element of the RAND model. Ultimately, though, we returned our focus to the "Purpose/Activity" element of the model, reflecting on how in most school-based reading tasks, the reader, text, and context are given, but readers must actively work to keep their purpose in mind.

Bringing the RAND model and the idea of reading with purpose to the forefront helped keep both me and my students focused on the elements of assigned reading that would bear the greatest fruit for our work together. More students were prepared for discussions, more were equipped with evidence for their essays, and more self-reported growth in their reading abilities at the end of the year.

CLOSING THOUGHTS ABOUT INQUIRY AND INSTRUCTION FOCUSED ON STUDENTS

As you can see, student-centered inquiries can lead down many different paths—sometimes different ones for different students. This work can be highly disciplinary or more intermediate, depending on what students need and prefer. As we help students become more aware of their competence, more connected to the material, and more able to make independent decisions about learning, we open new pathways for them to envision our disciplines as their own. This is also the first step in helping students begin to take ownership of a discipline so that they may re-envision the various norms within that given discipline.

Ultimately, returning to the self-determination theory mentioned earlier in this chapter, student-centered inquiry and instruction cycles can help us to shift students' sense of their own competence, autonomy, and relatedness in school and therefore their degree of investment in DL work. As a quick example, student interviews or focus groups with elementary students about science-based informational writing, placed alongside an analysis of student work products, may result in significant classroom changes. As a result of such a student-centered inquiry cycle, teachers might design shorter, more authentic scientific writing assignments that students feel more connected to, with a degree of choice in how they complete the tasks, all resulting in a greater sense of competence.

Such student-centered inquiry and instruction cycles can completely change how students view both themselves and the DL work that we ask them to complete. Although student-centered cycles of inquiry and instruction may not be the first cycles that teachers gravitate toward, they are an essential part of shifting toward a DL instructional stance.

PAUSE AND REFLECT

- After reading chapter 5, which student-centered inquiry questions may be most relevant to your discipline, classroom, department, or grade-level team?
- Which of the steps in the student-centered inquiry cycle would be easiest for you or your team to complete? Which would prove most challenging?
- Which student-level factors have caused questions or concerns for you and your school, especially postpandemic? How might these factors become the focus of new inquiry and instruction cycles for DL instruction?

- Who may be your best collaborators in designing, testing, and reflecting on new DL tasks?

TRY IT OUT

- On your own, or with a colleague, conduct an interview, survey, or focus group with students. Which literacy-focused or identity-focused elements may help you learn a good deal more about your students? How would knowing a bit more about your students and their individual and collective views of reading, writing, speaking, and content-focused work help you rethink your own teaching practices? Who may join you in this work?
- Look back across this chapter at Evan's, Jen's and Lindsey's, Sol's, and Karen's stories of delving more deeply into student-focused inquiry questions. In your opinion, what were the keys to success in these stories? What, if anything, could you borrow from their stories and try in your own classroom or school?

CONNECTING TO ILA'S STANDARDS 2017 FOR CLASSROOM TEACHERS

The International Literacy Association's *Standards for the Preparation of Literacy Professionals 2017* focus on the required skills and knowledge that classroom teachers (across grade levels) need in order to effectively design and refine classroom tasks that support students' reading, writing, and discussion skills.[12]

The standards that connect most closely to our own thinking about student-centered work can be found in Standard 3: Assessment and Evaluation; Standard 4: Diversity and Equity; and Standard 5: Learners and the Literacy Environment. From Standard 3, current and future classroom teachers are expected to continually observe students, analyze student work, and talk with students to learn more about how best to tailor instruction to meet their specific needs:

- 3.2: Candidates use observational skills and results of student work to determine students' literacy and language strengths and needs; select and administer other formal and informal assessments appropriate for assessing students' language and literacy development.
- 3.3: Candidates use results of various assessment measures to inform and/or modify instruction.

From Standard 4, current and future classroom teachers are expected to explore and honor students' various cultural, linguistic, and literate identities–bringing those identities into classroom work whenever possible:

- 4.1: Candidates recognize how their own cultural experiences affect instruction and appreciate the diversity of their students, families, and communities.
- 4.2: Candidates set high expectations for learners and implement instructional practices that are responsive to students' diversity.
- 4.3: Candidates situate diversity as a core asset in instructional planning, teaching, and selecting texts and materials.
- 4.4: Candidates forge family, community, and school relationships to enhance students' content and literacy learning.

Finally, from Standard 5, current and future classroom teachers are expected to have a deep understanding of motivation, engagement, and learning theories that influence how classroom instruction can best be tailored to specific students:

- For younger learners–5.1: Candidates apply knowledge of learner development and learning differences to plan learning experiences that develop motivated and engaged literacy learners.
- For older learners–5.1: Candidates demonstrate understanding of theories and concepts related to adolescent literacy learning and apply this knowledge to learning experiences that develop motivated and engaged literacy learners.

Note how these standards emphasize the need for teachers to know, understand, and attend to students' many identities, literacies, and lives at school versus lives at home. There is also a wise emphasis on forging strong school-home communication routines and partnerships. Assessment practices, both formal and informal, are key here. In order for teachers to know and respond to students' many identities and slowly grow their literacy skills, teachers must be both interested in uncovering students' multifaceted identities and open to incorporating those identities into the very fabric of classroom instructional practices.

CHAPTER 6

Culture as a Focus for Disciplinary Literacy Inquiry and Instruction

IN PREVIOUS CHAPTERS, we detailed the ways that focusing on students, the texts being used in lessons, or the literacy tasks in classrooms can be useful starting points for instructional shifts that incorporate disciplinary literacy (DL) skills. Broadening the scope a bit, a focus on the classroom or school context (the sociocultural context in the RAND model) can help to guide teachers to look at literacy instruction across disciplines in new ways and to develop approaches that are inclusive of and responsive to the variety of cultural contexts in which students and teachers find themselves, both within school and beyond. Inquiry cycles driven by curiosity about the role that context plays in literacy development for students may be guided by questions such as the following:

- How is my classroom context creating a meaningful, familiar, safe place where I can teach the literacies of a given discipline?
- What type of setting am I creating within my classroom to welcome a variety of voices and literacies into the space as valued participants?
- How can I use student voice and feedback to shape and inform my instruction?

- How do students experience my classroom culture? What role does student voice play in that culture? Who has voice and power? When and why?
- What aspects of my classroom or school promote or stand in the way of a culture of reading, writing, and speaking? Who has access to this culture, and who does not, and why?

An inquiry into the culture or context surrounding DL involves a teacher or team of teachers asking about the ways that their classrooms, schools, or larger communities support the development of DL skills. This includes first building a deep understanding of the culture around literacy in schools, and it requires also exploring how various content areas are constructed within districts and classrooms.[1] Disciplines within schools have cultures, and within those cultures, norms and values about literacy already exist.

Similarly, inquiry into culture and context asks teachers to investigate school and community contexts to draw on the existing capital, funds of knowledge, and strengths within those various communities–to build on them and to then develop DL skills and knowledge from that foundation. Funds of knowledge are the knowledge that communities already have that are embedded in the lives and routines of a given community.[2] The work of teaching responsively requires that we build spaces that sustain the cultures of students, build off of their funds of knowledge, and support them in developing critical ways of viewing the world.[3]

In this chapter, you will meet a number of teachers who have examined the context in which their instruction takes place, at the classroom, school, or district level. These examinations often involve the discovery of elements of culture they had yet to consider or had yet to capitalize on as an asset in the process of literacy development. For some, it meant discovering district-level practices that could be shifted in order to further develop literacy skills for certain students or populations, and for others, it meant thinking in new ways about how they may shift the culture and context within their own classrooms to support their intermediate and disciplinary literacy goals. In this chapter, you will meet:

- Marycruz Somes, a district-based ESL teacher who took a broad look into the experiences of English learners (ELs) in mainstream classrooms across her district
- Alejandra Muñoz, Martha Gammie, Katie Stowell, Ben Stein, and Dan Trahan, members of a middle school team who created lessons focused on discussion to be taught across all subjects

- Jimmy Aquino, a high school global history teacher who explored the culture of his students and the culture of doing history to build a classroom culture of criticality
- Jacqueline Hallo, Christina Collins, Sheila Jaung, Pamela Penwarden, John Padula, and Marisa Ricci, members of another middle school team who worked on increasing reading engagement and the culture of reading among sixth graders
- Kate Leslie, a high school social studies teacher who led a team in a revision process of their annual research paper
- Karen Engels, a third- and fourth-grade teacher who looked into the way that her library framed her classroom context and made shifts to make it more broadly inclusive and representative

We begin by setting the context with Marycruz Somes. Marycruz is a high school ESL teacher in Salem, Massachusetts, a district with a high percentage of ELs. In her role, she works as a coteacher in some classrooms and also teaches separate classes that are only for ELs. Her initial dive into questions of culture and how it framed and affected ELs came after the findings of a school-wide survey, noting that a low percentage of students were attentive during and invested in school. This led to further classroom-level investigations and, ultimately, new instructional practices within her own teaching.

MARYCRUZ SOMES
Making Space for Talk and Conversation for High School English Learners

I became very interested in this problem after seeing the unsettling data on student engagement coming from my last school-wide survey. According to the report, 21 percent of 639 respondents answered favorably to questions regarding how attentive and invested students were in school. Informal observations of ESL and non-ESL classrooms as well as conversations between ESL and non-ESL staff pointed out this problem too.

I asked [two colleagues] if they were willing to explore this problem more in depth and to look for solutions. They candidly agreed. Together we created a trajectory of work sessions, with clear outcomes for each one. We came up with our problem-of-practice statement, which was "Intermediate English language learners have trouble engaging in speaking activities in ESL classes. Teachers do not use high-interest speaking activities and do not use real-life events to make the discussions more meaningful for students." It was not easy to arrive at this statement. It involved a great deal of discussion with my colleagues, data analysis, and self-examination of our practice.

We reviewed the data regarding school engagement as well as disciplinary referrals, important data points for our work. We also came up with questions to survey our own students, and we analyzed the results. Keeping those data pieces and the informal classroom observations in mind along the way gave us the inspiration to join forces and try out something different in our classes.

Also, I started to be more observant and reflective when in other classes and in my own. I started noticing the need for ELLs to be more engaged in their classes. After being in a few mainstream classes as a coteacher, I noticed there was a pattern; the ELLs were too quiet. Sometimes it felt as if they were not even there. I noticed that a whole ninety-minute class would go by without hearing them talk or seeing them interacting with their peers. We are talking about classes with intermediate students—students who need ample opportunities to develop their proficiency in English in order to improve their ability in the target language—yet there were few or no such opportunities.

The observations prompted me to look more into my own teaching as well. They prompted me to pay more attention to how engaged my students were in my own ESL classes. I discovered that there was some disengagement in my classes too. I started paying more attention to the what and the how of my own teaching. I started connecting my curriculum to current events to make it more relevant to students. For instance, the essential questions in one of the units I needed to cover were, "What holds us together? What keeps us apart?" And there was so much discussion about gun control in our society at that time that it felt natural to bring this topic into the class. Slowly, I noticed that those disengaged students started perking up and being more willing to take risks in class.

The teaching idea that came out of this learning was the need for students to engage more frequently in activities that require them to hold rigorous, engaging academic conversations, such as Socratic seminars, debates, or any other discussion protocols. These are powerful speaking activities that we thought would impact student engagement and increase their speaking skills. Without any doubt, our ELLs need to speak more in classes, but they want to talk about issues that they care about, not about issues dictated in a textbook. I think that one of the problems with classroom motivation and engagement is that teachers rely heavily on textbooks or the curriculum and teach to the test. For this reason, the selection of relevant strong conversation/discussion prompts is crucial to increase engagement. Additionally, the idea of mixing up classes and team teaching came out of this learning as well.

In Marycruz's narrative, you can see how a focus on the school and classroom context allowed her to gain crucial insight into the literacy development of ELs, particularly in the domain of spoken language. Her inquiry led her not only to collaborate with others but also to develop new practices within her own classroom that allow for many rich speaking opportunities, in large part because they are connected to topics that matter to students and to a structure (Socratic seminar) that supports those conversations. This narrative illuminates many elements of the inquiry cycle, as they relate to DL instruction.

After determining a core topic for inquiry, namely ELs' engagement in school and, in particular, in classroom discourse, Marycruz entered Step #2 of the inquiry cycle, with a focus on building background knowledge. She used not only school-wide data that was available to her but also the input and expertise of colleagues who were also ESL teachers. Her collaborative work with colleagues resulted in new ideas for instructional approaches, such as Socratic seminar, utilizing current events as the focus for classroom conversation, and new team-teaching configurations. In testing these ideas, Marycruz noted that engagement in her classroom increased, particularly among ELs–a result that she is certain to now bring back to her colleagues in order to further refine their teaching ideas. Bolstered by early success, they are likely to be able to develop even more approaches that will support the literacy development of ELs.

In the remainder of this chapter, we outline the ways that teachers can consider the context and culture within their classrooms and schools and how these elements can support the development of DL skills. We ask you to consider the following questions across this chapter: *What are students' experiences in my classroom? How about in my school? How does a feeling and sense of culture help or hinder students' learning in literacy?* The five phases of the inquiry cycle will help you to ask and begin to answer these questions.

INQUIRY STEP #1: CENTERING CULTURE AS THE SUBJECT OF OUR INQUIRY WORK

As with the domain of tasks, teachers often have a bit more control of classroom and school culture than, for instance, the content of the curriculum. And, at the same time, culture is often elusive. What creates culture? Do we actually have control over it? Even within our schools? How often does the culture shift? Does my classroom culture always have to align with my school's broader culture? Do I need to constantly be shifting too?

When thinking about classroom culture, teachers are thinking beyond individual students. They are thinking about a group of students as a whole, or even about the whole school. This is the difference between thinking about differentiation, which generally occurs at the individual student level, and thinking at the global cultural level about issues that may affect everyone in the class or at least larger groups. Therefore, you may begin to ask culture-focused questions such as the following:

- Where do the students in my class come from?
- Who is represented in my classroom curriculum, and who is not?
- Does the culture in my classroom support students' voices and allow them to question what we do or what we learn? Or even question me as their teacher?
- Does my classroom culture allow me to learn about the backgrounds, funds of knowledge, and literacies of all of my students?

When you ask these questions, you are delving into the domain of culture. Importantly, shifting culture can help support DL instruction and shift the literacy learning that happens in your classroom.

It is important to recognize that asking these kinds of big questions can be hard. They can be daunting and nerve-racking. You might worry about what you will uncover. Know that it is natural to worry when you are on the brink of delving into a domain as big as culture. And culture is often hard both to uncover and to shift within classrooms and schools.[4] Schein famously commented that culture is simply *the way we do things around here*, meaning that it can become ingrained in the everyday, often to the point where it can feel invisible to members of a specific community.[5]

It can be hard to step back from the everyday routine in order to examine culture. For instance, why do you organize the furniture in your classroom a particular way? Why is your classroom library organized by genre instead of by author? Why do students sit in rows alphabetically? Why are groups of students always made up of four students? If you step back and consider these questions, your answer might be, "I'm really not sure." Or perhaps you might say, "Well, that's the way I learned," or "My colleagues all do it that way, so I do too." These answers all illustrate the tacit culture operating in your school or in your classroom. This culture lies beneath the surface and takes time to uncover.

Culture is important to consider not just because you should think about why your desks and chairs are set up the way they are but also because you should consider deeper questions, such as: which students' voices are more dominant in your classroom; whose experiences are represented in your classroom library; and which students and their families feel connected to the academic content and structure of school and which don't? These questions focus on equity and the ways that classroom culture can promote or hinder equitable learning experiences for students on a daily basis. Digging into questions of culture and the ways that culture shapes learning opportunities–both within literacy and beyond–also means digging into questions of equity and asking yourself how your own classroom practices can shift in order to ensure equitable outcomes for all students in your class or even school.[6]

You will remember that in the RAND model, context is the outermost encompassing layer. It represents the space in which all the inner work happens. So, in asking questions about culture and context, you are asking questions about how you, as a teacher, shape the space in which the other aspects of the DL inquiry and instruction model take place. How does your context support the students within it? How does the culture in your classroom support the enactment of different approaches to learning? How do the various cultures that students bring with them to school shape the culture of your classroom or school? How does your culture dictate choices about which literacy activities and texts your students use and interact with? The answers to all of these questions are shaped by context. In what follows, let's explore how different teachers have approached questions about culture and context within their own practice in ways that have shaped their literacy instruction.

INQUIRY STEP #2: BUILDING BACKGROUND KNOWLEDGE WHEN INQUIRING ABOUT CULTURE AND CONTEXT

As with the other literacy domains, it is important to build background knowledge about culture and context in order to make shifts that create inclusive literacy environments that respond to, represent, and inspire all students.

While building background knowledge about certain domains, such as texts or tasks, might be easily done through reading or watching videos, researching and learning more about classroom culture and context require broader exploration. When you are thinking about culture and context in a classroom or school, you are asking, in part, who is represented; what the backgrounds of the students are; and how students, as a whole, can have a voice.

To learn more about this, you may need to do some research into culture. Putting on an anthropologist's or sociologist's hat, you might spend time with students at recess or at lunch to observe patterns of communication, learning how students build relationships with each other, and what seems to make certain students feel included. You may extend that exploration into the community, learning about students in nonschool spaces. What is the culture among their sports teams, in their afterschool programs, in the community groups where they may volunteer? If you do this kind of research, you want to keep asking yourself which elements of the cultures you observe seem to invite students in, support them in growing, and build connections within each group.

To build background knowledge in the domain of context and culture, you may also turn to families in your research so that you can learn more about the experiences that make students feel at home, safe, and willing to take risks. Using what you learn and then approximating these conditions in your classroom are also likely to help build a classroom culture in which students are willing to push themselves, take risks, and build new DL skills.

Finally, turning to colleagues, as with some of the other domains we have already reviewed, is an ideal form of research. When teams of teachers come together, they can discuss their successes in building classroom cultures that are inclusive and representative, or compile an array of information that they may only have pieces of individually. They can also pinpoint areas where growth is needed and then work together on those areas. Developing strategies collectively often leads to exciting results in shaping or reshaping classroom or school culture.

To illustrate, we introduce you to a team of middle school teachers from the Lincoln School in Brookline, Massachusetts–Alejandra Muñoz, Martha Gammie, Katie Stowell, Ben Stein, and Dan Trahan. Working across disciplines with the same group of sixth graders, these teachers collaborated to reshape the culture around discussion in their middle school classrooms in order to center student voice.

LINCOLN SCHOOL TEAM PART 1
Developing a Culture to Support Authentic Discussion

When facilitating student discussions, we noticed common challenges across our content areas. For example, students rarely responded authentically to one another in classroom discussions; they often seemed to wait for their turn to speak and then delivered their prepared thoughts, and they struggled to hold a discussion with groups or individuals who disagreed with them without discussions turning into arguments or coming to a halt. Additionally, students did not use conversation starters such as "I believe," "What do you think," or "I have not heard _____ speak? _____, what do you think?" They also used no clarifying questions, such as "I heard you say _____. Am I getting that right?" And many students did not engage in classroom discussions at all because of fear of incorrectly responding and a lack of confidence in their participation.

Our work began with brainstorming questions and areas of inquiry such as the following:

- What do small group and intervention discussion norms look like?

- What do whole-class discussion norms look like?

- How can a set of discussion norms improve the quality of discussion?

- What are excellent small group strategies for discussion?

Then, in order to better understand the topic of academic discussion, we began to search for articles that related to the topic and reached out to other members of the district teaching community.

In our initial learning stages, we read the following articles:

- Michaels and O'Connor: "Conceptualizing Talk Moves as Tools"[7]

- Zwiers and Crawford: "How to Start Academic Conversations"[8]

- Feldman and Kinsella: "Practical Strategies to Improve Academic Discussions in Mixed Ability Secondary Content Area Classrooms"[9]

We also read other articles that related to discussion norms, content-area variations in academic language, and body language during discussion.

Upon returning to school in September, we each videotaped a class discussion based on subject matter that students were familiar with. We coded the data, looking for student participation, frequency of teacher input, and the use of academic conversation skills as outlined by Zwiers and Crawford in their article. We were able to identify areas of strength and create goals together.

Here, you can see that the middle school team from Lincoln used key strategies for research. First, they used each other, recognizing the specific struggles that their students had in building a classroom culture around discussion. They noted what was lacking in the discussions, and in doing this, simultaneously built goals for effective discussions. After creating some questions to guide their inquiry, they turned to experts on classroom discussion. Through reading articles, they were able to craft a shared understanding of the culture that they wanted to build around classroom discussion. Finally, they studied their own practice. Using video, they captured students' discussions and were able to pinpoint where the culture of discussion was already present (even if only a little bit) and what they wanted to try next to further build classroom cultures that supported strong discussion.

INQUIRY STEP #3: IDEA GENERATION ABOUT SHIFTING CULTURE AND CONTEXT

After building background knowledge about culture and context, it is time to generate new ideas for shifting the culture within your classroom. Regarding the domain of culture, there are three main approaches to developing these new ideas, which mirror some of the strategies used to generate new tasks found in chapter 4.

First, teachers may *adopt* already-proven approaches to building classroom culture. As in the example from Lincoln School, teachers may see, in one of their colleagues' classrooms or in a shared text, a strategy that is quite effective at bringing in all student voices. Simply adopting that approach would be a solid starting point for making a cultural change in one's own classroom.

Next, teachers may *adapt* a variety of culture-building approaches. In certain instances, teachers see an approach to building a strong and inclusive culture in one classroom that won't quite work in their own context. Perhaps it is an idea used with older students that needs adaptation to be effective with younger students. Or perhaps it needs to be more systematized to be effective in a given classroom or school. Depending on the degree and nature of changes needing to be made, adapting ideas for developing classroom and school culture can be an incredibly effective approach.

Finally, teachers may utilize *aspirational* culture-building approaches. Sometimes teachers can't quite find the right model for the type of classroom culture that they want to build. In that instance, they may take an aspirational approach to shifting or building classroom culture. This involves creating a strong vision for where they want the culture to be and (ideally working with others) trying out many different approaches to achieve the imagined outcome. It may take a while to achieve the aspired outcome. This can be a process involving lots of iteration and revision, but sometimes it is the best and most exciting path to follow.

To illustrate, we introduce Jimmy Aquino, a global history teacher at Multicultural High School in Brooklyn, New York. He describes focusing on *adapting* his history curriculum to the particular students he teaches, in the city where he grew up and was raised.

JIMMY AQUINO
Adapting by Connecting the Culture of History to the Culture of the Students

The administration wanted us to do a project-based learning (PBL) activity. And at first, I had no idea what to do with PBL, but I had 3D printers. So, I was able to create a mask project with the students. I thought, "What if I have my students research symbols, European symbols, Indigenous symbols from North and South America, and African symbols and what they mean?" Then, I had students create masks using these different symbols. First, they had to decide which European, Indigenous, and African symbols they would implement in the draft of their mask, and they had to show all three cultures. The masks were based on which cultures they felt they were more connected to, and mixing all three cultures gave them an idea of the complexity of their own culture. Students learned that they are all of different Latin American and Caribbean nations, but they all were also of European, Indigenous, and African descent. Now the masks are all over the school, and through that process of creating masks based on European, Indigenous, and African descent, students began to uncover which cultures they identify with in their own lives, and I was glad to see lots of connections to Indigenous and African cultures. Through this work students also began to realize that Spanish and English are colonial languages as we unpacked the various cultures.

Here we see Jimmy working to really understand students through exploring cultures, in a way that the global history curriculum requires. Through this work, he creates a culture of engaging in history in ways that focus on exploring forces such as colonialism. His teaching here capitalizes on the wide funds of knowledge that students bring into global history and uses these funds to learn even more. This task builds classroom culture in terms of how Jimmy's students approach history from a critical stance and allows students to bring a wide range of cultures into the global history classroom simultaneously.

Just as Jimmy's work illustrates the adaptive approach to culture building, the eighth-grade teaching team at the Baker School in Brookline, Massachusetts—Jacqueline Hallo, Christina Collins, Sheila Jaung, Pamela Penwarden, John Padula, and Marisa Ricci—illustrates the aspirational approach to building culture within their eighth grade. After giving students a survey on reading engagement and realizing that students did not have a habit of reading, nor did they see themselves (as a group) as readers, the team designed a multifaceted approach to building a culture of reading, trust, and engagement among the rising eighth grade.

BAKER MIDDLE SCHOOL TEAM
Developing a Culture of Reading among Eighth Graders

After several summer meetings, our DLI [Disciplinary Literacy Initiative] team and two local business owners developed a year-long plan for incoming eighth graders. During each quarterly term, students would spend a day at The Makery (a local makerspace), rotating through stations that included an interactive read-aloud, a literature circle meeting, book talks to introduce newly published YA books and upcoming literary events, and a writing workshop. They would also have independent reading time and an extended period in The Makery's workshop to design and create an art project that connects to our literacy initiatives. The Brookline

Booksmith's (a local bookstore) YA team would lead some of our discussions during The Makery trips as well as help us to select other required reading books for future visits. We are also considering inviting local writers, community activists, artists, and parents to participate in future "Community Literacy Project" days.

To create a community of engaged readers, we needed to dedicate time at the beginning of the year to building our eighth-grade community. We hope that after giving students opportunities to build relationships with their teachers and with each other, they will be enthusiastic participants in our authentic literacy discussions about identity and community. To accomplish this, we decided to start the year with a ropes course field trip so that students and teachers would have a chance to connect outside of the classroom. This trip has been a highlight of eighth grade in past years because of its collaborative and community-building nature. Consequently, we decided it would be a great tool to help us build relationships with our new students. Traditionally, we ended the year with this trip, but now it is slated to happen during the first week of school.

The eighth-grade team at the Baker School came together in order to imagine the type of engaged reading culture that they hoped for among their students. Without any clear models to adopt or adapt, they invented an aspirational model and put into place creative structures to enact the model and to jump-start the cultural shift that they envisioned.

INQUIRY STEP #4: IDEA TESTING—IMPLEMENTING NEW APPROACHES TO SHIFTING CULTURE AND CONTEXT

Testing new ideas for building or shifting classroom or school culture can feel rather daunting. Culture isn't built in a day, and it doesn't shift in a day. It is therefore important to give yourself time and to create reasonable benchmarks. For instance, if you are working on creating a culture where more students share their opinions, you may want to gather baseline data over a few days to see who seems to share more and who shares less or not at all. Then create a reasonable goal that would mean you have had some success in shifting these patterns. When you think about your new ideas to meet that goal, you also need to ask, "How long might this reasonably take?"

As teachers, we often hope for quick and easy results. When thinking about culture and making noticeable shifts in culture, long term, incremental results are the goal. Thus, it is important to employ a variety of strategies to consider the results of your culture-building or culture-shifting efforts. We name a few such strategies here:

- **Using classroom data**
  If you have gathered initial baseline data, such as which students participate and when, choosing a future midpoint or endpoint time to gather the same set of data will give you a good check-in on the results of your efforts.
- **Talking to students**
  If you are making shifts that focus on a sense of belonging, ownership, or engagement among students, checking in with students themselves about the results of your changes is a great way to discern and measure progress. Individual interviews or small focus groups with students can be conducted relatively quickly and will provide an enormous amount of information.
- **Talking to families and community organizations**
  You may be working on culture with the hope of building more engagement, and that engagement could emerge both at school and at home. Perhaps, like the teachers from Baker, you are working on building reading engagement. Checking in with families in order to see what they are seeing and hearing at home is a great way to check on the results of your culture-shifting efforts. Similarly, check with the community organizations where your students spend time. How are they seeing DL skills come to life? What shifts might they see in their students as a result of cultural shifts you have made within your classroom?
- **Observing in other school spaces**
  Just like you can learn about the cultures that are often most supportive of various students in spaces outside classrooms or schools, you can also check in on your culture-building efforts in those spaces. Are students bringing new literacy strategies into other spaces in their lives (e.g., afterschool activities, volunteer jobs, and so on)? Have the numbers of your ELs, for instance, who joined the school newspaper increased as a result of your efforts to bring their voices to the fore in your classroom? Investigating non-classroom or out-of-school spaces can provide great insight.

Kate Leslie, a high school social studies teacher at Brookline High School in Brookline, Massachusetts, illustrates how she and her team gathered student input to both develop and test new ideas for history research papers at her school.

KATE LESLIE
Using Student Input to Build a Responsive Research Paper

When the Social Studies Literacy Team commenced, we all identified the research paper project as a dilemma that we wanted to explore and try to improve. We agreed that the project was valuable and had the potential to teach our students critical literacy skills. However, we also could tell that it wasn't working in its current form. Too many students were being left behind. We wanted to figure out what was going wrong: What needed to change about the structure of the project to help more students be successful? What DL skills did we need to teach more explicitly—or in a different manner—in order for students to become proficient?

Instead of guessing the answers to these questions, we decided to set up focus groups with our current students to gain their insights into the project. Each of the members of the Social Studies Literacy Team met with four to seven of our own students outside of classroom time in order to get their opinions about the research project. We started by polling their opinions about the previous year's research project. What had gone well? What had been frustrating? We learned some incredibly helpful information, including the following insights:

- Students wanted a lot of freedom in their topic choice, even if that meant that it was harder to find sources.

- Students disliked the online note-gathering program called NoodleTools that teachers had been requiring that they use for research. This was causing many students to procrastinate note-taking.

- Students reported that one of the most useful things that teachers could do was meet with them one-on-one more often.

- Students also reported needing more time for the project. They wanted a chance to really work on each step of the research process, instead of feeling forced to rush through to just get it done.

Armed with this information, the Social Studies Literacy Team restructured our own research paper assignment, lengthening it to a four-month endeavor. We built in more time for explicit skill lessons, and we set aside class time for one-on-one meetings with students. We also decided to have students write reports on their research topics before trying to write a thesis-driven paper so that they could see the difference in the two styles. However, the smartest thing we decided to do was to continue to hold focus group meetings.

Our next round of focus group meetings was midway through our own research paper assignment. In this second round of interviews, we asked students what had been going well, what had been frustrating, and what had been the hardest aspects of the research process. Again, we gained invaluable feedback:

- We learned that students had enormous trouble conducting deep research on their topics because they struggled to find sources beyond superficial encyclopedia articles and basic database articles. We had never considered that finding good sources could be a major barrier for our students.

- We also heard students report that deciding on a thesis statement was one of the hardest steps of the research process. Unfortunately, this was also the research step that teachers felt the least equipped to help with. This made us realize that more one-on-one student/teacher meetings were desperately needed at this time in the research process.

We continued with the research process, making changes according to what students reported that they needed during the focus group interviews.

You can see how Kate's example ties together both idea testing, in which social studies teachers utilized new ideas based on student feedback, and check-in strategies. Though this vignette may seem to be one about task, in which the social studies team adjusted the research paper task, it also illustrates the way that Kate and her team made specific adjustments in how they listened to student voices and then taught according to student feedback. Creating curriculum that is responsive to students' needs is a key example of how teachers can shift the culture within their classrooms or schools and how they can do this in ways that support powerful DL development.

Similarly, the middle school teachers from the Lincoln School used their research to build a shared curriculum about discussion. Once they were able to try out this new curriculum over time, they were able to see distinct shifts in the classroom culture around discussion. Let's revisit the Lincoln team (from earlier in this chapter) to hear a bit more.

LINCOLN SCHOOL TEAM PART 2
Settling into New Discussion Practices

We then taught five lessons in which we introduced the discussion norms, watched our discussion videos and reflected on our new norms, practiced active listening, explored body language, and introduced protocols for effective turn-taking and participation. We worked as a team to implement these lessons in our classes and helped students make connections across their content area classes by using common language and practices.

Some of the outcomes of our work include improvement in active body language, use of paraphrasing sentence frames independently, more active listening for understanding and responding to classmates authentically, support of ideas with evidence, and improved eye contact, confidence, and use of academic vocabulary. It was evident by student conversation at the end of the year that students were able to transfer the learning they had done in other classes about discussion into other settings with scaffolding. Students began to regularly respond to one another's ideas and engage in more cohesive conversation about the content. Additionally, students reported feeling more confident sharing their ideas, and some of the students who used to talk more commented that they felt less pressured to talk first or continue talking and felt better when allowing others to share.

Here, we see how the Lincoln School teachers found distinct shifts in their students' engagement during discussions. As they looked back on their idea-testing process, they could confirm that the lessons that they codesigned and each taught across different subject areas shifted the culture in their classrooms to one in which students could engage with each other more productively and more authentically around the content. For them, idea testing also gave them the confidence to continue this work throughout the year with their students.

INQUIRY STEP #5: REFLECTING AND REVISING IDEAS FOR SHIFTING CULTURE AND CONTEXT

Once you have tried out new ideas and also used the tools mentioned in Step #4 to consider the results of your efforts to shift the classroom/school culture or context, it is then important to step back and reflect. What has gone well? What might you still want to change? What is your evidence telling you? Often this is when you start to see the takeaways from your work and to reflect on how you will move on to the next steps of your process, whether it is continued work on shifting culture and context, or focusing on other areas that can also impact DL instruction and skills.

Karen Engels, a third- and fourth-grade teacher at the Graham and Parks School in Cambridge, Massachusetts, illustrates how she made shifts to address the sense of community and representation in her classroom as well as the results of these efforts.

KAREN ENGELS
Using Literature to Build Classroom Representation and Inclusivity

Recently I realized that while my classroom library and curricular resources consciously reflected many of the cultures of my students, I had very little representation from South Asian authors. I used the South Asian Book Award website to help me identify a few possibilities and decided to add *Tiger Boy* by Mitali Perkins, set in the Sundarbans on the border between India and Bangladesh, as a book club choice for our fourth-grade character unit. On the first day of the book club meeting, a student from Bangladesh said in wonder, "There are Bangla words in this book!" and his face was just radiant. We positioned him as our "expert" on the setting, and throughout our discussions of the book, he explained many of the cultural allusions, from the geography of mangrove forests to the Bangladeshi value of education and the cultural context of a more authoritarian schooling system than we have in the United States. This led to many other immigrant students in the classroom comparing and contrasting their schooling experiences around the globe with the education system in America and allowed for each of those students to bring a uniquely valuable perspective to the discussion.

In Karen's story, we can see the direct result of her choices to expand the representation of South Asian authors in her classroom instruction. The sense of belonging among immigrant students within her classroom was directly and noticeably affected. Her example illustrates how attention to culture and creating a sense of belonging and representation within a classroom can relate directly to improved literacy engagement and outcomes for students.

CLOSING THOUGHTS ON INQUIRY AND INSTRUCTION FOCUSED ON CULTURE

As we end this inquiry into the role of culture in DL instruction, we want to leave you with a few reminders. First, remember from the RAND model that culture represents the surround. The other three domains that we have discussed in this book (texts, tasks, and students) are close to the teacher or close to the student. They can feel easier to wrap your head around. Culture is, by nature, more fluid and shifting. And it exists (often invisibly) all around us. It is not always the easiest domain to consider shifting. When you are making changes to enhance your DL instruction, considering shifting culture can be both a challenge and a necessity.

Recognizing that it is challenging, we recommend that most teachers start with shifts that are a bit more concrete first. Once you have built some routines and stamina with DL inquiry and instruction work, by making shifts in texts and tasks, or by exploring student-focused issues, you may then wish to investigate culture. At the same time, don't ignore culture. Too often, we tend to stop tinkering after making more concrete shifts, such as varying the literacy tasks that we give our students. Yet, if we don't create a classroom culture where all students feel that their voices are heard and that their identities are seen and noticed, those new tasks may be effective for only a handful of students. This may leave behind quieter voices or students who feel disconnected from school or certain subjects within school. Shifting culture can produce powerful, equitable effects, and those effects can ripple into the other domains that we review in this book.

PAUSE AND REFLECT

- After reading chapter 6, which culture-focused inquiry questions may be most relevant to your discipline, classroom, department, or grade-level team?
- Which of the steps in the culture-focused inquiry cycle would be easiest for you or your team to complete? Which would prove most challenging?
- Which aspects of your classroom or school culture already support DL development? Which aspects would you want to enhance to further support DL development?

- As you look back at the vignettes in the chapter, which seem to resonate for you? Which provide an entry point for your own inquiries?
- Thinking about culture usually means thinking about equity. What does this mean in the context of your classroom? Your school?

TRY IT OUT

- On your own, or with a colleague, try spending some time with students outside of the classroom. This could be in the lunchroom, during a sports practice, during an extracurricular activity, or even at a local community center. What is the culture like among students in these spaces? How are students supported, seen, and engaged differently than within your school or classroom? How can you take aspects of those cultures into your own school or classroom?
- Look back through the story of the Lincoln middle school team. What were their particular successes? What led to those successes? What else would you suggest they do to keep building a culture of deep discussion and collaboration among their middle school students?

CONNECTING TO ILA'S STANDARDS 2017 FOR CLASSROOM TEACHERS

The International Literacy Association's *Standards for the Preparation of Literacy Professionals 2017* focus on the required skills and knowledge that classroom teachers (across grade levels) need in order to effectively design and refine classroom tasks that support students' reading, writing, and discussion skills.[10] The standards that connect most closely to our own thinking about culture can be found in Standard 4: Diversity and Equity and Standard 5: Learners and the Literacy Environment.

From Standard 4, current and future classroom teachers are expected to "examine their own culture and beliefs; set high expectations for their students; learn about and appreciate the cultures of their students, families, and communities to inform instruction."[11]

This general standard is then broken into four elements:

- 4.1: Candidates recognize how their own cultural experiences affect instruction and appreciate the diversity of their students, families, and communities.

- 4.2: Candidates set high expectations for learners and implement instructional practices that are responsive to students' diversity.
- 4.3: Candidates situate diversity as a core asset in instructional planning, teaching, and selecting texts and materials.
- 4.4: Candidates forge family, community, and school relationships to enhance students' literacy learning.

From Standard 5, current and future classroom teachers are expected to create socially and academically safe and literacy-rich environments in response to their specific students' many identities and in which all students can thrive:

- 5.1: Candidates apply knowledge of learner development and learning differences to plan learning experiences that develop motivated and engaged literacy learners.
- 5.4: Candidates create physical and social literacy-rich environments that use routines and a variety of grouping configurations for independent and collaborative learning.

Note how these standards emphasize the need for teachers not only to know, understand, and attend to students' many identities but also to create larger social and intellectual communities within their classrooms that help students learn and develop. The move for a teacher from a student-centered (chapter 5) to a culture-centered (chapter 6) focus for inquiry and instructional work requires the widening of that teacher's instructional and cultural lens. It requires not only getting to know individual students but also gaining familiarity with the broader community. While this is not necessarily easy work, it is rewarding for all involved and often results in more authentic, effective literacy learning experiences for students.

CHAPTER 7

Leading and Supporting Disciplinary Literacy Work Across Contexts

BY THIS POINT IN THE BOOK, we hope you have a strong sense for the range of disciplinary literacy (DL) inquiry and instruction entry points you may adopt in your own work. You may make one small or big change; you may make many. It's possible that you may engage in this work alone, consulting this book and then making changes accordingly as you plan and reflect on your curriculum. Alternately, you may carry out your inquiry work with a team. Together, your team may wrestle with the scope of work, asking questions such as the following: "Is this the right place to start?" "Are we going too fast too soon?" "Are we doing enough?" "Are we taking on *too* much?" Determining when and how to start DL professional learning initiatives was reviewed extensively in our previous book *Investigating Disciplinary Literacy*, which we strongly recommend reading if you are wrestling primarily with questions of how to begin and maintain a larger DL project.[1] We also dig into three cases of professional learning in chapter 8 of this book to paint a picture of what this learning may look like.

However, an important reminder to highlight here is that, no matter where you start your own DL inquiry and instruction work, it is necessary to consider the ways in which your particular school and district context may support (or perhaps limit) your efforts. Professional learning research has begun to uncover, over the past two decades, the many ways in which school and district contexts shape teacher professional learning and related shifts in teaching.[2] In a nutshell, this body of research highlights what many educators have long known—teaching and learning are human endeavors and thus subject to contextual differences across schools and districts. While demographic information may be comparable across schools, we each know that every school's context is unique because its students, teachers, and leaders are unique.

In our own work, we have found that context matters greatly when teachers shift toward disciplinary literacy instruction. In fact, when it comes to DL inquiry and instruction, context plays an even larger role than with other curricular initiatives due to DL's relative novelty in the world of education and the degree to which it reflects unique teacher, student, community, and disciplinary interests and qualities. Perhaps the best disciplinary literacy work is that which connects directly with students' lives (see chapter 5) as well as with the larger cultural and community interests within which each school is situated (see chapter 6). As a result, we urge you to take time early and often within your DL investigations and experiments to consider the ways in which your own context shapes your work and how you can ensure, over time, that your DL learning and enactment align with contextual factors and needs.

For example, in a school that grants teachers lots of autonomy, anyone hoping to integrate DL practices into the curriculum might easily find a way to do so, since curriculum and instruction are under their control. Alternately, teachers working in a school with a scripted literacy curriculum may have to work hard to find one or two very small shifts that they can make to begin integrating new practices into their curriculum. Both efforts represent a positive shift. And both represent a shift that is responsive to school context.

In this chapter, we prompt this contextual thinking by sharing longer cases of leaders and teachers who attended carefully to contextual factors as part of a move toward disciplinary literacy instruction. Throughout the chapter, we present vignettes aimed alternately at leaders, teachers, and teacher leaders who individually and collaboratively can best support DL learning and implementation from their various positions within the school. Specifically, we lean into the particulars of each school or district context and the specific strategies and stances that leaders and teachers can take to facilitate the success of disciplinary literacy in those contexts. Recognizing that many readers of this book are educators who do not hold formal leadership roles, we also offer guidance and questions to consider for those hoping to partner with school or district leaders to put disciplinary literacy into practice, recognizing the critical role of partnering with leaders in this work.

You will see, as you read, how the questions outlined in the tables throughout this chapter can serve as guides for shifting teaching and learning in ways that respond to various elements of school culture and context. Specifically, we outline five ways that you may specifically analyze and harness the power of context to bolster your DL work, each of which contains reflective questions that may be of particular utility to educators holding specific roles in schools:

- partnering with school leaders (questions for formal and informal leaders)
- analyzing and navigating school culture (questions for teachers and others)
- focusing on timing (questions for teacher leaders, coaches, and others)
- focusing on students' unmet needs (questions for teachers and others)
- balancing classroom-level changes with larger school or district initiatives (questions for all)

Each item in this list offers strategies for grounding DL work in schools. Additionally, each also offers a lens through which to consider DL work. For instance, how can school leaders help to deepen the understanding of and commitment to DL work within a given school? Utilizing these strategies as a lens through which first to consider disciplinary literacy contextually and then to begin to design and implement disciplinary literacy strategically will bolster your success with this work.

PARTNERING WITH SCHOOL LEADERS TO SUPPORT DISCIPLINARY LITERACY WORK

One of the most important contextual factors for any educator to consider when launching into DL inquiry and instruction work is the stance, support, and vision of their school leaders. While secondary school leaders often have deep experience in one or two disciplines (e.g., mathematics, science, physical education, visual art, etc.), it is the rare secondary school principal or assistant principal who feels confident delving into the nitty-gritty of every discipline represented across a comprehensive middle or high school. Furthermore, many secondary leaders do not have a deep professional background in literacy instruction, as compared to many elementary school leaders. At the elementary level, school leaders are often former elementary teachers who are well versed in literacy instruction as well as multiple disciplines and developmentally appropriate practices; however, elementary principals rarely feel confident supporting deeper DL work within and across those disciplines. Even school leaders who are interested in and supportive of DL efforts may need support themselves in understanding the goals and possible rewards of DL work.[3]

Across disciplinary literacy projects that we have led or researched, one of the key determinants of success was the ways in which school leaders partnered with teachers in learning about DL and collaboratively tackling DL inquiry and instruction. Learning from those projects, we have found three broad areas in which the stance and actions of school leaders have propelled and sustained the work.

1. Partnering with Teachers and Participating Fully to Bolster Content and Process Knowledge

In this section, we speak more directly to those in schools who hold formal leadership roles. One of the first and most important moves a leader can make to bolster DL inquiry and instruction work is to participate shoulder-to-shoulder with teachers in early DL professional learning experiences. Whether attending professional learning workshops, bringing in outside experts to the district, or even simply reading a core text or set of articles together—when a leader participates in some or all of the professional learning work alongside teachers, it signals a strong commitment to and investment in the work. Furthermore, these leadership actions build leaders' individual capacity related to DL teaching and learning, which can support classroom walk-throughs, formal and informal classroom observations, and leadership efforts to spread DL work within and across schools.

2. Collaboratively Creating Holding Environments to Support the Work

Leaders wishing to support DL work may be well served by focusing on creating holding environments in which teachers can collaboratively, iteratively, and intentionally engage in DL inquiry and instruction. A holding environment is "a nurturing context in and out of which we grow, and can be a relationship, a series of relationships, carefully designed collaborative practices, or a complex organization like a school."[4] A leader establishes a holding environment through both words and actions, including messaging early and often to all faculty that a focus on DL is a core goal of the school's work; creating the space and psychological safety for teachers to collaborate, learn from experts and one another, and pilot new practices without fear of reproach; observing teachers not for evaluation purposes but for the purpose of learning and sharing successful approaches across classrooms. Leaders who focus on intentionally creating holding environments build capacity for teachers to engage in authentic and deep professional learning about DL and beyond.

3. Providing Time, Resources, and Financial Support

Finally, leaders can strengthen DL initiatives directly, in the form of providing time, resources, and financial support. Leaders can ensure that teachers have time set aside to collaborate. If teachers are gathering after school hours to collaborate, small stipends may assist and bolster the work. Leaders can also allocate funds for professional learning and instructional materials, student texts and supplies, and to attend online or in-person professional learning opportunities (e.g., conferences, webinars, online courses, etc.).

The leadership moves outlined here not only support DL inquiry and instruction efforts but can guide the work directly. For an illustration of this type of DL leadership work, consider the case of Eric Curl, former Holly Middle School principal in Oakland County outside Detroit, Michigan. In this case, based on a series of conversations with Eric, you can see the ways in which Eric partnered with teachers and teacher leaders, created effective schoolwide holding environments to sustain a DL focus, and invested time, resources, and financial support over a period of years.

ERIC CURL
Leading DL Professional Learning as a Principal

Eric's understanding of DL was rooted in his own experiences as a high school social studies teacher in the same district where he became a middle school principal. He remembered hearing that "everybody needs to [teach] reading and writing" and was hesitant about a "one-size-fits-all approach to literacy." It was that early experience that he harkened back to when he became principal of the middle school and began to take ownership of professional learning work. He sought a "sweet spot of professional development that is not only able to be used across the building, but that all teachers see relevance in."

The notion of this "sweet spot" is what drew him, during his third year as a principal, to state-sponsored work around disciplinary literacy in 2018–2019. As he learned more about disciplinary literacy as a theoretical framework and instructional approach, he thought: "Gosh, this is something that we can all learn together, but all chart our own paths utilizing our disciplinary specialties to really capture our kids' attention and turn them into, you know, mini-apprentices within our fields!"

From that moment of realization, Eric began the process of setting a mission and goals around adopting a DL instructional approach for his school. He began by first approaching his "advisor team" (i.e., his schoolwide instructional leadership team, comprising his assistant principal, school counselor, special education representative, and two teacher leaders from each content-area academic department). He began the work of mission-building by asking members of that team to think back to why they "became a social studies or a science or a technology teacher . . . to center our passion for the subjects that we chose."

In August of 2019, soon after introducing the notion of disciplinary literacy to his advisor team and reading an article together about DL to further explore the topic, Eric was able to bring his advisor team to a state-sponsored, two-day DL professional development workshop. This workshop further introduced the essentials of disciplinary literacy as an instructional approach. The workshop was centered around new state-designed DL practice documents, which provided further encouragement for Eric and his team that they were heading in the right direction in terms of a building-wide focus for literacy instruction.[5]

One of the entry points to DL instruction that Eric and his team first encountered during that pivotal August 2019 summer workshop was the question formulation technique (QFT). The QFT routine is certainly not new, but its new application in classrooms as an entry point to DL work is being explored across states. This process encourages students to engage in rounds of questioning around particular disciplinary content: fostering divergent, convergent, and metacognitive thinking. Students are supported in crafting "focus questions" about content, similar to "essential questions" from the Understanding by Design framework. At the heart of the QFT routine is active exploration of disciplinary content, using the habits of mind and ways of working within that specific discipline—which is also at the heart of DL work.

Emerging from that workshop, Eric and his team were newly energized around the notion of "activating and engaging students as doers in our disciplines and not passive receivers of content." Eric and his advisor team came back to their school ready to design and lead their own professional learning series for the 2019–2020 school year around disciplinary literacy. As Eric said, "The piece that I know our staff latched onto the most was inquiry and questioning." He intentionally tried to keep his DL focus on those two big ideas: inquiry and questioning. He and his advisor team saw it as their best way of encouraging a schoolwide focus on DL instructional practices.

Across the 2019–2020 school year, Eric set aside three hours per month to specifi-cally help staff focus on DL inquiry and questioning, and the QFT routine specifically. He invited a DL expert to provide state-sponsored professional development to support the launch of the initiative in September of 2019, during their first school-based professional development day of the school year. It was in that first session that Eric and the facilitator helped the entire staff craft their professional learning "driving question" for the year: "How do we begin to use disciplinary literacy as a way to strengthen students as doers in our disciplines?"

Importantly, though most of the faculty were energized and excited by this profes-sional development direction, there were some challenges: "There were a few [teachers] that were concerned, like, 'Oh, hey, we're just gonna beat them over the head with QFT'?" It was at this point, early in the 2019 school year that Eric made it clear—establishing trust and clarifying his mission—"I'm not asking you to just do this for a compliance thing . . . I'm asking you to really think about what compelling pieces . . . What prompts, what phenomenon can you use with your students to have them generate legitimate questions you know that they're interested in learning?"

However, the professional learning story doesn't end there. Across our conversations with Eric in 2020–2021, despite Eric's insistence that not as much DL or inquiry-based work was occurring across the pandemic (as the school toggled between fully remote and hybrid modalities in 2020–2021), evidence from classrooms told a slightly different story. According to Eric, teachers across disciplines showed evidence of developing new instructional practices in both remote and hybrid modalities that mirrored some of the DL and inquiry-based professional learning from the previous year. For instance, teachers were curating and utilizing digital text sets to encourage students to read widely and develop focus questions around discipline-specific topics in English and social studies. Math and science teachers were inviting disciplinary experts into their classrooms via Zoom to talk with students about discipline-specific habits of mind and real-life experiments in STEM fields. As Eric said, "On a positive note, the remote and hybrid teaching allowed for . . . another layer of interaction that students can have with either experts or material that they didn't have before [because] our kids didn't have computers . . . now every kid has a computer. We didn't have this [learning management system] where you can have resources—now everybody has access to it."

After seeing the ways that teachers utilized DL strategies in their hybrid and fully online classrooms, looking toward the 2021–2022 school year, Eric was far more optimistic about re-engagement in schoolwide learning about DL instructional practices. With new teacher interest in digital text sets and the utilization of technology to support the curation of resources and the asking/answering of discipline-specific questions, Eric was poised to harness that interest and return to a schoolwide focus on DL in the summer and fall of 2021. "We're going to get back to that idea of how we can utilize the practices of disciplinary literacy to activate our students as doers in each discipline . . ."

In this case, you can see how Eric systematically created a focus for the DL professional learning initiative, rooted in teachers' own identities and care for student learning. He created time and space for teachers to learn together. He attended professional learning alongside them and then later led some of the professional learning alongside teacher leaders. In his classroom observations and conversations with teachers, he kept a steady focus on DL, even as the global COVID-19 pandemic created multiple disruptions for his carefully crafted professional learning plans. In reflecting on Eric's case, consider the questions posed in table 7.1 about ways in which formal and informal school leaders can support larger DL inquiry and instructional work.

ANALYZING AND NAVIGATING SCHOOL CULTURE

To further illustrate the importance of school culture as an element of the larger context within which DL work takes place, we turn to teacher and leader Chris Norkun. Chris was a high school English teacher at Salem High School in Salem, Massachusetts, when we first met. He described the ways that school context shaped his own slow shifts toward more intermediate and discipline-specific literacy instructional practices. He had to spend time getting to know his students

TABLE 7.1   Leadership questions to ask when starting DL work

	Questions that individuals and/or teams might ask
Who are the formal leaders supporting our work?	Will principals, assistant principals, curriculum directors, district-level leaders, or other formal leaders be an ongoing part of our investigations and work? How can we involve them together or alternately over time? What, if any, permissions or invitations may need to be secured at the outset of an initiative?
Who are the informal leaders supporting our work?	Will teacher leaders, instructional coaches, special educators, interventionists, librarians, or other informal school leaders be an ongoing part of our investigations and work? How can we involve them together or alternately over time?
What existing supports do we want to utilize that may need to be negotiated with leaders?	How can we make good use of existing professional learning time and structures (e.g., PLC time; team meeting time; departmental meeting time; afterschool or release-day professional learning time; etc.)? What, if any, permissions or invitations may need to be secured at the outset of an initiative in order to utilize existing time and structures?
What, if any, new professional learning supports may we need to negotiate with leaders?	What, if any, upfront and/or ongoing professional learning supports may we need to request (e.g., permission and funding to attend conferences, online professional learning opportunities, etc.)? Which, if any, outside experts do we need to consult up front and/or over time in order to support our inquiry and instructional work?
What resources do we need to begin and/or sustain our work?	What, if any, upfront and/or ongoing professional learning materials and resources may we need to request (e.g., copies of professional learning texts focused on DL or literacy within each discipline; student-level resources related to disciplinary literacy work; etc.)?
How can we involve and communicate with leaders over time?	Which leaders should we regularly be communicating with about our investigations? How often should we be sharing our findings (e.g., weekly or monthly with teacher leaders and coaches; quarterly with principals and curriculum directors; etc.)? Which leaders should we regularly invite to play an active role in our investigations? What is the best timing for these collaborations (e.g., inviting instructional coaches to observe, co-teach, and support monthly teacher reflection sessions; inviting school principals to participate in larger unconference professional learning days where teachers share work across content areas and grade levels; etc.)?
How can we help leaders to share resulting work widely?	What roles are formal and informal leaders able to play in terms of sharing classroom-level successes across classrooms and across schools? What is the best format for sharing work (e.g., district-level teacher-led unconferences around DL; school and district newsletters and spotlights on teacher work; cross-classroom and cross-school classroom walkthroughs and debriefs; etc.)?

For more guiding questions such as those listed here, please see Dobbs et al., *Investigating Disciplinary Literacy: A Framework for Collaborative Professional Learning* (Cambridge, MA: Harvard Education Press, 2017).

as well as the broader context of a new school when he moved from an independent school to a public school. Taking the time to get to know the context and recognizing the kind of instruction that he wanted to provide for all students allowed him, ultimately, to make deep shifts in his practice. This strategy of taking time to understand and then be responsive to a school culture is one that educators in all roles can use.

CHRIS NORKUN
Shifting Notions of Instructional Goals in Private and Public High Schools

The dilemma that prompted me to try something new was the culture shock of transitioning from eight years in private school education into urban public school education. The pedagogy I used in private school was developed by the private school culture, where entrance exams and interviews ensure that a majority of the students shared the same dispositions and academic skills. The schools in which I worked wanted students to experience a college seminar model as high school students, so we all ran our classes similarly: assigning a lot of homework, teacher-led Socratic seminars or lectures on content, and assigning a culminating essay or test to see if students learned the content. Humanities teachers rarely taught reading and writing skills, as our students already displayed high levels of literacy in order to get into the school. What we did was expose them to as much literature as possible and assign the essay prompts we all wrote while in college. I got really good at teaching students in this culture. Students would do a lot of homework, come to class to listen to a lecture with a handful of student contributions, write long papers, and see teachers during office hours to get coaching on the reading and writing.

Then I made a move into an urban high school, and within the first two weeks, I realized I had a major dilemma. Not only was my classroom management terrible, but I also realized I was very weak at teaching discrete literacy skills. I didn't have any intentionality in what I was doing, and my classes were a mess. I was perpetually frustrated with my students, and they were perpetually frustrated with me. And, of course, I blamed everything and everybody except myself, while nothing was changing in my classroom.

The first thing I did was to fall back on my ability to relate to students. Those skills I developed in private school teaching and athletic coaching translated between types of schools. I feel like by the time we hit the end of the first marking period, students got a sense of who I was, and I was able to whip up some basic policies and procedures to restore calmness to my classrooms. I was able to refine these basic policies and procedures throughout that year and hold everyone together enough to cross the finish line (things like assigned seats, what to do when the bell rings, a bathroom policy, how to pass in materials). These types of procedures were not required in private school because of the small class sizes, homogeneity, and the threat of being kicked out if students could not fit in to cultural norms.

The other part of the dilemma, my instructional pedagogy, was much more challenging to address. Once I was able to consistently get students to sit in their seats and use their voices at appropriate volumes, students then either refused or did not have the skills to do the activities I assigned. So, I asked people in my PLC what they used. That was the moment when I learned how to function in and perpetuate a public school model of mediocrity. My team filled me up with fill-in-the-blank notes, graphic organizers that had prompts and clues that read like a child's scavenger hunt (e.g., What does the character say in the third paragraph on page 52?), crossword puzzles, and poster projects. I know this is all very mediocre-at-best pedagogy, but that shift allowed me to really start working through my dilemma because now I had some sense of calmness in the room and a change in workflow. Students began submitting the aforementioned trivial activities, and I could assign grades. Each class and I started doing something that kind of resembled a traditional public school routine. Toward the end of that first year in public school, I knew that what I expected my private school students to do was vastly different than what I expected my public school students to do. I hated that and brought this up with my department chair. She listened and supportively suggested three courses for me to take the following year.

The first class was called "Classroom Management That Works," and the second class was called "SLATE: Second Language Acquisition for Teachers of English." Both of these courses were offered through our district—the first class I completed online over the summer, and the second class was a standard graduate-level night course I took during the fall. The third class was another online class called "Content Area Literacy" offered through UVA-Wise that I completed during the second semester. Those three classes changed my pedagogy. My classroom management drastically improved that second year due to a year's worth of learning on the fly, asking my PLC for support, picking and choosing various things my colleagues did, and learning all about rituals and routines via the online course.

The SLATE course was an experiential learning course supplemented with plenty of reading on best practice methodology. I quickly realized that my high school English teachers did exactly what I did my first year in public school—they assigned reading for homework, administered various reading quizzes to begin class, went over the quizzes, answered clarifying questions, and then gave us work time to start the next night's reading. Then, we handwrote essays—some in class and some at home. I only knew what I knew at that point. The SLATE course was the first time I learned about the gradual release method of "I do, we do, you do," which allowed me to build from all of the handouts my PLC gave me. I didn't want to do a scavenger hunt, so I had to reflect on what I really wanted students to do—and then show them how to do it.

Soon, I was able to create handouts and note catchers that started to support skill development versus content acquisition-through-scavenger-hunt worksheets. I started front-loading vocabulary with Frayer boxes and then realized that was the type of homework students would do. Workflow changed again as students produced different types of work; student engagement increased as I was able to start making literacy skills concrete; classroom culture continued to improve as I fine-tuned rituals and routines and discovered ways to make learning evident to students as they built and developed new literacy skills.

I remember the "Content Area Literacy" course set me up with the value of planning a "before, during, and after" literacy experience every time students read. I remember learning about the value of a model/exemplar for everything (reading, writing, speaking, listening, and academic behavior expectations). Somewhere that year, I picked up various ways to use sentence and discourse starters to help model and support student writing and speaking skills. The final piece was a hard look at curriculum and realizing just because I read something in college or grad school didn't mean everyone had to read it. I started learning more about my students' interests and finding texts to match.

I look back and realize how lucky I was to survive that first public school experience. I also realize that both the private schools and the public school lacked a sustainable way to foster an innovative and evolving definition of "pedagogical excellence" within their unique ecosystems. In both my private school career experience and that first public school career experience, I adjusted my practices pretty quickly to find some level of student success and cultural normalcy for my work. But I ended up rapidly growing into "teaching like a veteran" teacher of that school. I hit that status rapidly without being able to develop an eye for what could be beyond that pedagogical model. So even though I was working on the original student-centered dilemma, I grew complacent once I saw myself as a "veteran" inside each ecosystem and fostered my own normalcy bias for what I was going to do and for what students were going to do.

Chris's experience of adjusting his curriculum, first in response to what other teachers did at his new school and then ultimately in response to what he wanted for all students, represents the end of a long process of self-reflection, questioning, inquiry, learning, and iteration. Ultimately, Chris was coming to know the culture in his new school and making appropriate adjustments in his instruction to be responsive to that culture and to best meet his goals for students. We share with you some questions that can guide a similar process for you as you are figuring out how to launch into DL work, whether to do this work alone or with others, the scale at which you may want to dive in, and the existing capacity for taking on this work.

As you consider these questions, think about whether you may be taking on this work as an individual teacher or with a team. Also, recognize that *there is no one right way to do this work!* If you work in a school that is under extreme pressure to raise test scores and are required to use a curriculum tailored to that need, we don't suggest that you discard that guidance or that curriculum. Instead, think about how you can add on, adjust, and make initial changes around the edges. As Chris notes, sometimes simple routines and more basic or intermediate literacy work must be tackled first, before making the leap into DL inquiry and instruction. Slowly, you will build your capacity to engage in DL work. Then, as you and your colleagues begin to see results in the classroom, you may make incremental changes while others build trust in the fact that these shifts can produce the accountability outcomes they are looking for (such as increased test scores).

If you find yourself in a school where there is great excitement, capacity, and space to take on DL work, we still recommend that you consider the scale of work in the beginning. Taking on too much too soon can lead to confusion, fatigue, and doubt. Find the sweet spot where you can make a few big changes and gather data to see the effect. Then your shifts toward DL may swiftly spread across the school. But just because there is great interest and space to make changes doesn't mean you should make every change all at once. As you consider your starting point, the shifts you are making, and how you are thinking about your results and successes, the questions in tables 7.2 and 7.3 may serve as useful guides.

TABLE 7.2   Cultural and contextual questions to ask when starting DL work

	Questions individuals might ask	Questions teams might ask
Professional learning experiences / Existing knowledge	What professional development, professional reading, or other learning experiences have I already had around literacy or disciplinary literacy? What can I build on and not repeat?	What professional development, professional reading, or other learning experiences has this team had (or have most of us had) around literacy or disciplinary literacy? How can we build on existing knowledge?
Needs assessment	What kinds of assessments have I used lately that let me know where my students stand in terms of their literacy skills in my discipline/a particular discipline?	Has our team conducted a needs assessment recently that we can draw on? What does it tell us about students' literacy skills in our discipline?
Strengths and weaknesses	What are my strengths and weaknesses related to literacy teaching and learning?	As a team, what are our strengths and weaknesses in terms of literacy teaching and learning?
Outside factors	Are there choices or factors outside my control (such as a required curriculum that doesn't match student needs and interests, or assessments that don't do what I need) that shape my literacy instruction? Are there ways I can still use or shift these?	Are there school-level or district-level factors outside the team's control (required curriculum or assessments) that shape our literacy instruction? Are there ways that we, as a group, can use or shift these?
Expertise	In which literacy domains (e.g., vocabulary, comprehension, writing) do I have greatest instructional expertise? How might these areas of expertise guide my early classroom experiments?	Are there different levels of expertise among the individuals on our team? Within our larger school/grade level/department? How can we best activate these various sources of expertise?
Shared focus	If I checked in with other teachers or my students and their families, would they agree on the strengths and weaknesses that I've identified to target in my practice?	Would those beyond our team agree on the strengths and weaknesses that we've identified? What might our students and their families say?
Readiness	What areas of my practice am I most ready to target?	Are the right people on the team? Are they the ones most ready to engage in DL professional learning and instructional change?

For more guiding questions such as those listed in this table, please see Dobbs et al., *Investigating Disciplinary Literacy* (2017).

TABLE 7.3   Logistics that may need attention when starting DL work

	Questions individuals may ask	Questions teams may ask
Timing	When can I logistically work on this? When can I do the reading, thinking, and planning necessary? How will I carve out time for this individual work?	When will we, as a team, be able to work together and in which formats (e.g., PLCs, collaborative planning/learning time, teacher leaders, instructional coaching, teacher access to professional materials, with expert consultants, and so on)?
Structures and scale	What structures can I put into my days so that I am certain to work on this? Where in my practice or curriculum do I want to begin this work (what is the scale at which I'll start)?	Which new professional learning structures and resources would we need to put into place before we begin a large-scale initiative?
Choosing the right structures	Given how I teach, the context of my classroom, and the context of my school, what new structures for implementing DL instructional practices will be most effective?	Given the school context, what new structures for learning about and implementing DL instructional practices will be most effective for our team?
Inquiry experiences	Have I done inquiry work like this before? If so, do I feel comfortable digging right in? If not, what do I need to do (or whom do I need to turn to for support) in order to start this kind of professional learning and instructional change?	What experience do teachers on the team have with inquiry work? Are there structures that might best support this work (new or familiar structures)? Can teacher leaders help to facilitate this work? Is the team familiar with protocols that could help us work together effectively?
Skills for scaling up	Are there leadership skills I could hone in order to support the scaling-up process? Or literacy skills I could still build to support this process?	Are there skills and knowledge, in the area of literacy or in the area of leadership, that we may need to build, as a team, before scaling up this initiative?

For more guiding questions such as those listed in this table, please see Dobbs et al., *Investigating Disciplinary Literacy* (2017).

Being able to ask the right questions about your desire to shift toward learning about and implementing disciplinary literacy instruction is vital. Asking and answering these questions allow you to gauge the best moves to make.

IT'S ALL IN THE TIMING

As you'll see in the next vignette from Jay Wallace—an elementary math coach and teacher in Wakefield Public Schools in Wakefield, Massachusetts—sometimes the shift toward more authentic and discipline-specific content and literacy work requires time. It requires iterative conversations among teachers, teams, and perhaps coaching colleagues. DL inquiry and instruction work can vary greatly, in terms of timing, depending on contextual factors. In an environment that supports coaching, teaming, and frequent consultation of colleagues, then you may be well positioned to move more quickly and efficiently.

As you read Jay's vignette, consider similarities in timing between Jay's work and the work of middle school social studies teacher Eileen Woodford (see chapter 4). Remember that Eileen worked with a team by first focusing on general literacy strategies. After nearly a year, the team was ready to make more specific and noticeable changes in their curriculum. Even after a year of learning about and dabbling in DL instruction, though, Eileen was nervous to implement a brand-new way of teaching and assessing her students (remember that she ultimately found great success with a new debate format to help teach ancient civilizations). We want to acknowledge that some of this nervousness will always exist, even after long stretches of collaborative inquiry. Yet, because Eileen waited for the right time to scale up her work, the changes resulted in deep and engaged student learning.

Similarly, you will see how after a year of district-sponsored initiatives introducing more authentic math conversations and hands-on reading, writing, and calculating tasks in elementary math classrooms, one fourth-grade teacher was still a bit uncertain. However, through multiple coaching conversations with Jay, co-planning opportunities, trying in-class experiments, and carefully analyzing the results, the positive effects of discipline-specific literacy work emerged. Just like the encouragement Eileen received from her team, Jay's coaching work paved the way for faster and richer classroom experimentation than might otherwise have been possible. Timing and support were critical.

JAY WALLACE PART 1
Building Teacher Background Knowledge and Confidence

I spent a lot of time this year working with an enthusiastic fourth-grade teacher. She was interested in trying out new tasks that would get her students to engage with math in ways that were visual and rooted in developing conceptual understanding. One of the school goals was improving mathematical discourse, and she understood that some tasks were better at getting students to discuss and share their thinking than others, so we often spent time improving tasks from the district's math program or creating our own.

One morning we were discussing fractions and her students' understanding of mixed numbers and improper fractions. She talked about how some of her students did not see how a mixed number (a whole number with a fractional part) could refer to the same amount as an improper fraction (e.g., 1½ versus 3/2). She was questioning whether to simply teach the students the conversion algorithms so that they would be able to perform the necessary calculations. Concerned about this, I posed a thought experiment.

"There are two students. One can generate equivalent fractions by drawing a picture of the fraction and dividing or combining parts within the picture. This student has no understanding of the simple algorithm, and it takes her longer than using an algorithm. Sometimes she makes mistakes because her process is so involved. Another student knows the algorithm to find equivalent fractions. She can crank out equivalent fractions quickly and efficiently but has no conceptual understanding of what those fractions represent. Both students score well on an exit slip for generating equivalent fractions. Can you predict how each student might perform on a pretest that involves adding two fractions?"

Our conversation led to the conclusion that, while knowing the algorithm will help students in the short term, developing conceptual understanding will support future learning. Students will of course learn the algorithm but only after they have a solid conceptual understanding. We decided to look into discussion and hands-on lessons that may further develop students' conceptual understanding of fractional parts, one that would be a good jumping-off point to discussing mixed numbers and improper fractions.

I began by doing a little research. At this point, I felt like the teacher had made a real leap in terms of her understanding of developing mathematical ideas in students, that is, concept first, then procedure. It was now my turn to find or create something that met our needs. I consulted a personal favorite, *Elementary and Middle School Mathematics* by Van de Walle, Karp, and Bay-Williams.[6] The book suggested that students often do not see mixed numbers as a whole plus a fraction and need that convention explained, but they should develop their own understanding of these numbers as smaller units within wholes. Using Cuisenaire rods and conversation starters, an adaptation of an activity from the text, we co-planned and developed Part 1 of a new lesson.

In this snapshot of Jay's work with a fourth-grade math teacher, you can see several important elements of the inquiry and instruction model in action, as well as the critical role of timing. Together, Jay and the fourth-grade teacher spent time articulating the instructional challenge at hand–students' fragile knowledge of representing and working with improper fractions and mixed numbers. From that identified challenge, the pair targeted classroom discussion and the use of manipulatives as new, discipline-specific tasks that may better support students in developing both deeper mathematical content knowledge and the language to express this knowledge and understanding. Instead of sending the teacher to hunt down dozens of online articles on best practices in mathematics discussions (building her background knowledge in isolation), Jay was able to support her quickly and collaboratively in a few ways:

- through a coaching conversation and hypothetical case example, which helped the teacher pinpoint "concept first, then procedure" as a new instructional goal
- through reiterating the district and school-wide focus on (and power of) class discussion as a task primed to help students surface each other's misconceptions and solidify new understandings
- by consulting a well-known text (*Elementary and Middle School Mathematics*) for already-established routines and procedures that may help students better solidify their conceptual and procedural understandings
- by co-planning a new lesson together, filled with new opportunities for students to solve problems

While the teacher may have come to some of these same instructional conclusions on her own, through her own reading and solo investigations, consulting a well-versed colleague (in this case, a math coach) sped up the inquiry and instruction process. It allowed for greater comfort in tinkering with new practices sooner rather than later.

Notice in Part 2 of this vignette how Jay video recorded a portion of the resulting lesson, further speeding along and supporting teacher reflection.

JAY WALLACE PART 2
Testing and Documenting New Ideas in a Fourth-Grade Math Classroom

The next day, we posed Part 1 of the problem to the students. Students were each given a bag of Cuisenaire rods. Each bag had different arrangements of rods, and only one rod was labeled with a fraction. For example, there could be six rods, some large, some small. One, in between the others in length, would be labeled 2/5. The task for students was to identify the total amount in the bag and describe it as a fraction.

The students were reminded of the mathematical and discussion norms they had been taught, which were posted on anchor charts around the room. The students quickly engaged, and while some worked more quickly than others, the conversations developing in small groups were impressive. Students asked "why" questions in their small groups, as they had been taught to do by the classroom teacher. Some questions we overheard included these:

- "Why don't you just stack them next to the big one?"

- "Why did you write that?"

- "Okay, why does this make sense?"

After the lesson, the teacher and I debriefed. We were very interested in the language the students used to explain their thinking. We were so impressed that we ended up video recording a segment of the discussion. Here is the transcript of just one minute we recorded. It starts right after a student asked, "Can you explain using a mathematical argument?"

Student A: "Because it said on our card that the red rod = 6/6. So, we knew that it equals one. And if we put both of these up, it equals two. And the whole . . . ah, 5/6 wasn't a whole, so we had to add 1/6 to make it 6/6. Then we added the 2/6 and then, four of them, four of the uh 1/6 to get 6/6. Then we had two left over.

Student B: Is 2/6 the larger fraction? What's the fraction?

Student A: So . . . the fraction is, well, it can't really be, yes it can be. The 2/6 we combined it with four of the 1/6 so it became 6/6.

Student C: Why did you put those two on top?

Student A: Because that's how it became 6/6.

Student D: Because that is 1, and this is 1.

Although this group of students reported their solution as both a mixed number and an improper fraction, it was clear from the discussion that many other students now needed a more explicit opportunity to describe the total as an improper fraction and see the equivalence with a mixed number describing the same total. Based on this understanding, we developed a Part 2 to this lesson, where students would be given a bag of rods and asked to generate a single equivalent fraction to the mixed number provided in the bag. Specifically, they would be asked, "How many unit fractions are in the bag? Remember that unit fractions are the smallest unit like 1/5 or 1/4." Students would be encouraged to develop a strategy that is replicable, to give them an opportunity to develop their own procedure.

This lesson, for me, illustrated the value of students working together and using explicit mathematical discourse to explain their thinking, giving kids a chance to develop their own understandings in the context of a group doing a rich mathematical task. The coaching piece that really worked for me was the conversation we had prior to the lesson. The teacher and I had a chance to consider a problem of practice and make a plan to address it. This teacher was willing to engage in a risky conversation that challenged her thinking.

In table 7.4, we provide guiding questions that may help you to think carefully about the timing of particular inquiry and instructional activities, which may be particularly relevant for teacher leaders or instructional coaches, or those teachers taking a lead role in supporting DL efforts in their schools. Furthermore, in chapter 8 we provide additional examples of how educators (including teachers, teacher leaders, coaches, and school leaders) can partner to engage in this kind of DL inquiry and instruction work.

TABLE 7.4   Questions to ask about the timing and need for disciplinary literacy work

	Questions individuals might ask	Questions teams might ask
Student needs	Do most of my students have a need for more support with DL skills or literacy skills more broadly?	Is there widespread agreement, within the team and beyond, that students need more support with DL skills or literacy skills more broadly?
Shared understanding	Do I have a clear understanding of what "disciplinary literacy" means to me and in my classroom?	Do we all share a similar understanding of what "disciplinary literacy" means, from which we can launch our work?
Willingness	Am I really ready to try something new in my classroom, knowing that there will be lots of mistakes and missteps along the way?	Are we at a place, as a team, or as a school, where there is broad-based interest in and willingness to engage in change processes around DL?
Moving toward readiness	Is there anything I need to work on first to then be able to shift toward DL (e.g., shoring up basic or intermediate literacy skills, familiarizing myself with fundamental concepts in my field, and so on)?	Is there anything that the team might need to do in order to create more buy-in? Are there other change processes afoot that need to be finished before launching into DL learning and change? Is there a need to build more shared understanding of our school's strengths and needs regarding DL?
Addressing a need	Do I know which needs disciplinary instruction will address? Are there unmet needs that will begin to be addressed when I start to make these changes to my instruction?	Are there unmet needs within the school that our team can pinpoint and begin to address through DL instructional practices?

For more guiding questions such as those listed in this table, please see Dobbs et al., *Investigating Disciplinary Literacy* (2017).

IDENTIFYING STUDENTS' UNMET NEEDS

Often, when diving into DL professional learning, teachers discover previously unidentified and unmet needs among their students. For instance, elementary teachers may realize, as they ask their students to record close observations in a science class, that students don't know how to observe, let alone observe closely. High school teachers, supporting students with research projects in history, may realize that, although students have many passions they hope to pursue through research, the actual process of conducting research is one that is unknown to them. Often, beginning to think about disciplinary literacy uncovers other areas of need. Asking the types of questions provided in table 7.4 can help you begin to determine students' unmet needs (and associated gaps in teacher knowledge) that you may want to address in the process of developing and implementing DL instruction. Of course, this might look different, depending on your role as a teacher, coach, specialist, or leader. In fact, sometimes this work happens outside of the K–12 context altogether.

To illustrate, let's see how Jessica Scott, an associate professor at Georgia State University, worked to create a summer experience in STEM for deaf and hard-of-hearing (DHH) students.[7] This work led her to uncover aspects of her students' learning experience that were both unique to the DHH population of students and missing from their current curricula. For example, DHH students are not likely to have ever met someone in the STEM fields who is also DHH, making it a challenge for these students to envision themselves entering STEM fields.

JESSICA SCOTT
Discovering Deaf and Hard-of-Hearing Students' Unmet Science and Literacy Needs

I started my work with a summer STEM program for deaf and hard-of-hearing (DHH) adolescents because of a number of factors. The first was that my graduate study and research experiences piqued my interest in how older bilingual (American Sign Language [ASL] and English) DHH students make sense of academic texts written in English. My background has always been in English and literacy with bilingual DHH students, and moving into work that was still literacy oriented but existed within a specific discipline was interesting to me. The second factor was work I had done on summer learning opportunities for young DHH students. Findings from this work indicated that, like hearing students, DHH children may experience a summer loss in key literacy skills when they are not in school, which I believe results from a lack of summer learning opportunities that are fully accessible to DHH youth.[8] The final factor was that the executive director of the Georgia Center for Deaf and Hard of Hearing (GCDHH) expressed interest in developing a collaborative relationship with our program at the university to provide an academically oriented summer program for DHH teens around the state. We held our first camp in summer 2017.

As a researcher, my first instinct with any dilemma is to read about it. I started looking into what literature existed on the topic of STEM education for DHH students in elementary and secondary settings. Unfortunately, the literature in this area was extremely limited. Between 1995 and 2017, I could find only sixty-seven articles that addressed DHH students in the STEM areas at all, and a number of them looked into the experiences of college-age rather than K–12 age students. In my quest for information, I found that my best resources ultimately were human resources. The team I work with currently includes (1) a STEM education researcher and former science teacher; (2) a former science teacher who worked with DHH students, is Deaf himself, and is currently pursuing his PhD in science education; (3) the executive director of GCDHH, who is Deaf and works on summer programming for deaf youth, and (4) future teachers of the deaf in the master's program at my university working as graduate research assistants. I have come to rely on our interdisciplinary group to bring knowledge and ideas that can enhance or better my own.

Our goal with the STEM program was always to provide hands-on, engaging, and linguistically accessible opportunities for learning. The teens who came to our camp were mostly students with inherent interest in STEM topics, but every year, we have had a few campers who are looking for opportunities to be out of their house and with DHH peers during the summer months and do not have any particular interest in STEM. This has meant that our activities had to balance the knowledge and motivation of those two groups. We incorporate as much experiential learning as possible, including science experiments, field trips, and opportunities to engage with peers and adults. In particular, I believe it is important for this population to engage with DHH peers and adults who are linguistically and culturally competent and who might serve as role models. We built everything around the 4Cs (critical thinking, creativity, communication, and collaboration) and 5Es (engaging, exploring, explaining, elaborating, and evaluating) to keep our focus on understanding and communication of ideas rather than memorization of information or rote task performance.[9]

The STEM summer camps over the years have been an exciting mix of experiential learning and connecting with DHH peers and mentors, all using accessible language with fluent language models. The main camp instructor since the inception of the camp has been a Deaf science teacher, and we had visitors from the National Technical Institute for the Deaf and Gallaudet University who came to run activities. When interacting with hearing science students and scientists, we have teams of skilled interpreters to facilitate communication. The campers have had the opportunity to learn how to complete and analyze DNA extractions, how to do basic coding through Arduino, how 3D printers work, and how to use 3D printers to make small objects. We have also taken field trips and behind-the-scenes tours with working scientists. For example, the students had the opportunity to go behind the scenes at the Georgia Aquarium to learn about their conservation programs, to take a guided tour at the Chattahoochee Nature Center, and to visit the Fernbank Science Center and Observatory. One of our most exciting events, though, was when the campers met Deaf adults who worked in STEM areas—including college professors, NASA engineers, and NASCAR-trained automotive technicians.

Over the course of the program, the students were placed in partnerships with the purpose of debriefing after activities to discuss what they learned, what they enjoyed about the activity, and which future careers might be related to what they had done. This gave campers the opportunity to interact with each other and the adults around them to process what they learned. Each year as the last event of the camp, the pairs present what they have learned and how their thoughts about STEM and working in STEM fields has changed over the course of the week. Georgia State University employees, members of the Deaf community, and their families typically attend the event.

My takeaways from this project are numerous. First, it has reinforced my beliefs about the importance of having access to DHH peers and adults who can support learning and, in some cases, serve as role models. The teens who came to our camp shared that the only Deaf scientist they had ever met before was their science teacher in the high school. It was a powerful experience to see them interacting with successful DHH and Deaf adults working in STEM. Over the years, we have had two students who attended the camp who had been raised orally and used primarily spoken language to communicate. Each of them demonstrated in their own ways the impact that being in this community of DHH peers had on them. At one point during the final presentations in 2018, an audience member asked one of the students, "What does it feel like to be with other kids who are deaf like you are?" and he responded, "I feel . . . free." In 2021, the second student began the week using only spoken language, having learned no ASL previously. By her exit interview, she was using a mix of both ASL and English—five days of ASL immersion had a huge impact on her language use with us!

I also took away from this project the importance of providing summer opportunities for learning that are accessible to all students. While DHH students are frequently thought of as a special case because of their communication needs, summer is a great time for all children to explore ideas and develop interests that may be important for their futures. For such opportunities to be accessible—whether this means linguistically, culturally, or physically—is important.

We are already at work planning our program for next year. We will be looking for grant funding to support our activities and will continue to collect data about the students who attend the camp and how their scientific thinking and connection to STEM changes over the course of the program. I also plan to continue my work in DL with DHH children specifically related to their reading and writing abilities.

Jessica's case illustrates an important element of DL inquiry work—the need to create new spaces for learning when we discover that they are missing. It is not always the case that we can simply refine what has already been done; sometimes we need to create something entirely new, as was the case here. Jessica was able to build a new space that met a unique need for her students, such that meeting a fellow deaf scientist became as important as developing and growing science and literacy skills across the summer.

While refinement of current instructional practices and classroom spaces is always an important part of DL inquiry and instructional work, we must also look for opportunities to build new spaces that extend beyond classrooms as well. The Baker Middle School team's work (highlighted in chapter 6) with the Community Literacy Project is another example of creating new, outside-of-school spaces to support DL work when needed.

BALANCING CLASSROOM-LEVEL CHANGES WITH LARGER SCHOOL OR DISTRICT INITIATIVES

Finally, as you think about starting any type of change process, whether it's making a small shift in one area of your instruction or starting fresh to develop an entirely new curriculum, it is important to think about your changes in relation to the larger school community and context. It is also important to think about changes to incorporate DL in relation to other initiatives, as any given school usually has a number of change initiatives underway at the same time. Table 7.5 provides some guidance on questions you might ask to strike a balance here. You don't want to carve out a scope for your work that is so big that you begin to experience initiative overload.

TABLE 7.5 Situating DL change work within the context of larger initiatives

- *In what ways does this initiative interact with and come into balance with other work in my/our school community?*

	Questions individuals might ask	Questions teams might ask
Balancing with other initiatives	How does the work I'm trying to do around DL complement and/or compete with other school-wide improvement efforts I am invested in?	How does work around DL complement and/or compete with other school-wide improvement efforts that individuals or our entire team may be invested in?
Personal balance	Is the timing right for this work? Will I feel balanced professionally if I take on these changes now? Or am I in danger of experiencing initiative overload or burnout?	Is the timing right for this work for our team? Will this initiative provide professional balance for those involved? Or are we in danger of experiencing initiative overload or burnout?
Energizing work	What aspects of this work energize me? Does this work play to my strengths? Or how can I shape the work to play to my strengths and growing edges?	As a team, does this work energize us? How does it play to the strengths of the group? How does it push us toward our growing edge, as a group and as individuals?
Aligning with the community	Does my beginning work around DL align with the priorities of the school community?	Does the work of the team around DL align with the priorities of the school community?
Blind spots	What are my blind spots as I begin this work? What am I not considering?	What are our collective blind spots as a team? What else are we not considering?

For more guiding questions such as those in this table, please see Dobbs et al., *Investigating Disciplinary Literacy* (2017).

We believe that taking time to carefully ask yourself these questions as you launch into disciplinary literacy work is crucial. At the same time, it is also important to recognize that you will likely have to begin your work within some constraints. Some of these constraints might be rather large to begin with, such as a restrictive curriculum; while others might be small, such as finding the right afternoon to meet with your team. No matter, it is natural, when taking on new work, to have to navigate constraints. Even if you come to the work of DL instruction with great enthusiasm, learning to navigate constraints throughout the change process is a natural part of professional growth.

Since the first printing of this book in 2019, we have found that teachers and leaders have greatly appreciated asking themselves and each other the questions outlined in the tables in this chapter while reflecting on the related vignettes. This reflective work, up front and throughout DL professional learning initiatives, greatly assists in understanding and navigating contextual differences in schools and districts. When educators consider context in terms of leadership, culture, timing, student needs, and balancing initiatives, they are far better positioned to design and enact DL professional learning that is the right size for their circumstances. Ultimately, these considerations then lead to substantive changes in teaching and learning. When we each dig into learning about and developing new practices inside a scope that is meaningful and reasonable, then we can start to make impressive, substantial changes that will result in tangible benefits for students.

PAUSE AND REFLECT

- After reading chapter 7, which contextual factors in your school and district seem most critical for you to consider as you embark on DL inquiry and instructional work?
- Which questions highlighted in the tables spread throughout this chapter—both individual and team-level questions—seem most important for you to answer first?
- Which of the vignettes featured in this chapter resonated most for you? Which parts of the vignettes provide ideas for starting places in your own DL inquiry and instruction work?

TRY IT OUT

- On your own, or with a colleague, take a look at the questions in the tables spread across this chapter. Choose at least three questions to begin with, and journal some initial responses. Which questions push your thinking most? Which make you nervous? Which, if any, might you need to ask of your school leaders?
- Choose another question or two from the tables in this chapter. First try to answer the questions alone, as an individual. Then ask/answer the same questions with a colleague or team. How did the experience of answering the questions alone and with colleagues change your thinking or your planned next steps?

The Professional Learning Systems and Structures Needed to Bring Disciplinary Literacy to Life

THE DISCIPLINARY LITERACY (DL) practices outlined in this book represent, for many educators and possibly for you too, a departure from comfortable, familiar teaching practices. This is often true particularly for secondary teachers, who may see themselves first as content-area experts and for whom thinking about literacy instruction in their content may be new. Any time that an instructional shift is needed or wanted, it is critical that teachers have sufficient opportunities for professional learning to support change. Thus, in thinking about adopting or adapting DL instruction, your work must go hand in hand with careful thought and planning for the professional learning that will support instructional shifts.

As any educator will tell you, professional learning is, more often than not, a frustrating experience.[1] Too often, educators experience mandatory professional learning that is not relevant to their grade or content area or that does not directly address the needs of their students. And too many teachers, including some who share stories of doing DL work in their own classrooms, work alone to achieve these goals outside of their school's professional learning structures.

To streamline and systematize professional learning, many districts turn to large-scale providers who, while they may address important ideas, quickly enter and exit a context, providing workshops or seminars that are impersonal, too broad, or only begin to introduce new ideas without the necessary follow-up.

Research has taught us that teacher professional learning, to be effective, must look different than traditional experiences. The "consensus model" for effective professional learning frames the experience as context specific, ongoing, collaborative, and supported over time by coaches or other experts; further, it creates opportunities for teacher input and expertise.[2] In addition, we know that it is critical to gather input about professional learning needs from teachers themselves, as opposed to designing and conducting professional learning from needs assessments based only on static measures such as student learning data or fidelity of curriculum implementation.[3] Teacher voice is, ironically, an all-too-often ignored component of designing and implementing effective professional learning.

Since teachers must learn across their careers, there is ongoing inquiry in the field about the most effective approaches to professional learning.[4] However, most work around professional learning focuses wholly on design as opposed to teacher voice and input. In our own work around DL professional learning, we believe that it is critical to center teacher voice, both in the design process and in the implementation process. Creating flexible approaches that can adapt to teachers' needs and include their voices at all points is crucial. This helps us to frame the foundational tenets of DL professional learning, in contrast to much of the work and thinking that is currently taking place regarding effective professional learning.

We distinguish between large-scale professional learning ventures and more hyper-local DL professional learning endeavors (see table 8.1) to emphasize the

TABLE 8.1   Large-scale versus disciplinary literacy professional learning features

Large-scale professional learning features	Disciplinary literacy professional learning features
Focus on including the right design elements/characteristics	Focus on teacher input to inform design
Focus on developing and implementing programs	Focus on teachers' espoused learning needs and interests
Focus on scale	Focus on contextual needs including organizational supports and constraints
Often comprise static elements	Adaptive, encouraging iteration

fact that DL professional learning is often qualitatively different than the professional learning initiatives that leaders may have been a part of before or those in which teachers have traditionally participated. Teacher voice, expertise, authority, and agency are central to the work of DL professional learning, and it is critical to bring this framework to the table as individuals, schools, or districts design DL professional learning processes and approaches.

THREE DISTINCT APPROACHES TO DISCIPLINARY LITERACY PROFESSIONAL LEARNING

In our 2017 book, we introduced a model for DL professional learning that combined three critical elements: professional learning communities (PLCs), inquiry, and teacher leaders.[5] This robust model leans into the idea, framed above, that the best professional learning is collaborative and context specific. Additionally, it exemplifies the key features of DL professional learning: placing teachers' expertise and knowledge of practice at the center of the learning; using inquiry as a cornerstone; and encouraging teachers to build on existing knowledge to generate, try out, and iterate new ideas for practice. Finally, the model recognizes the need for guidance in professional learning work, relying on teacher leaders to be "lead learners" in this work.[6]

In this book, we broaden these ideas slightly to build out a flexible and responsive framework for DL professional learning. We recognize that not all DL professional learning will occur within a comprehensive model such as the one we described in our 2017 book. At the same time, we believe that it is still critical to honor the intention behind all three elements of that model.

Thus, the professional learning that we describe here is *collaborative, founded in inquiry*, and *guided*. Notably, these three elements embody the tenets of effective DL professional learning, in that they center teacher voice, localized needs, and an adaptive approach. In generalizing the three critical components of DL professional learning, we hope to present a nimble approach for you to use when designing professional learning opportunities to support DL instructional practice. Taking a more meta perspective, this shift also represents our own alignment with the call for professional learning to be flexible and context specific. We elaborate on each of the three core elements next.

THREE CORE ELEMENTS OF DL PROFESSIONAL LEARNING

Collaborative

DL professional learning is most effective when it is collaborative, as collaboration helps educators to co-create and share ideas.[7] Collaborative learning opportunities create a sounding board for each educator, and they build collective capacity and efficacy.[8] Similarly, teacher collaboration ensures that the work is responsive to contextual needs.

Founded in Inquiry

Inquiry allows educators to enter a space of not knowing. Through asking questions and turning the lens back on their individual or shared practice, with a focus on learning as opposed to critique, a unique and flexible opportunity for learning and growth opens. An inquiry-oriented stance is particularly important given that DL remains a relatively new field of research and practice and thus requires invention and adaptation as opposed to simply adoption.[9] Additionally, in the current context of education, in which teachers are more often asked to implement rather than design solutions, inquiry centers teacher expertise and frames educators as the creators, not simply implementors, of new practices. Finally, inquiry centers teachers' curiosities and allows each educator to follow the questions about DL practice that intrigue or confuse them the most.

Guided

For any group to collaborate effectively, some guidance and a sense of direction are necessary. Knowing where to turn or whom to turn to for guidance and structure is critical in this work. Guidance and structure may come in the form of a co-created plan between two teachers taking a deep dive into DL work. The pair of teachers, committing to learning about and trying out DL practices, may create a shared calendar for themselves so that they can stay on track and hold each other accountable for their learning work. Alternately, a peer may be chosen from among a schoolwide team beginning to learn about disciplinary literacy. That teacher leader may then co-create agendas with various group members and facilitate team meetings. The group will then know that they can rely on the teacher leader to provide critical structure and guidance over time. Finally, in some cases, external facilitators and experts for a school- or district-wide DL initiative may support teams in getting started and sustaining their DL inquiry and collaborative work.

In what follows, we lay out three composite case studies of DL professional learning approaches. These models illustrate the ways that learning about disciplinary literacy can be responsive to questions of need, scale, and resources, including time. These composites build on our experiences across many projects in a variety of contexts, and they are intended to form a jumping-off point for you as you are considering how to dive further into DL professional learning. These composite cases are intended for individual educators and also for school leaders considering different DL professional learning models for their schools. Similarly, the examples can be used by district-level leaders, who may be considering ways to introduce and expand DL and design the necessary attendant professional learning. Each model is collaborative, grounded in inquiry as the cornerstone of the professional learning process, and guided–following the key components of DL professional learning that have emerged from our ongoing work in the field.[10]

Since inquiry cycles form the central component of each of the professional learning models for DL that we outline here, it is important to first remember the steps of the inquiry cycle, which we use to guide each of the following professional learning models (see figure 2.2 in chapter 2). Next, we illustrate the key features of each step of the inquiry cycle, for each DL professional learning model presented here (see table 8.2).

MODEL #1: PAIRED SELF-STUDY

In model #1 collaboration may take the form of two teachers joining together to dig further into DL learning and practice. No matter your position or role in a school, this case is an option for just about anyone. Perhaps you are a teacher reading this book who may seek out a colleague to work with, diving into this learning together. In this instance, the teachers would serve as each other's supports and guides as they dive into inquiry around a chosen element of DL practice. Read on for a composite case that describes how this model may play out.

TABLE 8.2   Inquiry cycle steps for three different DL professional learning models

Inquiry step	Model 1: A teacher pair	Model 2: A school-based book study	Model 3: A comprehensive, district-based initiative
1. Defining an inquiry question	Shared work between teacher pair	Collaboratively generated—expert facilitator (teacher leader or other-wise) critical to the process	Collaboratively generated; likely differs by grade-level or content-area teams; chosen facilitator critical to the process
2. Building back-ground knowledge	Teacher-driven deep dive	Team-driven deep dive, with guidance from expert facilitator	Deep dive driven by each team; guidance provided by expert facilitators
3. Collaborative idea generation	Teacher pair duo (occasional ideas branch off individually, too)	Within the book study group (occasional ideas branch off individually, too)	Within each team (occasional ideas branch off individually, too)
4. Individual idea testing	Teachers undertake this independently, with their own students	Undertaken independently by teachers with their own students	Undertaken independently by teachers with their own students
5. Shared reflection and idea revision	Teacher duo, together	Book study team, together	Grade-level or content-area teams together; occa-sional cross-team opportunities too

Parsing Out Inquiry in Model #1: A Composite Case with Diego and Alana

Alana and Diego both teach fourth grade. Alana has heard a bit about disciplin-ary literacy and is interested in exploring further, as she thinks about how to support students' literacy learning both in ELA and across other content areas. Alana decides to invite Diego into this exploration. After browsing through this book, they agree to inquire into the area of text to guide their DL learning and experimentation. Diego and Alana decide to give themselves two weeks to skim the early portions of this book and to then explore the text chapter (chapter 3) with a careful eye. Both annotate the chapter, coming away with ideas and questions. At their next meeting, they help each other to make meaning of DL overall and begin to build shared meaning about how working with texts can be a key element of DL practice. After supporting each other in building this shared knowledge, they decide to capture some possible inquiry questions, with a focus on text. They craft the following questions:

- Whose voices are represented in our classroom libraries?
- How do our classroom libraries help support students' literacies as related to other content areas?
- Are there ways that we could use text sets to build DL skills among our students?
- How are we using vocabulary to support student engagement with text?

After considering these inquiry questions, Alana and Diego discuss which question to pursue and decide on the first so that they can build a better understanding of whose voices are represented in their classroom libraries (*Step #1 of the inquiry cycle*). Both previously had a sense that their libraries needed some work, but they weren't sure how to guide those changes. This inquiry question will help provide some additional information to support shifts in their classroom library content.

To build some background knowledge (*Step #2 of the inquiry cycle*) about classroom libraries and how they can be a scaffold for DL learning, Alana and Diego agree to take a few weeks to do some independent research and learning. Diego begins his exploration by talking with other teachers in the building to learn how they have made decisions about what to put in their classroom libraries and how students responded to the library content. He begins to unearth a few patterns, noting that some teachers focus on volume, filling their libraries with as many books as possible, while others focus on content, paying attention to the ways that the stories and characters in their classroom library books echo the experiences of students in their classrooms and in the school community. Others focus on ensuring that their books represent a mix of fiction and nonfiction, across a broad array of topics.

Alana looks to voices in the field to build a stronger understanding of the role of classroom libraries in DL development among students. She reads articles from the American Library Association, seeks out recordings of presentations made at the National Council of Teachers of English annual conference, and explores blogs of educators and authors digging into questions of representation among books for elementary students. She also digs into Bishop's concept of windows, mirrors, and sliding glass doors, which frames the idea that books should provide all students with reflections of themselves, opportunities to learn about and explore the experiences of those who are different from themselves, and the opportunity to imagine themselves in new and different worlds.[11]

Alana and Diego are excited to bring back what they have learned for their next meeting. They share how they each explored their inquiry question and all that they had learned. Excited by what they hear from each other, they begin to generate new ideas to try out with their own classroom libraries (*Step #3 of the inquiry cycle*). Their idea generation process includes many possibilities, including the following:

- Systematically exploring their libraries to surface and highlight the racial and cultural background of the main character of each book
- Determining the percentage of fiction vs. nonfiction books in their libraries
- Conducting a vertical library inventory, looking at grades below and above theirs, to consider the range among main character, genre, etc.
- Analyzing the lists students keep in their reading notebooks to catalog their reading across the year
- Introducing students to the idea of windows, mirrors, and sliding glass doors, and asking them to use that as a lens to analyze their classroom library content[12]

Diego and Alana are excited to dive into most of these ideas, but they decide to go with the final idea, as it involves students most directly. They spend a bit of time brainstorming how they could plan for and then enact this idea and then agree to take a few weeks to try out lessons in their classrooms before coming back together.

During the ensuing three weeks, both Diego and Alana introduce the idea of windows, mirrors, and sliding glass doors to their students, and they engage students, in a number of different ways, both with the framework and in applying the framework to the books they have previously read, books in their classroom library, and more (*Step #4 of the inquiry cycle*). At this point, both teachers are excited for their next meeting to share what emerged during the idea testing phase of the process. As they begin to share about what unfolded in their classrooms when they introduced this framework and put it into action with students, both teachers realize that their students have displayed a new level of excitement about books when asked to analyze book content and characters. Diego's students made graphs of the racial and ethnic background of main characters to capture disparities. Alana's students interviewed each other about how it felt when they read a book with a main character who looked like them or had life experiences similar to them. Both Alana and Diego notice that their students who are Black, Indigenous, and People of Color (BIPOC), in particular, were invested and engaged in this work. These students were most eager to pursue next steps, such as adding new books to their classroom libraries, doing a similar inventory in the school library, or reaching out to publishers about whose voices were most represented in books.

This engagement, in particular, was exciting to Diego and Alana, and so they wanted to continue this work. Both teachers recognized that idea testing and reflection (*Steps #4 and #5 of the inquiry cycle*) may iterate a few times, driven by a single inquiry question. They spent the next month continuing their inquiry into the use of the Bishop framework with their students, resulting in letters to publishers, the creation of a student advisory group to work with the school librarian, and ongoing consultation among both teachers and their students about planned new acquisitions for their classroom libraries. At the end of that month, when Diego and Alana came together to reflect once again (*Step #5 of the inquiry cycle*), they both expressed a new understanding of the importance of their classroom libraries and a commitment to both revising their library content and creating open dialogue with students about this content. Classroom libraries became a more dynamic and critical "member" of their classroom communities. At the end of this inquiry cycle, Alana and Diego agreed that it was an invigorating process that took them in directions that they could not have predicted. At the end of the day, they left with a much deeper understanding of the role of texts in their students' literacy learning and a commitment to continuing their inquiry in this area as well as digging into other areas of DL instruction.

MODEL #2: A SCHOOL-BASED BOOK STUDY

In model #2, you might decide with a team at a school or with a teacher leader to create and then lead an optional book study to delve further into DL learning and practice. Teachers may be invited, across content areas, to opt into the book study, with the book provided for them and possibly a small stipend to compensate for their time. In this instance, the teacher leader who convenes the group, or a chosen team leader, could provide support and guidance to the team as they dive into inquiry around a chosen element of DL practice. Read on for a composite case that describes how this model may play out.

Parsing Out Inquiry in Model #2: A Composite Case at Hurston Middle School

At Hurston Middle School, the principal and literacy coach are interested in sharing about disciplinary literacy with teachers across content areas with the hopes of shifting instruction to include this new approach. From experience, they know that a simple professional learning session during a regular faculty meeting will not drum up much interest; neither will a mandate for all teachers to engage in ongoing DL professional learning. In order to strategically seed the idea across the school, they instead design a model for a shared book study, using this *Disciplinary Literacy Inquiry & Instruction* book as an anchor. Specifically, they invite teachers from across the school who they think might eventually become early adopters of DL practices, or at least early cheerleaders of the idea. Each teacher will receive a stipend to participate in bi-weekly book group meetings after school hours, across the fall semester. The literacy coach plans to facilitate the meetings, and ultimately eight teachers agree to join. The resulting team has representation across content areas, including specialists, and across sixth, seventh, and eighth grade. Many of those invited have been eager participants in recent professional learning initiatives at the school, so the principal and literacy coach are optimistic about the group.

Prior to their first meeting, the literacy coach, Ana, asks group members to read the first two chapters of this book to build background knowledge about disciplinary literacy. Though some group members struggle to differentiate DL from content-area literacy or the idea of literacy across the disciplines, the first meeting serves as an opportunity to build shared knowledge and understanding.[13] As they focus on a locally agreed upon definition of disciplinary literacy, different team members offer potential examples. An eighth-grade math teacher proposes reading graphs as an example of disciplinary literacy in math. A sixth-grade social studies teacher describes her use of the claim-evidence-reasoning routine and explains how this builds literacy skills specific to history and social studies, particularly with a focus on utilizing text-based evidence. Similarly, a librarian who works with all grades in the middle school proposes that effective use of databases to find relevant texts and articles for research projects represents a library-specific DL skill. Finally, two science teachers, after a small breakout conversation, share the work that they had begun by pulling out key vocabulary from each unit to pre-teach prior to digging into the unit. These teachers explain that their textbook highlights key vocabulary in the midst of the text of each unit, but they have found that students struggle to learn and then use this new vocabulary along the way. They had just tried out the idea of pulling out the vocabulary ahead of time and teaching it to students so that they entered the unit with the relevant vocabulary knowledge already in place. This approach to DL, similar to the others, resonates with the group.

Once it is clear to Ana that the group has a strong understanding of disciplinary literacy, she asks them to spend some time before the next meeting thinking about an inquiry topic that they may want to pursue, after re-reading sections about collaborative inquiry in the book. Ana also asks that teams of two group members read and become experts on each of the core chapters of the book: texts, tasks, students, and sociocultural context–to teach other members of the team during the next meeting.

The next group meeting involves not only a jigsaw so that each group member is able to build an understanding of the four core chapters of the book but also a far-ranging conversation to decide on an inquiry topic for the larger group (*Step #1 of the inquiry process*). Ana is careful to ensure that each teacher's discipline may fit well under the umbrella of the larger inquiry question. She wants each teacher to leave the meeting with a clear idea about how to pursue the question first through further research and then in practice. Possible inquiry topics are far ranging and include these questions:

- How do we help our students to be more interested in reading?
- How do we integrate students' technological savvy with teaching our content to them?
- In what ways can student choice be more central in our teaching and assessment?
- How can we support our students in engaging with each other about what they are learning?
- How might we better connect with community members and community resources to support different aspects of our curriculum and thus student learning?

Though it is clear that the group could generate inquiry topics for the entirety of a meeting, a quick straw poll shows great interest in investigating the idea of students engaging with each other.

Before the next meeting, Ana provides group members with various resources on peer-to-peer engagement. These include reciprocal teaching, classroom discussion, Socratic seminars, online discussion tools, and more. Each group member reads about the slices of the topic that most interest them (*Step #2 of the inquiry process*), and when they come back together to meet, they share what they have learned and begin to co-create ideas that they may try out in their classes. The group ultimately agrees to focus on discipline-specific student-generated and student-led discussions (*Step #3 of the inquiry process*). Some group members plan to try this out using a classroom-based modality, while others want to experiment with online discussion tools. In both models, group members agree to see how it works to have students generate discussion topics related to what they are learning and then facilitate the discussion for each other using discipline-specific language and talk routines. Though some group members are nervous that this is a big leap, as most classroom discourse is currently teacher centered, they are also eager to try this out and to see how students respond.

As each group member tries out a variety of strategies for exploring their inquiry question, Ana also urges them to return to the chapters on tasks and students to further support the instructional approaches that they are designing. Some group members pair up to design lessons using student-driven discussion, and others try out ideas independently (*Step #4 of the inquiry process*). All are able to draw heavily on the resources provided by Ana and the ideas in the suggested book chapters. When they come together for their next meeting, each group member shares the strategies that they tested around student-led discussions. The excitement among the group is evident, as many group members eagerly note the ideas that colleagues tried, interjecting thoughts about how they might revise colleagues' ideas for their own subject areas and grade levels.

After extensive sharing about the various approaches that each group member used to increase student engagement via student-led discussion (*Step #5 of the inquiry process*), the group makes a collective decision to continue with the idea testing process (*Step #4 of the inquiry process*). In particular, they want to focus on two areas: modality and management. Some teachers had, in their initial idea testing, worked on increasing students' engagement with each other live, through in-class discussions. Others, however, utilized virtual modalities, such as online discussion boards, for their ideas. The group now wants to swap approaches, with each member trying out ideas in the modality that they had previously not explored. This, they hypothesize, will add even more to the collective inquiry when they next come together. Group members also want to work on management strategies, in tandem with their focus on student-driven discussion. Educators are excited by their initial outcomes around discussion and also note their struggles with management, as the experience felt a bit "wild" or "loose" to some educators. Working on both increasing engagement with their content, as well as supporting students in doing this in productive ways, was a shared goal among the group. After this meeting, Ana, the literacy coach, is excited by the ideas generated by each group member, seeing new possibilities for engagement among and for students, in a variety of content area classrooms and grade levels. She is encouraged that group members want to continue the idea testing portion of the inquiry. She hopes that the next meeting's discussion and reflection will then help to ground the group as they dive into a new inquiry focus.

MODEL #3: A COMPREHENSIVE SCHOOL- OR DISTRICT-BASED INITIATIVE

In model #3, a school or district leader may decide that DL learning and instruction are critical components of a school or district's goals. As a leader, you may gather a design team and work with external consultants to craft a professional learning plan for disciplinary literacy that is responsive to contextual needs, including teachers' capacity for learning and implementing new practices. Teams of teachers may be invited to apply to participate together to create natural holding environments for the work. Each team may then be led by a team-chosen teacher leader, who would convene the group and provide ongoing support and guidance to the team as they dive into inquiry around a chosen element of DL practice. Each team leader could also act as a liaison to school or district leadership or to external consultants to contribute to and hold the big picture around DL professional learning.

Parsing Out Inquiry in Model #3: A Systems-Level Approach

This model of DL professional learning is a systems-level approach. Districts wanting to invest in DL instruction may take on this approach across schools at the same level (e.g., all middle schools; all secondary schools; all high schools)

FIGURE 8.1   The seven-step framework for designing and implementing
larger-scale disciplinary literacy professional learning projects

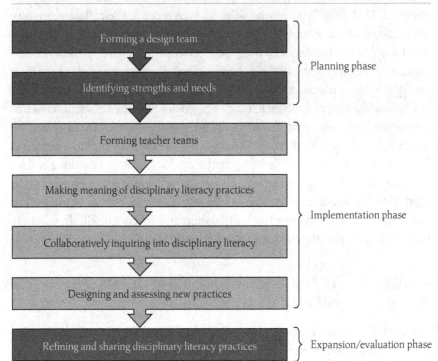

Source: Adapted from Dobbs et al., *Investigating Disciplinary Literacy* (2017), p. 49. Reprinted with
permission of Harvard Education Press.

or, in the instance of a smaller district, across all schools, PK–12. Given the comprehensive nature of Model #3, it is critical to lean into the design process to
thoughtfully build out the structures that will support DL professional learning,
recognizing the unique assets of the district or school community. We have written extensively about this third model in our book *Investigating Disciplinary Literacy*, and thus we present only key highlights of the model here.[14]

Model #3 proceeds in three phases (see figure 8.1): a planning phase
(Steps #1–2), an implementation phase (Steps #3–5), and an expansion/eval-
uation phase (Step #7). Compared with Models #1 and #2, Model #3 involves
different players at different phases of implementation, starting first with a
smaller planning team, moving then to broad engagement among educators, and

then again focusing on evaluation and expansion with a potentially smaller group or a team that is tasked with sustaining and institutionalizing the practices developed in the initiative.

Model #3 is appropriate for schools or districts who have already begun experimenting with DL practices and now know that they are ready to take this work to scale. It is most effective to implement this model when there is existing capacity across a school or district for collaboration among educators. When a school has tried out some work around disciplinary literacy using a version of Model #2, then Model #3 may be the natural next step, if there is excitement and buy-in for the initial DL work. If a school or district is hoping to weave DL practices into the instructional culture of a school or district, across grades and content areas, taking the time and resources necessary for Model #3 is likely the most effective approach, as this model involves a ground-up creation of ongoing, collaborative professional learning—the very type of learning that is most likely to lead to long-lasting instructional change. We invite readers interested in large-scale DL professional learning to explore the processes fully outlined in our 2017 book.

CONTEXTUALLY RESPONSIVE PROFESSIONAL LEARNING

The three models for DL professional learning here are intended as examples of how educators may design and choose the most appropriate type of DL professional learning, given the particulars of their circumstances. Of course, it is critical to adapt these ideas for the unique elements of any given context so that DL professional learning experiences are contextually responsive.

Throughout this chapter, we present the particulars of three models as a jumping-off point for design and implementation work. These models begin to illustrate the ways that DL professional learning is available and possible for educators in a variety of settings and circumstances. Similarly, leaders considering incorporating DL practices across their schools or districts can look to these different models to figure out the right fit for their school or district. In some instances, starting small is optimal, while in others, a comprehensive approach to DL professional learning is the right place to start. Importantly, this chapter is intended to illustrate the idea that DL professional learning can be effective using a number of different models, particularly in concert with careful attention to some of the contextual circumstances described in the previous chapter (see chapter 7). Undertaking DL professional learning work need not be overwhelming, nor must it be the singular professional learning focus of a teacher, team, school, or district.

As long as those hoping to design and delve into DL professional learning keep the three key elements of the process in focus, it is possible to build a responsive professional learning approach. Collaboration, a foundation in inquiry, and the opportunity for ongoing guidance and support are the critical components of DL professional learning. As illustrated in the three models described in this chapter, these are flexible components and will necessarily look and play out differently according to context and scale. Centering these elements will ensure that the professional learning that educators experience, focused on DL instruction, embodies high-quality professional learning and is thus most likely to have a lasting impact on instruction and student learning.[15]

PAUSE AND REFLECT

- After reading chapter 8, what type of approach to DL professional learning seems like the right fit for you or your school at this point in time?
- What might be the first step toward determining where to start with DL professional learning?
- Who might be excited to step into the role of lead learner for DL professional learning in your school or district?[16]

TRY IT OUT

- Gather a few other educators to discuss the possibility of collaborating on DL professional learning. What excites them? What seems like a good model, given your context and capacity?
- Consider the three proposed models for DL professional learning introduced in this chapter. Knowing your own school or district context, begin to sketch out a DL professional learning plan, based on the ideas presented here. What could the different components of the plan be? What existing structures or strengths could the plan draw on? How might the core elements of collaboration, inquiry, and guidance play a role in the plan?

CHAPTER 9

Co-constructing the Future That Teachers and Students Need

AS WE COME TO THE END OF THIS BOOK, it is important for us to return to some of the ideas introduced in chapter 1. We have written this book both for teachers and leaders already interested in taking on disciplinary literacy (DL) inquiry and instruction work and for those who have just begun to consider the possibilities that DL work may hold. We have also written this book for educators, like ourselves, who find themselves a bit tired when faced with an onslaught of strategies, tips, tricks, and professional learning experiences that feel far from being "professional" or about real "learning."

All too often in schools today, and certainly in many online education communities, effective teaching and learning work are presented as simple and straightforward—just adopt this, or try that. For anyone who has spent time in a classroom and worked elbow to elbow with students, we know that this is just not the case. Instructional improvement work is incremental, challenging, and often only possible with great support from colleagues, coaches, and mentors.

We have created the second edition of this book for those educators who know that there is no quick solution or simple recipe that leads to transformed teaching, learning, and schools. This is a book for those who wish to engage deeply in investigating texts, tasks, students, and sociocultural elements in their schools, in order to design context-specific DL teaching and learning routines. Across this book we have offered numerous windows into the classrooms of teachers across grade levels and content areas, not to hold those classrooms up as perfect models but to illustrate how rigorous thinking, collaboration, and iterative refinement can lead to truly amazing student learning.

We each, as teachers, researchers, and writers, have come to DL inquiry and instruction work in different ways, and for each of us, engaging in this work means something slightly different now, in the middle of 2024, having lived through a global pandemic and the societal questioning of the purpose of schooling. Thus, we end this book by sharing a bit more about our own original entry points into DL (what we "used to think") and what this work means to us now ("now we think") as we wrestle with how to best support teachers, leaders, and students as part of our own reflective journeys.

FOR JACY
Finding Connections Through Disciplinary Literacy Means More Now Than Ever Before

Working as a middle school literacy specialist and coach, I was always surprised at how disconnected and isolated teachers were from one another. Teachers focusing on art, English, history, math, physical education, science, and so on each operated in a silo, and yet they shared the same students and encountered many of the same teaching and learning challenges. In my earliest coaching work, I tried to focus everyone's attention on content-area literacy, those intermediate and general literacy strategies that theoretically could be shared across all classrooms. I imagined that those strategies would bring teachers together, foster collaboration, and even create more consistency for our young adolescent students who were just learning how to transition from classroom to classroom across their day. However, most of our content-area literacy experiments fell flat. While they produced modest student achievement gains in some classrooms, they flopped in others. They certainly didn't create engaging, authentic connections between students and content, teachers and their students, or classrooms and the wider community. I was left feeling like a bit of a failure as a coach.

Now, many years later, by rethinking and reframing the work around DL, rich connections to teachers' and students' local communities, and both honoring and critiquing the ways in which each discipline provides a lens through which to view the world, I have been able to see some of the successes that I had hoped for earlier in my career. In coaching teams of teachers around the DL ideas presented throughout this book, I have seen classrooms transform. Teams of teachers across disciplines have come together around common disciplinary and cross-disciplinary goals. Unlike my early thinking that the common goal was lockstep use of intermediate strategies executed with fidelity across all classrooms, I realize now that the real common goal is apprenticing students into the disciplinary ways of reading, writing, and thinking that each of us prize in our respective domains. Furthermore, some of the richest conversations in classrooms occur when we invite students to ask questions about the limits of each discipline's worldview, who benefits from particular modes of communication, and the role of gatekeeping within each field. These are the conversations that help students forge both disciplinary and transdisciplinary identities, particularly for adolescents navigating a more complex postpandemic landscape.

Across the pandemic, teachers and leaders found one another in virtual spaces (whether in Zoom breakout rooms, via online conference discussions, or sharing questions and ideas on social media). Collaboration within and across disciplines has never mattered more, with teachers seeking expert advice from one another as often if not more frequently than turning to lauded experts, many of whom weren't grappling with the new realities of teaching in online and hybrid learning environments. And so, we offer this book to those teachers and leaders who want to continue those peer-to-peer collaborations, who are coaching one another through disciplinary and cross-disciplinary inquiry and instructional experiments. Now, in all of our professional work, we focus on adult inquiry leading to new classroom instruction, all in service of meeting students' context-specific needs. I wish I'd had this book in hand at the beginning of my coaching career!

FOR CHRISTINA
Reframing Professional Learning

When I was a teacher, I hated professional learning. Slick speakers would come from outside our school, district, city, and even state to show us deck after deck of slides purporting to help us "solve the problem" of low achievement for so many of our students. I always wanted to scream at them, "You don't know anything about us! I have no control over anything you are discussing! I am not sure you've ever met a kid before!" And most often, "My kids are not a problem!"

I hated the implication that they, and in turn we as teachers, were just a problem to be solved, fixed, or erased. My students were people I wanted to teach to envision themselves as readers and writers and a full spectrum of possible selves in all sorts of future roles, if they didn't already. I resented the implication that my students were so often treated as failing or "at-risk," when I knew them to be brilliant, funny, and kind, with rich visions for their own lives. I wanted them to consider the work of people who participate with books, both in formalized literary criticism sorts of ways and in other creative and expressive ways too. And I love my discipline—I make meaning and understand the world because I love English and reading and writing. I wanted professional learning to help me to do that work better.

Now, I'm not certain that the speakers who came to talk to us felt similarly, but because of the gulf between their teaching and my classroom, I felt a huge distance that didn't make space for my expertise or the expertise of my students. And I wanted to bridge that distance but didn't know how. As I've gotten into learning more about professional learning, I've tried to remember that feeling that I had and how much I, as a teacher, wanted to do my work better. Since then, I've tried to build tools to help teachers do their work better, addressing their own questions and dilemmas, as no one helped me address mine. And over time, I've come to realize that the work is more effective when we let everyone bring their expertise and ideas to the table and learn with and from each other how we might build more supportive and productive spaces for and with students.

FOR MEGIN
Cutting Across Disciplinary Distinctions

In what was probably my favorite year as a fifth-grade teacher, I found myself sitting amid piles of papers and piles of books, looking at what was exciting my students the most in their reading and writing. Though we had interesting discussions and writing going on about fictional books, my students were lit up with excitement and passion about the nonfiction books that were set out all over the classroom. They were incensed when they read about the injustices perpetrated against people of Japanese descent during World War II. They were enraged to learn of the specific ways that African American people were still being robbed of basic civil rights, so many years after the launch of the Civil Rights Movement in this country. And they were angry about the history of apartheid in South Africa that they read about. These represented just a few of the issues about which my students felt passionate. As I looked at their work, it became clear that, though we were asked to teach literacy and social studies and reading, I needed to merge my instruction in these domains in order to follow my students' passions. With that, the Justice Project was born.

My students researched issues of justice and injustice that inspired them to action. They made connections between their own histories—those of immigration, poverty, resilience, and community-building—and those they were reading about in various nonfiction texts. They learned how to use their general writing skills and to shape them through a disciplinary lens to report on important issues of justice and to convince others to take action. This work excited my students more than anything else that year. And it served as the spark for my own continued work to find strategies for supporting teachers in breaking down their teaching in order to find what truly interests students and to then layer on the disciplinary lenses that will push those interests further and deeper.

Many years ago, in my fifth-grade classroom, I was able to carve out space to follow students' interests, passions, and inquiries. This led to a vibrant interdisciplinary space that also allowed for their growth as disciplinary learners and thinkers. In 2024 students' voices continue to lift up, as they ask critical questions about inequities in our society, about the ways that normative models have fallen short in serving all members of our communities, and about the purposes of schooling, both now and in the future. DL empowers students as learners, just as it empowers teachers to learn, design, invent, and iterate. DL opens up spaces for students to bring their vital questions—about rights, belonging, injustice, and agency—to the table, through different disciplinary lenses. In so doing, these students are building the knowledge and disciplinary discourse that will most certainly reshape the contours of their communities, both disciplinary and otherwise. Perhaps now, more than ever, DL teaching and learning is a critical lever for justice in schools.

LESSONS LEARNED

As you can see, this work is deeply personal for each of us and for the teachers with whom we've collaborated and highlighted throughout this book. As a result of our work with teachers and leaders across contexts, we have built and refined our framework for inquiry that focuses on improving instruction by helping teachers ask careful questions, use the expertise that already exists in their schools, and build new instructional strategies that will work for particular students in particular schools. Ultimately, our inquiry and instruction framework situates teachers as the deciders, completely capable of determining if and when to keep new ideas or to keep working and developing. Having written about designing and enacting DL professional learning work before, we now sum up a few of the broader lessons we have learned, both over time and in the years since the publication of the first edition of *Disciplinary Literacy Inquiry & Instruction*.[1]

TEACHERS SHOULD STILL TAKE THE LEAD— MORE SO NOW THAN EVER

In response to the COVID-19 pandemic, school systems by and large seem to have reverted to a variety of one-size-fits-all solutions. Except, now, postpandemic, these one-size-fits-all solutions are being met by teachers who are newly and rightfully skeptical about the ways in which generic solutions don't support adaptive change in an era of disrupted schooling. This is a troubling trend, because in our own research and experience we have found that, when provided the opportunity and support, teachers can and will build the instructional tools that their students need to achieve high levels of literacy. In fact, teachers' peer-to-peer collaborations during the pandemic are a prime source of evidence to this point. It was teachers, themselves, who created, shared, and collaborated on the most important resources used to support students in the midst of the disruption.

Some of the tools that teachers develop may involve using and applying strategies we already know a great deal about, while other tools in some disciplines will need to be built. For example, research and practice literature has a great deal to teach us about literacy work in disciplines such as social studies but far less about literacy in others.[2] Similarly, much of the work conducted thus far about disciplinary literacy has focused on secondary grades–though we have seen how this work can be incredibly beneficial for students in elementary grades, as illustrated by some of the cases in this book and beyond. Teachers will certainly be the ones who generate the best approaches to this work and who will be able to nimbly adapt strategies for younger or older learners. Investing in teacher decision-making and collaboration must be part of the answer to the question of how best to prepare students for an ever-changing and increasingly complex society.

THE SUPPORT OF LEADERS IS CRITICAL—ENGAGE DEEPLY AND THEN STEP BACK

While we have always known that both formal and informal leaders can support DL inquiry and instruction work, the roles of leaders have become even clearer in the past handful of years. When leaders engage deeply in DL professional learning work–attending professional learning sessions with teachers, sitting in on teacher-led meetings to learn more about instructional experiments, co-creating DL initiatives, and creating spaces for teachers to share practices across classrooms and schools–DL inquiry and instruction work can flourish and produce systemic changes.

However, an important realization emerged for us in the intervening time between the first and second edition of this book. Sometimes the most important leadership move is *stepping back*. Once DL inquiry and instruction work is underway, formal school leaders may best serve the initiatives by giving teachers time and space to engage in inquiry, try new instructional strategies, and iterate on their own. As the world of education postpandemic seems to tilt once more toward top-down leadership moves, we encourage leaders of schools and teams to provide the tools, resources, and time that teachers need to design excellent context-specific DL practices.

COLLABORATION HAS ALWAYS BEEN ESSENTIAL— BUT NOW WIDESPREAD INVESTMENT IN TECHNOLOGICAL TOOLS CAN HELP

We are reminded again and again that collaboration is one of the essential ingredients in moving disciplinary literacy work forward. However, there is much improvement to be made, and at times, this fact can be overwhelming and can prevent us from taking the time to deeply consider our own practices alongside those of colleagues.

Fortunately, one of the many lingering effects of the global pandemic is a new investment in and competence with videoconferencing and other virtual communication tools. When time is limited, and when collaborating across classrooms, buildings, and districts feels difficult, we must remember the skills we developed when strategically using Zoom, Google Meet, and a variety of digital tools to collaborate and capture classroom experiences through audio and video across the

COVID-19 pandemic. While we all have experienced "Zoom fatigue" at times, we must remember the powerful collaboration opportunities that exist in the virtual spaces we created throughout 2020–2022. For many of us, regular virtual check-ins with trusted colleagues may be the best way to keep DL inquiry and instruction work moving forward.

WE OFTEN WIND UP SOMEWHERE OTHER THAN WHERE WE EXPECTED—AND THAT'S OKAY

It can be easy, when engaging in inquiry work, to have an idea or strategy that we are predisposed to think will work. But careful inquiry work asks us to be open minded and to listen carefully to students, even when our best ideas don't go as planned. This is why iteration is critical. We must be open to tinkering, trying new things, taking risks, and attempting new approaches. It can be challenging to open ourselves up in this way, to each other and to the chance that our ideas may not work. But it is this openness that lets us be responsive to students, to invent new practices, to better communicate our disciplines, and to know whether what we are changing is indeed making a difference.

These lessons still hold true, but at the end of the day, we have designed this book to have two major takeaways that we haven't found in other approaches. These keys aren't prescriptive. They aren't a silver bullet that will change everything immediately. Instead, we hope this book helps you find tools to approach the dilemmas that you want to address, to create change thoughtfully, systematically, and in ways that fit your school, classroom, and students. We still believe this is the way to refine and improve our teaching.

FOCUS ON WHAT YOU CAN CHANGE—SMALL CHANGES ARE OFTEN BIG CHANGES IN DISGUISE

If your school has a set curriculum, perhaps you can't immediately change student tasks, or perhaps your texts are not as interchangeable as you may like. What our approach gives you is strategies to find a way to improve, beginning with what *can* be shifted and doing so in a systematic and careful way. With the groups we have coached, we have strategically focused on what can be changed in a particular classroom or school and for particular students.

Authentic and effective professional learning is a process of teachers carefully observing what is and is not working and for whom; a process of systematically choosing, answering, and responding to particular circumstances in a specific space and context; a process of considering what levers are actually available to pull in any given place. Over time, our small classroom changes become bigger systemic changes, if and when they are documented and shared deliberately.

When it comes to DL questions, we've found that considering inquiries grounded in texts, tasks, students, or cultural context can give us effective approaches to making change. This entire framework resituates teachers as the experts, the people most likely to design and refine instruction that will make a real difference for students in the twenty-first century.

CONSIDER YOUR DISCIPLINE—BOTH STRENGTHS AND LIMITATIONS

Throughout our work in schools, we have focused on disciplinary literacy as a means of understanding how different content areas may be better accessed by students. We do this because we see this approach as a bridge between students, with their distinct interests, preferences, and goals, and the roads they may pursue into different fields in the future. For us, the disciplines are the tools we hope to equip our students with so that they can consider a broad array of potential pathways and perhaps try on various future identities through our teaching. The literacy of the disciplines is about much more than just reading and writing. Instead, this type of literacy is about communities and how they behave.

However, while it is important to highlight and teach the powerful ideas and languages of each discipline, it is also critical to help students begin to notice and critique the limitations of each historical discipline. Each discipline has codified ways of constructing knowledge and communicating, and sometimes those codified ways of knowing and doing are more artifacts of societal norms and biases than they are inherent to the disciplines. Therefore, it is increasingly important to provide students with the language and tools to be disciplinary insiders as well as critics of the disciplines, informed consumers and producers who understand and question the various ways that the disciplines have been historically created and bounded. Situating students as creators within the disciplines, utilizing their own literacies, is critical to the revisioning of disciplines in the future. This leads us to an additional idea about disciplinary literacy that we have been thinking about more and more throughout the past few years.

CRITICAL DISCIPLINARY LITERACY FOR EQUITY AND SOCIAL JUSTICE

Disciplinary literacy is certainly about making the communication routines of various content areas and disciplinary experts more explicit for students, with a goal of providing students with more access to and greater opportunities within various professional fields. We believe this to be absolutely true. Yet, we also constantly hear colleagues and scholars talking about the need for more women scientists or writers of color or any number of ways to demographically diversify adult professional communities. Given that the productive, successful future of our new global society requires a deep investment in a diverse and equitable citizenry, we invite you to take a both/and approach in teaching your students important DL skills and habits while also inviting critique and revision of the disciplines themselves.

The disciplines, at least as they currently exist in the academy, have been constructed by those in power, who are predominantly white, cis, straight men with economic capital. This means that the modes of communication within the disciplines have been shaped by those who share these identities. Passing on normative ways of knowing from generation to generation, within a discipline, creates both a sense that those in a discipline are insiders, but also that those who are not are outsiders. As we teach disciplinary ways of knowing and working to students as novices, we can and should also ask them to think critically about these communities and how they have perpetuated the very hierarchies we are hoping to help our students someday dismantle. We must create disciplinary spaces in which students are insiders in ways that include their funds of knowledge, literacies, and cultural identities.

Here, we illustrate the emerging idea of critical disciplinary literacy through two examples:

In ELA the literary canon can be narrow in terms of which stories are held up as literature and whom these stories represent. In our view, a critical DL approach must question this canon—asking questions about who is represented and how to help students understand both the broader societal issues facing authors and their contexts as well as students' own modern interpretations. Moving from these questions into discussions about the identities, linguistic habits, and types of narratives that are and are not represented in canonical literature helps students to build a critical lens. This represents the beginning of deconstructing systems that center whiteness and marginalize other identities. The goal here is to support students as they learn how not only to participate in existing disciplinary communities but to ultimately work to shift the communication norms within those disciplines to be more inclusive of multiple identities, literacies, and cultures.

In another example, a facet of DL often explored by teams and teachers is that of how language is used in various content areas. School language reflects the traditional ways that knowledge is produced in different disciplinary communities. We want students to have access to these different registers of language in order to participate in various disciplinary communities, but we also want to be wary of an approach that conveys, intentionally or not, that academic registers are without normative cultural influence. They are not. They are gatekeepers, keeping people of many different cultural, linguistic, and socioeconomic backgrounds out of those disciplinary communities.

Again, we believe that teachers must take a both/and approach. First, support students in understanding the normative language of a particular discipline—both how that language came to be normative and how it works. However, that must go hand in hand—concurrently—with explicit discussions about language that critique the narrow literacies of the disciplines, asking questions and inventing new ways to communicate in the disciplines using a variety of literacies. Teachers must create new spaces in classrooms to discuss language in a critical way, to ask hard and necessary questions about how we might shift perceptions of language to avoid reifying problematic systems that frame some as belonging and others as outsiders to a discipline.

No matter what point you are at in your learning about and enactment of DL practices, we invite you to consider the ways that your teaching can take on a critical lens. As you support students in developing the language and habits of mind of the disciplines, think about why you are giving them these lenses. Be explicit with students about this. Conversations with students, even our youngest students, can reveal for them the power structures embedded within our society and the way that literacy, writ large, can act as a gatekeeper to many different academic communities. Simultaneously, equipping them with the skills needed to enter a variety of disciplines and the critical lenses needed to then transform those disciplines, making them more welcoming and expansive in their views and ways of working, represents the true potential that we see in the next phase of DL learning in schools.

DISCIPLINARY LITERACY WORK RESPONDS TO THE CURRENT MOMENT(S)

Occasionally in our work, we are asked whether disciplinary literacy has already *had its moment*, whether it is time to move on to something else, particularly when thinking about adolescent literacy. However, we believe now, more than ever, that disciplinary literacy responds to the current moment(s) in education. In fact, we believe that it responds to both current and enduring questions in the field. As we come to the end of this final chapter, we return once again to the words of Jenee Uttaro and Jenelle Williams, whom you met in the preface. They consider the current and enduring relevance of disciplinary literacy and how it fits into broader discourses about teaching literacy that are happening in this moment.

Here Jenelle speaks to the ways that disciplinary literacy responds to current conversations in the field around the science of reading and also builds on a wide body of research into literacy development:

> **Jenelle:** I think people are conflating the science of reading with the simple view of reading. And they are not one in the same. I think Nell Duke and Kelly Cartwright's article, where they're really pushing back against the simple view of reading, evaluating the literature base that has come since the simple view of reading, and then proposing the active view of reading, is critical for us.[3] What I appreciate about what they lay out is the true complexity of what we're really talking about. And so, if people are framing it like you're either doing the science of reading—which is not a thing you can do; it's a research base—or you're doing disciplinary literacy, then that tells me a lot about the level of understanding someone is bringing to the conversation.
>
> Because when we talk about the true science of reading, the body of research, it includes executive function, cultural experiences, background knowledge, motivation, and engagement. Yes, all of those foundational phonological skills and concept of print and all of those things are part of it too. But all of these other things as well, and reading

strategies, and more! So, if we're talking about disciplinary literacy, I think it is the science of reading, but what we've pulled from it are the applicable portions of research for adolescents. And that's the piece that I think is really important, especially with so many of the conversations about what the kids don't have, or what they lost during the pandemic. The reality is that students are different. Students have come to us different from before, because they've had different experiences. So, I think it's really important for those of us that work in adolescent literacy to keep pushing back on: (A) the fact that science of reading does not just mean phonics, and (B) that in disciplinary literacy we pull from that wide body of research.

Just as Jenelle speaks to the ways in which disciplinary literacy can provide us with an expansive perspective on the science of reading, including the ways in which DL work has a deep foundation in research, Jenee speaks to the ways in which DL learning and instruction is inherently adaptive and supports systems-level change:

> **Jenee:** In this book Jacy, Christina, and Megin talk about Heifetz and how disciplinary literacy work is adaptive work.[4] What was so great about the disciplinary literacy project I did with them was that once we were done, we then moved to a conversation with K–8 schools. We had those schools and educators come on board to say, "Oh my gosh! What are they doing at the high school? How can we continue this conversation across all levels?" And granted, system-wide impact is still something that we're working toward. But the fact is that the work could grow across the entire district. Because, you know, disciplinary literacy work begins in PreK. It begins with two- and three-year-olds. And we were focused at the high school. This is systems-level work, challenging adaptive work.

Jenelle and Jenee highlight the ways that DL inquiry, learning, and instructional practice build on the deep history of adaptive change work in schools. At the same time, their words make it evident how relevant disciplinary literacy is at this current moment. As such, disciplinary literacy represents a critical component of the ongoing work of school change as well as a crucial lens to bring to current dilemmas in the field.

A FINAL NOTE

We hope, in this book, you have found the tools with which to better approach instructional improvement in your classroom or school and to see the potential in disciplinary literacy to provide a pathway toward that improvement. We can teach students about our disciplines in such a way as to give them access and ultimately to make them aware that they have the power to change these communities to be accepting and more diverse. We hope the classroom stories and related strategies in this book give you a strong starting place to analyze and refine your own instruction or instruction across your school, with the goal fostering a stronger community.

Ultimately, the approach we describe in this book is designed to help us work toward reculturing schools, honoring and building on the expertise of teachers and creating a stronger system of collaborative adult inquiry that leads to teaching all of our students more effectively. We must show students what we love *and* question about various disciplines, about literacy practices, and about learning. This approach is grounded in the expertise of teachers, in the power of literacy to help students find and create their own selves and futures, and in the hope that is required to keep working toward improvement.

Further Reading on Disciplinary Literacy

RESOURCES FOR BUILDING A SCHOOL-WIDE CULTURE AND SET OF PRACTICES AROUND DISCIPLINARY LITERACY

- *Best Practices of Literacy Leaders: Keys to School Improvement* (2nd ed.), edited by Swan Dagen & Bean, 2020
- *Collaborative Coaching for Disciplinary Literacy, Strategies to Support Teachers in Grades 6–12* by Elish-Piper, L'Allier, Manderino, & DiDomenico, 2016
- *Disciplinary Literacies: Unpacking Research, Theory, and Practice*, edited by Ortlieb, Kane, & Cheek, 2023
- *Disciplinary Literacy in Action: How to Create and Sustain a School-Wide Culture of Deep Reading, Writing, and Thinking* by Lent & Voigt, 2018
- *Doing Disciplinary Literacy: Teaching Reading and Writing Across the Content Areas* by Gabriel, 2023
- *Investigating Disciplinary Literacy: A Framework for Collaborative Professional Learning* by Dobbs, Ippolito, & Charner-Laird, 2017

RESOURCES THAT DISCUSS DISCIPLINARY LITERACY ACROSS GRADE LEVELS (K–6 AND 5–12)

- *Digitally Supported Disciplinary Literacy for Diverse K-5 Classrooms* by Colwell, Hutchinson, Woodward, & Bean, 2020
- *Disciplinary Literacy and Gamified Learning in Middle School Classrooms: Questing Through Time and Space* by Haas, Tussey, & Metzger, 2022
- *Engaging Students in Disciplinary Literacy, K-6: Reading, Writing, and Teaching Tools for the Classroom* by Brock, Goatley, Raphael, Trost-Shahata, & Weber, 2014
- *Literacy Instruction with Disciplinary Texts: Strategies for Grades 6–12* by Lewis & Strong, 2020
- *Literacy in the Disciplines: A Teacher's Guide for Grades 5–12* by Wolsey & Lapp, 2016
- *Read, Write, Inquire: Disciplinary Literacy in Grades 6–12* by Spires, Kerkhoff, & Paul, 2020
- *Teaching Disciplinary Literacy in Grades K-6* by Lupo, Hardigree, Thacker, Sawyer, & Merritt, 2022

RESOURCES THAT FOCUS ON ONE OR MORE CONTENT AREAS

- *Adolescent Literacy in the Academic Disciplines: General Principles and Practical Strategies* edited by Jetton & Shanahan, 2012 (ELA, math, science, social studies)
- *Building Students' Historical Literacies: Learning to Read and Reason with Historical Texts and Evidence* (2nd ed.) by Nokes, 2022 (social studies)
- *Content Matters: A Disciplinary Literacy Approach to Improving Student Learning* edited by McConachie & Petrosky, 2009 (ELA, math, science, social studies)
- *Developing Readers in the Academic Disciplines* (2nd ed.) by Buehl, 2017 (ELA, math, science, social studies)
- *Literacy and History in Action: Immersive Approaches to Disciplinary Thinking, Grades 5–12* by McCann, D'Angelo, Galas, & Greska, 2015 (social studies)
- *Reading and Writing in Science: Tools to Develop Disciplinary Literacy* by Grant, Fisher, & Lapp, 2015 (science)

- *This Is Disciplinary Literacy: Reading, Writing, Thinking, and Doing… Content Area by Content Area* by Lent, 2015 (ELA, math, science, social studies)

RESOURCES FOR SUPPORTING LANGUAGE DEVELOPMENT IN THE DISCIPLINES

- *Academic Conversations: Classroom Talk That Fosters Critical Thinking and Content Understandings* by Zwiers & Crawford, 2011
- *Building Academic Language: Meeting Common Core Standards Across the Disciplines* (2nd ed.) by Zwiers, 2014
- *Common Core Standards in Diverse Classrooms: Essential Practices for Developing Academic Language and Disciplinary Literacy* by Zwiers, O'Hara, & Pritchard, 2014
- *Content-Area Conversations: How to Plan Discussion-Based Lessons for Diverse Language Learners* by Fisher, Frey, & Rothenberg, 2008
- *The K-3 Guide to Academic Conversations: Practices, Scaffolds, and Activities* by Zwiers & Hamerla, 2017
- *Teaching Vocabulary to English Language Learners* by Graves, August, & Mancilla-Martinez, 2013
- *They Say, I Say: The Moves that Matter in Academic Writing* (5th ed.) by Graff & Birkenstein, 2021
- *Words Worth Using: Supporting Adolescents' Power with Academic Vocabulary* by Townsend, 2022

READILY AVAILABLE ARTICLES WE HAVE USED TO INTRODUCE DISCIPLINARY LITERACY TO TEACHERS

- "Analysis of Expert Readers in Three Disciplines: History, Mathematics, and Chemistry" by Shanahan, Shanahan & Misischia, 2011. In the *Journal of Literacy Research*, 43(4), 393–429.
- "Disciplinary Literacy: Adapt Not Adopt," by Gillis, 2014. In the *Journal of Adolescent & Adult Literacy*, 57(8), 614–23.
- "Disciplinary Literacy: Just the FAQs" by Shanahan & Shanahan, 2017. In *Literacy in Every Classroom*, 74(5), 18–22.

- "Disciplinary Literacy Through the Lens of the Next Generation Science Standards" by Houseal, Gillis, Helmsing & Hutchison, 2016. In the *Journal of Adolescent & Adult Literacy, 59*(4), 377–84.
- "Does Disciplinary Literacy Have a Place in Elementary School?" by Shanahan & Shanahan, 2012. In *The Reading Teacher, 67*(8), 636–39.
- "Doing and Teaching Disciplinary Literacy with Adolescent Learners: A Social and Cultural Enterprise" by Moje, 2015. In the *Harvard Educational Review, 85*(2), 254–78.
- "Layering Intermediate and Disciplinary Literacy Work: Lessons Learned from a Secondary Social Studies Teacher Team" by Dobbs, Ippolito, & Charner-Laird, 2016. In the *Journal of Adolescent & Adult Literacy, 60*(2), 131–39.
- "Teaching Disciplinary Literacy to Adolescents: Rethinking Content-Area Literacy" by Shanahan & Shanahan, 2008. In the *Harvard Educational Review, 78*(1), 40–59.
- "What Is Disciplinary Literacy and Why Does It Matter?" by Shanahan & Shanahan, 2012. In *Topics in Language Disorders, 32*(1), 7–18.

ONLINE DISCIPLINARY LITERACY RESOURCES WE RECOMMEND

- Annenberg Learner free online modules introducing disciplinary literacy in the four core subject areas (ELA, history, math, science)
  - http://www.learner.org/series/reading-writing-in-the-disciplines/
- Literacy in the Disciplines Blog (featuring free articles and webinars by researchers and teachers alike)
  - http://literacy6-12.org/
- Michigan's 6–12 Disciplinary Literacy Task Force (featuring essential practice documents, free online courses, and relevant blog posts)
  - http://www.gomaisa.org/organizations/general-education-leadership -network-geln/6-12-disciplinary-literacy-task-force/
  - Direct link to free courses: http://www.edupaths.org/catalog?Search =disciplinary%20literacy

Are My Students Doing Disciplinary Literacy?

KEY:

N = Not Yet (This practice is not yet present.)
O = On the Way (There is evidence that this practice is in development and partially enacted.)
Y = Yes (This practice is present and being enacted.)

TEXTS			
N	O	Y	
☐	☐	☐	Are the texts authentic (i.e., reflective of disciplinary language and thinking)?
☐	☐	☐	Do the texts represent the discipline in a way that builds toward or mirrors thinking of professionals within the discipline?
☐	☐	☐	Do the texts provide multiple entry points for students?
☐	☐	☐	Is there variety within and among the texts, while still presenting meaningful, discipline-specific content?
☐	☐	☐	Do the texts represent multiple identities, languages, cultures, funds of knowledge, and literacies?
☐	☐	☐	Do the texts connect with students' lives, cultures, communities, and languages specifically?

TASKS

N	O	Y	
☐	☐	☐	Are students engaging in authentic tasks that build toward or mirror those of particular disciplines?
☐	☐	☐	Are students given opportunities to act as scientists, think like mathematicians, reason like historians, and so on, as opposed to just learning about how others engage in this work?
☐	☐	☐	Are students given opportunities to think about power and authority within the disciplines, including who may be included and who may be excluded from normative views of a discipline?
☐	☐	☐	Are students immersed in the work of the disciplines in an age-appropriate manner?
☐	☐	☐	Are students experiencing tasks that allow them to identify with the discipline and see it as a potential for postsecondary education or career?
☐	☐	☐	Are students given opportunities to create within the disciplines and to see new ways that they may contribute to the discipline?

STUDENTS

N	O	Y	
☐	☐	☐	Are there opportunities for all students to engage in disciplinary literacy instruction? Are learning experiences differentiated to meet different needs and create multiple entry points?
☐	☐	☐	Are there opportunities for all students to see their backgrounds and experiences represented in the materials used to build disciplinary literacy knowledge and skills?
☐	☐	☐	Are disciplinary literacy learning opportunities designed to engage all students through a variety of learning modalities?
☐	☐	☐	Are students invited to bring their own life experiences and literacies to their learning in the disciplines?
☐	☐	☐	Is knowledge of students—gained from families, community organizations, and students themselves—used as a component of the curriculum in order to deepen student engagement?

CULTURE

N	O	Y	
☐	☐	☐	Are students supported in developing the skills to engage with each other in meaningful ways around discipline-specific skills and content?
☐	☐	☐	Do the cultures within classrooms and schools make space for all students to feel recognized and included? How is voice shared within classrooms and schools?
☐	☐	☐	Are classrooms spaces where all students feel known and that their identities, cultures, and literacies are welcomed as they learn in the disciplines?

☐ ☐ ☐   Are there explicit opportunities within the curriculum to build community and connection among students while also teaching them discipline-specific literacies?

EQUITY

N   O   Y

☐ ☐ ☐   Are there opportunities for students to consider gatekeeping in relation to various disciplines?

☐ ☐ ☐   Are teachers and students finding ways to question and push back on the established norms of literacy within various disciplines?

☐ ☐ ☐   Is the instruction making space for those who are often underrepresented in various disciplines to see themselves in and enter into those disciplinary communities?

☐ ☐ ☐   Is the instruction making space for students from all backgrounds to see the potential for both entering and shaping/reshaping disciplinary communities?

Though this checklist is not exhaustive, nor is it the only way to answer these questions, it can serve as a starting point for thinking about disciplinary literacy instruction. You may use it yourself, reflecting on your own instruction. A team of teachers may decide to use the checklist as they observe in each other's classrooms. Individuals or teams of teachers may use it while looking at videos of teaching found online. Or individuals, teams, coaches, and leaders may use it as they take learning walks or participate in instructional rounds across a school or district.

We invite you to use this checklist flexibly and to redesign it in ways that work for you. The checklist could easily be turned into a rubric, or each question could be answered along a continuum. As you deepen your own understanding of disciplinary literacy and marry that with what you know about your context, you may want to add questions or adjust those that are here.

NOTES

Foreword

1. R. A. Heifetz, A. Grashow, and M. Linsky, *The Practice of Adaptive Leadership: Tools and Tactics for Changing Your Organization and the World* (Boston, MA: Harvard Business Press, 2009).

Preface to the Second Edition

1. Richard F. Elmore, ed., *I Used to Think…And Now I Think…: Twenty Leading Educators Reflect on the Work of School Reform* (Cambridge, MA: Harvard Education Press, 2011).
2. Timothy Shanahan and Cynthia Shanahan, "Teaching Disciplinary Literacy to Adolescents: Rethinking Content-Area Literacy," *Harvard Educational Review* 78, no. 1 (2008): 40–59.
3. Jacy Ippolito, Christina L. Dobbs, and Megin Charner-Laird, *Disciplinary Literacy Inquiry and Instruction* (West Palm Beach, FL: Learning Sciences International, 2019), 16.
4. Nell K. Duke and Kelly B. Cartwright, "The Science of Reading Progresses: Communicating Advances Beyond the Simple View of Reading," *Reading Research Quarterly* 56 (2021): S25–S44.
5. Shanahan and Shanahan, "Teaching Disciplinary Literacy to Adolescents," 43.
6. Christina L. Dobbs, Jacy Ippolito, and Megin Charner-Laird, "Layering Intermediate and Disciplinary Literacy Work: Lessons Learned from a Secondary Social Studies Teacher Team," *Journal of Adolescent & Adult Literacy* 60, no. 2 (2016): 131–39.

Chapter 1

1. Vicki Jacobs, "Adolescent Literacy: Putting the Crisis in Context," *Harvard Educational Review* 78, no. 1 (2008): 7–39.
2. Stephanie Harvey and Anne Goudvis, *Strategies That Work: Teaching Comprehension to Enhance Understanding* (Portland, ME: Stenhouse Publishers, 2000); Ellin Oliver Keene and Susan Zimmermann, *Mosaic of Thought: Teaching Comprehension in a Reader's Workshop* (Portsmouth, NH: Heinemann, 1997); Ralph Fletcher and JoAnn Portalupi, *Craft Lessons: Teaching Writing K–8* (Portland, ME: Stenhouse Publishers, 2007).
3. D. M. Ogle, "K-W-L: A Teaching Model That Develops Active Reading of Expository Text," *The Reading Teacher* 39, no. 6 (1986): 564–70; for quick access to a wide variety

of general comprehension strategies, see "Reading and Writing Strategies," http://www
.adlit.org/in-the-classroom/strategies.

4. Timothy Shanahan and Cynthia Shanahan, "Teaching Disciplinary Literacy to Adolescents: Rethinking Content-Area Literacy," *Harvard Educational Review* 78, no. 1
(2008): 40–59.

5. Shanahan et al., "Teaching Disciplinary Literacy to Adolescents," 40.

6. *Time to Act: An Agenda for Advancing Adolescent Literacy for College and Career Success*
(New York: Carnegie Council on Advancing Adolescent Literacy, 2010); *Common Core
State Standards* (Washington, DC: National Governors Association Center for Best
Practices and the Council of Chief State School Officers, 2010).

7. *Common Core*, 3.

8. Christina L. Dobbs, Jacy Ippolito, and Megin Charner-Laird, *Investigating Disciplinary
Literacy: A Framework for Collaborative Professional Learning* (Cambridge, MA: Harvard
Education Press, 2017).

9. Shanahan et al., "Teaching Disciplinary Literacy to Adolescents."

10. Christina L. Dobbs, Jacy Ippolito, and Megin Charner-Laird, "What Do We Mean
When We Say Disciplinary Literacy? Exploring a Messy Construct." (Poster presented
at the Annual Meeting of the American Educational Research Association, New York,
NY, April 2018).

11. Stephanie McConachie and Anthony Petrosky, eds., *Content Matters: A Disciplinary
Literacy Approach to Improving Student Learning* (San Francisco, CA: Jossey-Bass,
2010); Elizabeth B. Moje, "Developing Socially Just Subject-Matter Instruction: A
Review of the Literature on Disciplinary Literacy Teaching," *Review of Research in
Education* 31, no. 1 (2007): 1–44; Elizabeth B. Moje, "Foregrounding the Disciplines
in Secondary Literacy Teaching and Learning: A Call for Change," *Journal of Adoles-
cent & Adult Literacy* 52, no. 2 (2008): 96–107; Elizabeth B. Moje, "Doing and Teaching Disciplinary Literacy with Adolescent Learners: A Social and Cultural Enterprise,"
Harvard Educational Review 85, no. 2 (2015): 254–78; Shanahan et al., "Teaching
Disciplinary Literacy to Adolescents"; Timothy Shanahan and Cynthia Shanahan,
"What Is Disciplinary Literacy and Why Does It Matter?" *Topics in Language Disorders* 32, no. 1 (2012): 7–18.

12. Dobbs et al., "What Do We Mean When We Say Disciplinary Literacy?"

13. Jacobs, "Adolescent Literacy: Putting the Crisis in Context."

14. William G. Brozo, Gary Moorman, Carla Meyer, and Trevor Stewart, "Content Area
Reading and Disciplinary Literacy: A Case for the Radical Center," *Journal of Adoles-
cent & Adult Literacy* 56, no. 5 (2013): 353–57; Shanahan et al., "What is Disciplinary
Literacy and Why Does It Matter?"

15. Shanahan et al., "Teaching Disciplinary Literacy to Adolescents," 44.

16. *Standards for the Preparation of Literacy Professionals 2017* (Newark, DE: International
Literacy Association, 2018); Michael D. Toth, *Who Moved My Standards? Joyful
Teaching in an Age of Change: A SOAR-ing tale* (West Palm Beach, FL: Learning Sci-
ences International, 2016).

17. Brozo et al., "Content Area Reading"; Christina L. Dobbs, Jacy Ippolito, and Megin Charner-Laird, "Layering Intermediate and Disciplinary Literacy Work: Lessons Learned from a Secondary Social Studies Teacher Team," *Journal of Adolescent & Adult Literacy* 60, no. 2 (2016): 131–39.
18. Shanahan et al., "What Is Disciplinary Literacy?," 8.
19. Shanahan et al., "What Is Disciplinary Literacy?," 9.
20. Dobbs et al., "Layering Intermediate and Disciplinary Literacy Work."
21. Cynthia Brock, Virginia Goatley, Taffy Raphael, Elisabeth Trost-Shahata, and Catherine Weber, *Engaging Students in Disciplinary Literacy, K–6: Reading, Writing, and Teaching Tools for the Classroom* (New York: Teachers College Press, 2014); Jamie Colwell, Amy Hutchison, and Lindsay Woodward, "Digitally Supported Disciplinary Literacy in Elementary Instruction," *The Reading Teacher* 75, no. 4 (2022): 463–74; Cami Condie and Jacy Ippolito, "Encouraging Our Youngest Students to Think Like Scientists: Exploring Elementary Teachers' Experiences of Teaching Disciplinary Literacy," *Massachusetts Reading Association Primer* 44, no. 2 (2016): 6–14; Charlotte Frambaugh-Kritzer and Stephanie Buelow, "Problem Solving Like a Mathematician: Disciplinary Literacy Instruction in Elementary Mathematics," *Reading Horizons: A Journal of Literacy and Language Arts* 61, no. 2 (2022): 3; Anne Håland, "Disciplinary Literacy in Elementary School: How a Struggling Student Positions Herself as a Writer," *The Reading Teacher* 70, no. 4 (2017): 457–68; Jacy Ippolito, Cami Condie, Jaclyn Blanchette, and Cleti Cervoni, "Learning Science and Literacy Together: Professional Learning That Supports Disciplinary Literacy Instruction for Our Youngest Learners," *Science & Children* 56, no. 4 (2018): 91–95; Jacy Ippolito, Cami Condie, Christina L. Dobbs, Megin Charner-Laird, and Jaclyn Blanchette, "Planting Seeds: To Grow Science Disciplinary Literacy Skills We Must Layer Basic and Intermediate Literacy Skills Across K-12," *Massachusetts Reading Association Primer* 45, no. 2 (2017): 14–23; Timothy Shanahan and Cynthia Shanahan, "Does Disciplinary Literacy Have a Place in Elementary School? *The Reading Teacher* 67, no. 8 (2014): 636–39; Tanya S. Wright and Amelia W. Gotwals, "Supporting Kindergartners' Science Talk in the Context of an Integrated Science and Disciplinary Literacy Curriculum," *The Elementary School Journal* 117, no. 3 (2017): 513–37.
22. Shanahan et al., "Teaching Disciplinary Literacy to Adolescents."
23. Condie and Ippolito, "Encouraging Our Youngest Students; Ippolito et al., "Planting Seeds"; Ippolito et al., "Learning Science and Literacy Together."
24. Moje, "Doing and Teaching Disciplinary Literacy."
25. Moje, "Doing and Teaching Disciplinary Literacy," 258.
26. Christina L. Dobbs, Jacy Ippolito, and Megin Charner-Laird, *Investigating Disciplinary Literacy: A Framework for Collaborative Professional Learning* (Cambridge, MA: Harvard Education Press, 2017).
27. Angela Breidenstein, Kevin Fahey, Carl Glickman, and Frances Hensley, *Leading for Powerful Learning: A Guide for Instructional Leaders* (New York: Teachers College Press, 2012); Kevin Fahey, Angela Breidenstein, Jacy Ippolito, and Frances Hensley,

An Uncommon Theory of School Change: Leadership for Reinventing Schools (New York: Teachers College Press, 2019).

28. *Standards for the Preparation of Literacy Professionals 2017* (Newark, DE: International Literacy Association, 2018).

Chapter 2

1. Ronald A. Heifetz, Alexander Grashow, and Marty Linsky, *The Practice of Adaptive Leadership: Tools and Tactics for Changing Your Organization and the World* (Cambridge, MA: Harvard Business Press, 2009).
2. Heifetz et al., *Practice of Adaptive Leadership.*
3. Kevin Fahey, Angela Breidenstein, Jacy Ippolito, and Frances Hensley, *An Uncommon Theory of School Change: Leadership for Reinventing Schools* (New York: Teachers College Press, 2019).
4. Megin Charner-Laird, Jacy Ippolito, and Christina L. Dobbs, "The Roles of Teacher Leaders in Guiding PLCs Focused on Disciplinary Literacy," *Journal of School Leadership* 26, no. 6 (2016): 975–1001; Christina L. Dobbs, Jacy Ippolito, and Megin Charner-Laird, *Investigating Disciplinary Literacy: A Framework for Collaborative Professional Learning* (Cambridge, MA: Harvard Education Press, 2017); Christina L. Dobbs and Christine M. Leider, "A LangCrit Analysis of Teachers' Beliefs About Language Learning and Language Diversity," *Journal of Multilingual Theories and Practices* 2, no. 1 (2021): 25–46; Jacy Ippolito, Chrisina L. Dobbs, and Megin Charner-Laird, "Bridge Builders: Teacher Leaders Forge Connections and Bring Coherence to Literacy Initiative," *JSD* 35, no. 3 (2014): 22–26.
5. *Reading for Understanding: Toward an R&D Program in Reading Comprehension* (Santa Monica, CA: RAND Corporation, RAND Reading Study Group, 2002), http://www.rand.org/pubs/monograph_reports/MR1465.html.
6. Nell K. Duke and Kelly B. Cartwright, "The Science of Reading Progresses: Communicating Advances Beyond the Simple View of Reading," *Reading Research Quarterly* 56 (2021): S25–S44.
7. Dobbs et al., *Investigating Disciplinary Literacy.*
8. Marilyn Cochran-Smith and Susan L. Lytle, *Inquiry as Stance: Practitioner Research for the Next Generation* (New York: Teachers College Press, 2009).
9. Heifetz et al., *Practice of Adaptive Leadership*, 159–61.
10. Charner-Laird et al., "Roles of Teacher Leaders"; Dobbs et al., *Investigating Disciplinary Literacy*; Ippolito et al., "Bridge Builders."
11. Charner-Laird et al., "Roles of Teacher Leaders"; Ippolito et al. "Bridge Builders."
12. *Standards for the Preparation of Literacy Professionals 2017* (International Literacy Association, 2018).
13. *Standards for the Preparation of Literacy Professionals*, 5.

Chapter 3

1. Cynthia Shanahan, Timothy Shanahan, and Cynthia Misischia, "Analysis of Expert Readers in Three Disciplines: History, Mathematics, and Chemistry," *Journal of Literacy Research* 43, no. 4 (2011): 393–429.
2. M. A. K. Halliday and J. R. Martin, *Writing Science: Literacy and Discursive Power* (New York: Routledge, 1993).
3. Kimberly Lenters, "Resistance, Struggle, and the Adolescent Reader," *Journal of Adolescent and Adult Literacy* 50, no. 2 (2006): 136–46.
4. Emily Phillips Galloway, Joshua Fahey Lawrence, and Elizabeth Moje, "Research in Disciplinary Literacy: Challenges and Instructional Opportunities in Teaching Disciplinary Texts," in *Adolescent Literacy in the Era of the Common Core*, edited by Jacy Ippolito, Joshua Fahey Lawrence, and Colleen Zaller (Cambridge, MA: Harvard Education Press, 2013), 21.
5. Only textbooks used in classroom settings for didactic purposes that require unique disciplinary skills; for more, see Aaron Weinberg, Emily Wiesner, and Ellie Fitts Fulmer, "Didactical Disciplinary Literacy in Mathematics: Making Meaning from Textbooks," *International Journal of Research in Undergraduate Mathematics Education* (2022): 1–33.
6. Tools such as those provided by the Wisconsin Department of Public Instruction: http://dpi.wi.gov/reading/professional-learning/text-complexity; and by Michigan's Mission: Literacy: http://missionliteracy.com/complex-text.html.
7. Phillips Galloway et al., "Research in Disciplinary Literacy."
8. Jacy Ippolito, Christina L. Dobbs, & Megin Charner-Laird, "What Literacy Means in Math Class: Teacher Team Explores Ways to Remake Instruction to Develop Students' Skills," *The Learning Professional*, 38, no. 2 (2017): 66–70.
9. *Standards for the Preparation of Literacy Professionals 2017* (International Literacy Association, 2018).

Chapter 4

1. Margaret Mackey, "Who Reads What, in Which Formats, and Why?" in *Handbook of Reading Research*, 5th vol., edited by Elizabeth Moje, Peter Afflerbach, Patricia Enciso, and Nonie K. Lesaux (New York: Taylor & Francis, 2020), 99–115.
2. Tracy Linderholm, "Reading with Purpose," *Theory into Practice* 36, no. 2 (2006): 70–80; Tracy Linderholm and Adam Wilde, "College Students' Beliefs About Comprehension When Reading for Different Purposes," *Journal of College Reading and Learning* 40, no. 2 (2010): 7–19; Shenglan Zhang and Nell K. Duke, "Strategies for Internet Reading with Different Reading Purposes: A Descriptive Study of Twelve Good Internet Readers," *Journal of Literacy Research* 40, no. 1 (2008): 128–62.
3. Nadia Behizadeh, "Adolescent Perspectives on Authentic Writing Instruction," *Journal of Language and Literacy Education* 10, no. 1 (2014): 27–44; Nell K. Duke, Victoria Purcell-Gates, Leigh A. Hall, and Cathy Tower, "Authentic Literacy Activities for

Developing Comprehension and Writing," *The Reading Teacher* 60, no. 4 (2006): 344–55; Victoria Purcell-Gates, Nell K. Duke, and Joseph A. Martineau, "Learning to Read and Write Genre-Specific Text: Roles of Authentic Experience and Explicit Teaching," *Reading Research Quarterly* 42, no. 1 (2011): 8–45.

4. Gwynne Ellen Ash and Melanie R. Kuhn, "Meaningful Oral and Silent Reading in the Elementary and Middle School Classroom: Breaking the Round Robin Reading Addiction," in *Fluency Instruction: Research-based Best Practices*, edited by Timony Rasinski, Camille Blachowicz, and Kristin Lems (New York: Guilford Press, 2006), 155–72; Michael F. Opitz and Timothy V. Rasinski, *Good-bye Round Robin: 25 Effective Oral Reading Strategies* (Portsmouth, NH: Heinemann, 2008).

5. Gwynne Ellen Ash, Melanie R. Kuhn, and Sharon Walpole, "Analyzing 'Inconsistencies' in Practice: Teachers' Continued Use of Round Robin Reading," *Reading and Writing Quarterly* 25, no. 1 (2009): 87–103.

6. See http://www.breakoutedu.com.

7. See http://www.serpinstitute.org/sogen.

8. See http://sheg.stanford.edu/history-lessons/athenian-democracy-sac.

9. Shane Safir and Jamila Dugan, Street Data: *A Next-Generation Model for Equity, Pedagogy, and School Transformation* (Thousand Oaks, CA: 2021).

10. Safir et al., *Street Data*.

11. *Standards for the Preparation of Literacy Professionals 2017* (International Literacy Association, 2018).

12. *Standards for the Preparation*, 78.

Chapter 5

1. *Reading for Understanding: Toward an R&D Program in Reading Comprehension* (Santa Monica, CA: RAND Corporation, RAND Reading Study Group, 2002). http://www.rand.org/pubs/monograph_reports/MR1465.html.

2. Nell K. Duke, Victoria Purcell-Gates, Leigh A. Hall, and Cathy Tower, "Authentic Literacy Activities for Developing Comprehension and Writing," *The Reading Teacher* 60, no. 4 (2006): 344–55; Seth Parsons and Allison Ward Parsons, "The Case for Authentic Tasks in Content Literacy," *The Reading Teacher* 64, no. 6 (2011): 462–65.

3. Brian R. Belland, ChanMin Kim, and Michael J. Hannafin, "A Framework for Designing Scaffolds That Improve Motivation and Cognition," *Educational Psychologist* 48, no. 4 (2013): 243–70.

4. Colleen M. Fairbanks, Gerald G. Duffy, Beverly S. Faircloth, Ye He, Y., Barbara Levin, Jean Rohr, and Catherine Stein, "Beyond Knowledge: Exploring Why Some Teachers Are More Thoughtfully Adaptive Than Others," *Journal of Teacher Education* 61, no. 1–2, (2010): 161–71.

5. Belland et al., "Framework"; Phyllis C. Blumenfeld, Toni M. Kepler, and Joseph C. Krajcik, "Motivation and Cognitive Engagement in Learning Environments," in *The Cambridge Handbook of the Learning Sciences*, edited by R. Keith Sawyer (Cambridge University Press, 2005), 475–88.

6. Christina L. Dobbs and Christine M, Leider, "A LangCrit Analysis of Teachers' Beliefs About Language Learning and Language Diversity," *Journal of Multilingual Theories and Practices* 2, no. 1 (2021): 25–46; Allen A. Rovick, Joel A. Michael, Harold I. Modell, David S. Bruce, Barbara Horwitz, Thomas Adamson, Daniel R. Richardson, Dee U. Silverthorn, and Shirley A. Whitescarver, "How Accurate Are Our Assumptions About Our Students' Background Knowledge?" *Advances in Physiology Education* 21, no. 1 (1999): 93–101.

7. Robert J. Graham, "The Self as Writer: Assumptions and Identities in the Writing Workshop," *Journal of Adolescent and Adult Literacy* 43, no. 4 (1999): 358–64.

8. Jedda Graham, Ruth Tisher, Mary Ainley, and Gregor Kennedy, "Staying with the Text: The Contribution of Gender, Achievement Orientations, and Interest to Students' Performance on a Literacy Task," *Educational Psychology* 7 (2008): 757–76.

9. Christina L. Dobbs, Jacy Ippolito, and Megin Charner-Laird, "Layering Intermediate and Disciplinary Literacy Work: Lessons Learned from a Secondary Social Studies Teacher Team," *Journal of Adolescent & Adult Literacy* 60, no. 2 (2016): 131–39.

10. Daniel Koretz, *The Testing Charade: Pretending to Make Schools Better* (Chicago, IL: The University of Chicago Press, 2017).

11. Richard M. Ryan and Edward L. Deci, "Self-Determination Theory and the Facilitation of Intrinsic Motivation, Social Development, and Well-Being," *American Psychologist* 55, no. 1 (2020): 68–78.

12. *Standards for the Preparation of Literacy Professionals 2017* (International Literacy Association, 2018).

Chapter 6

1. Shai Frost, Roberta Buhle, and Camille Blachowicz, *Effective Literacy Coaching: Building Expertise and a Culture of Literacy* (Arlington, VA: ASCD, 2009); Cynthia Greenleaf, Ruth Schoenbach, and Lynn Murphy, *Literacy Practices That Adolescents Deserve: Building a Culture of Engaged Academic Literacy in Schools* (International Reading Association, 2014), http://www.literacyworldwide.org/docs/default-source /member-benefits/e-ssentials/ila-e-ssentials-8066.pdf; Linda Jacobson, "Building a Culture of Literacy: Ideas for Making Literacy the Foundation in Your School." *Literacy Today* 35, no. 1 (2017): 20–24, http://www.literacyworldwide.org/docs/default -source/ild/building-a-culture-of-literacy.pdf.

2. Norma González, Luis C. Moll, and Cathi Amanti, *Funds of Knowledge: Theorizing Practices in Households, Communities and Classroom* (Mahwah, NJ: Lawrence Erlbaum, 2006); Luis C. Moll, Cathy Amanti, Deborah Neff, and Norma Gonzalez, "Funds of Knowledge for Teaching: Using a Qualitative Approach to Connect Homes and Classrooms," *Theory into Practice* 31, no. 2 (1992): 132–41.

3. Allan Luke, "Critical Literacy: Foundational Notes," *Theory into Practice* 51, no. 1 (2012): 4–11; Django Paris and H. Samy Alim, eds., *Culturally Sustaining Pedagogies: Teaching and Learning for Justice in a Changing World* (New York: Teachers College Press, 2017).

4. Kevin Fahey, Angela Breidenstein, Jacy Ippolito, and Frances Hensley, *An Uncommon Theory of School Change: Leadership for Reinventing Schools* (New York: Teachers College Press, 2019); Edgar H. Schein, *Organizational Culture and Leadership*, 5th ed. (San Francisco, CA: Jossey-Bass, 2016).

5. Schein, *Organizational Culture*.

6. Paul Gorski and Katy Swalwell, *Fix Injustice, Not Kids and Other Principles for Transformative Equity Leadership* (Arlington, VA: ASCD, 2023).

7. Sarah Michaels and Catherine O'Connor, "Conceptualizing Talk Moves as Tools: Professional Development Approaches for Academically Productive Discussions," in *Socializing Intelligence Through Talk and Dialogue*, edited by Lauren B. Resnick, Christa S. C. Asterhan, and Sherice N. Clarke (Washington, DC: AERA, 2015), 333–47.

8. Jeff Zwiers and Marie Crawford, "How to Start Academic Conversations," *Educational Leadership* 66, no. 7 (2009): 70–73.

9. Kevin Feldman and Kate Kinsella, "Practical Strategies to Improve Academic Discussions in Mixed Ability Secondary Content Area Classrooms," December 2005, http://fliphtml5.com/fsnu/wnuz/basic.

10. International Literacy Association. *Standards for the Preparation of Literacy Professionals, 2017 Edition.* (Newark, DE: International Literacy Association, 2018).

11. *Standards for Preparation*, 80.

Chapter 7

1. Christina L. Dobbs, Jacy Ippolito, and Megin Charner-Laird, *Investigating Disciplinary Literacy: A Framework for Collaborative Professional Learning* (Cambridge, MA: Harvard Education Press, 2017).

2. Hilda Borko, "Professional Development and Teacher Learning: Mapping the Terrain," *Educational Researcher* 33, no. 8 (2004): 3–15; Anthony S. Bryk, Louis Gomez, Alicia Grunow, and Paul LeMahieu, *Learning to Improve: How America's Schools Can Get Better at Getting Tetter* (Cambridge, MA: Harvard Education Press, 2015); Quinn Hannan, and Lin Russell, "Coaching in Context: Exploring Conditions That Shape Instructional Coaching Practice," *Teachers College Record* 122, no. 10 (2020): 1–40.

3. Jacy Ippolito and Douglas Fisher, "Instructional Leadership in Disciplinary Literacy," *Educational Leadership* 76, no. 6 (2019): 50–56.

4. Eleanor Drago-Severson and Jessica Blum-DeStefano, *Tell Me So I Can Hear You: A Developmental Approach to Feedback for Educators* (Cambridge, MA: Harvard Education Press, 2017), 52.

5. See http://www.michigan.gov/mde/services/academic-standards/literacy/literacy-in-michigan-and-essential-practices.

6. John Van de Walle, Karen Karp, and Jennifer Bay-Williams, *Elementary and Middle School Mathematics: Teaching Developmentally*, 10th ed. (Upper Saddle River, NJ: Pearson, 2020).

7. When referring to the fact of reduced or absent access to sound, the terms "deaf" or "DHH" will be used. When referring to individuals who are culturally Deaf and use American Sign Language (ASL), "Deaf" will be used.

8. Jessica A. Scott, Hanah Goldberg, Carol McDonald Connor, and Amy R. Lederberg, "Schooling Effects on Early Literacy Skills of Young Deaf and Hard of Hearing Children," *American Annals of the Deaf* 163, no. 5 (2019): 596–618.

9. "The 4Cs Research Series," P21, 2017, http://p21.org; *BSCS 5Es Instructional Model* (Colorado Springs, CO: Biological Sciences Curriculum Study, 2006), http://bscs.org/reports/the-bscs-5e-instructional-model-origins-and-effectiveness.

Chapter 8

1. *Teachers Know Best: Teachers' Views on Professional Development* (Seattle, WA: Bill and Melinda Gates Foundation, 2014).

2. Hilda Borko, "Professional Development and Teacher Learning: Mapping the Terrain," *Educational Researcher* 33, no. 8 (2004): 3–15; Linda Darling-Hammond, Maria E. Hyler, and Madelyn Gardner, *Effective Teacher Professional Development* (Palo Alto, CA: Learning Policy Institute, 2017); Thomas R. Guskey and Kwang Suk Yoon, "What Works in Professional Development?" *Phi Delta Kappan 90*, no. 7 (2009): 495–500.

3. Darling-Hammond, et al., *Effective Teacher.*

4. Heather C. Hill and John Papay, *Building Better PL: How to Strengthen Teacher Learning* (Research Partnership for Professional Learning, 2022), http://annenberg.brown.edu/sites/default/files/rppl-building-better-pl.pdf.

5. Christina L. Dobbs, Jacy Ippolito, and Megin Charner-Laird, *Investigating Disciplinary Literacy: A Framework for Collaborative Professional Learning* (Cambridge, MA: Harvard Education Press, 2017).

6. Megin Charner-Laird, Jacy Ippolito, and Christina L. Dobbs, "The Roles of Teacher Leaders in Guiding PLCs Focused on Disciplinary Literacy," *Journal of School Leadership* 26, no. 6 (2016): 975–1001.

7. Borko, "Professional Development"; Darling-Hammond et al., *Effective Teacher.*

8. Michael Fullan, *All Systems Go: The Change Imperative for Whole System Reform* (Thousand Oaks, CA: Corwin Press, 2010); Alma Harris, "System Improvement Through Collective Capacity Building," *Journal of Educational Administration* 49, no. 6 (2011): 624–36.

9. Victoria Gillis, "Disciplinary Literacy: Adapt not Adopt," *Journal of Adolescent & Adult Literacy* 57, no. 8 (2014): 614–23.

10. Charner-Laird et al., "Roles of Teacher Leaders"; Dobbs et al., *Investigating Disciplinary Literacy.*

11. Rudine Sims Bishop, "Mirrors, Windows, and Sliding Glass Doors," *Perspectives: Choosing and Using Books for the Classroom* 6, no. 3 (1990).

12. Bishop, "Mirrors, Windows."

13. Timothy Shanahan and Cynthia Shanahan, "What Is Disciplinary Literacy and Why Does It Matter?" *Topics in Language Disorders* 32, no. 1 (2012): 7–18; Thomas DeVere

Wolsey and Diane Lapp, *Literacy in the Disciplines: A Teacher's Guide for Grades 5–12* (New York: Guilford Press, 2016).

14. Dobbs et al., *Investigating Disciplinary Literacy.*

15. Borko, "Professional Development"; Darling-Hammond et al., *Effective Teacher*; Guskey et al., "What Works?"

16. Megin Charner-Laird, Jacy Ippolito, and Christina L. Dobbs, "Teacher-Led Professional Learning," *Harvard Education Letter* 30, no. 3 (2014): 6–8.

Chapter 9

1. Christina L. Dobbs, Jacy Ippolito, and Megin Charner-Laird, *Investigating Disciplinary Literacy: A Framework for Collaborative Professional Learning* (Cambridge, MA: Harvard Education Press, 2017); Jacy Ippolito, Christina L. Dobbs, and Megin Charner-Laird, *Disciplinary Literacy Inquiry and Instruction* (West Palm Beach, FL: Learning Sciences International, 2019).

2. Esther A. Enright, William Toleda, and Katherine Landau Wright, "Advancing Civics-Specific Disciplinary Writing in the Elementary Grades." *Journal of Writing Research* 15, no. 1 (2023): 41–71; Yongjun Lee, Laura M. Lemanski, Megan M. Van Deventer, and David G. O'Brien, "Leveraging Collaborative Expertise: Social Studies Teachers' Perspectives of Disciplinary Literacy Instruction," *Literacy Research and Instruction* 60, no. 3 (2021): 220–41; Thomas M. McCann, Rebecca D'Angelo, Nancy Galas, and Mary Greska, *Literacy and History in Action: Immersive Approaches to Disciplinary Thinking, Grades 5–12* (New York: Teachers College Press, 2015); Jeffery D. Nokes, *Building Students' Historical Literacies: Learning to Read and Reason with Historical Texts and Evidence,* 2nd ed. (New York: Routledge, 2022).

3. Nell K. Duke and Kelly B. Cartwright, "The Science of Reading Progresses: Communicating Advances Beyond the Simple View of Reading," *Reading Research Quarterly* 56 (2021): S25–S44.

4. Ronald A. Heifetz, Alexander Grashow, and Marty Linsky, *The Practice of Adaptive Leadership: Tools and Tactics for Changing Your Organization and the World* (Cambridge, MA: Harvard Business Press, 2009).

ACKNOWLEDGMENTS

WE WANT TO ACKNOWLEDGE and thank all of the people who have helped us to bring the second edition of this book to life.

First and foremost, we would like to thank all of the amazing educators who contributed their stories to this second edition project, including Christopher Alba, Jimmy Aquino, Christina Collins, Lisa Collins, Alisa Conner, Eric Curl, Martha Gammie, Rich Giso, Jacqueline Hallo, Rachel Hayashi, Karen Engels, Sheila Jaung, Jasmine Juo, Kate Leslie, Evan Mousseau, Alejandra Muñoz, Chris Norkun, Julie Padgett, John Padula, Pamela Penwarden, Jennifer Rappaport, Sol Rheem, Marisa Ricci, Jessica Scott, Marycruz Somes, Ben Stein, Katie Stowell, Dan Trahan, Jay Wallace, and Eileen Woodford. We have learned so much from talking and working with each of you!

Second, we would like to express our gratitude to Jenee Uttaro and Jenelle Williams. Your foreword to this second edition is inspiring and provides amazing insights to guide readers into the text. Both of you have bolstered our work and collaborations for years. We look forward to learning with you and from you for years to come.

We would also like to acknowledge and thank Meg Bowen, Rhonda Fiechuk, and all of our friends at Learning Sciences International, for helping to bring the first edition of this book into existence.

Simultaneously, we are so grateful to Jayne Fargnoli, Molly Grab Cerrone, Laura Clos, and all of our friends at Harvard Education Press. Working on this second edition with HEP has felt like "coming home" in so many ways–thank you for that opportunity.

Last, we would like to thank all of our students, readers, teachers, mentors, and colleagues who we have learned from and with for decades. We are humbled at how our respective professional networks have grown exponentially over the years, and we look forward to many more years of collaboration ahead.

ABOUT THE AUTHORS

JACY IPPOLITO is a professor in leadership and literacy at the McKeown School of Education at Salem State University (Salem, MA), where he currently co-directs graduate programs in Educational Leadership and the Center for Educational Leadership at SSU (CEL@SSU). Jacy's research, teaching, and consulting focus on the intersection of literacy coaching, educational leadership, adolescent literacy/critical disciplinary literacy, and school reform. For more about Jacy's work, or to connect with him directly, please visit www.visualcv.com/jacyippolito.

CHRISTINA L. DOBBS is an assistant professor and program director of English Education for Equity and Justice at Boston University. Her research focuses on adolescent writing development, supporting culturally and linguistically diverse students, critical disciplinary literacy, and teacher professional learning. Additionally, Christina conducts research about the experiences of women of color in the academy and works to combat censorship and support intellectual freedom in American schools.

MEGIN CHARNER-LAIRD is a professor in leadership and elementary education at the McKeown School of Education at Salem State University (Salem, MA). Currently, she co-directs graduate programs in Educational Leadership and the Center for Educational Leadership at SSU (CEL@SSU). Megin's research focuses on school leadership, teacher leadership, critical disciplinary literacy, and the intersection of teachers' and leaders' practice with educational policy. Throughout her work, Megin focuses on the intersections between policy, research, and practice, and her teaching, research, consulting, and writing speak to this intersection.

INDEX